Yacht Charter Handbook

ROD HEIKELL

Imray Laurie Norie & Wilson Ltd
St Ives Cambridgeshire England

Published by
Imray Laurie Norie & Wilson Ltd
Wych House St Ives Huntingdon
Cambridgeshire PE17 4BT England
☎ +44(0)1480 462114
Fax +44(0)1480 496109
e-mail ilnw@imray.com
1997

ISBN 0 85288 383 8

British Library Cataloguing in Publication
Data.
A catalogue record for this book is available
from the British Library.

CAUTION
Whilst every care has been taken to ensure
accuracy, neither the publishers nor the
author will hold themselves responsible for
errors, omissions or alterations in this
publication. They will at all times be grateful
to receive information which tends to the
improvement of the work.

PLANS
The plans in this guide are not to be used
for navigation. They are designed to support
the text and should at all times be used with
navigational charts.

Printed at Bath Press Colourbooks Ltd
Blantyre, Scotland

Contents

Preface

People go on a yacht charter holiday for all sorts of reasons. For the simple pleasure of getting away from terra firma. For that sweet magic when the sea and the wind click in to give you the sail of a lifetime. For evenings ashore and nights afloat. For the parties. Some are sent away to become human again after a stressful time at work. Or re-establish some sort of contact with a wife or partner and children. Some just can't do without it for no good reason they can put their finger on.

The intention of this book is to smooth your way from the first decision to go on charter to finally ending up at your chosen destination. For whatever reasons you decide to sign up for a yacht charter holiday, there follows after that decision, a whole lot of practical things you need to decide on and to do. It would be nice if having once decided to go, you were magically transported to that yacht sitting at anchor in a picture postcard bay, but it doesn't work like that. If it is all to be an enjoyable process, a little initial research and planning will go a long way to making it as hassle free as it can be. Finding the right company to book with, the sort of yacht suited to your needs and a destination that suits your sailing skills and inclinations, is not always as straightforward as it might seem. This book will guide you through the whole business as gently as possible.

One thing is certain. Sailing holidays can be addictive and the pleasure of waking up on board after the first night is something that may plague your dreams for years to come. I don't hold with all that old cynicism of 'been there, done that, seen the movie'. Every time I get on a boat some strange chemistry afflicts my neurones and turns me from western schizoid man into a human being with a bit of time to think about things which don't revolve around timetables and diary appointments. Conrad once said something along the lines of ... a boat is not a slave, give her your all, your love, your skill and she will carry you for as long as she is able. On a yacht charter out there you can capture some of that and shrug off the supermarket cynicism which eats into our land-based lives so often.

Have some fun!

Acknowledgements

Thanks to Chris Doyle and Nancy Scott for the section on the Caribbean. To Elaine Thompson at Yachting World for photos and advice. To Robin Paine at the Moorings UK for information on the bonding minefield. To Pat Collinge at Sunsail for photos. To Barry Nielson at Sailing Holidays for beer and gossip. To Mike Moseley at Templecraft for the digitised diagrams of charter boats. To Odile for putting the initial directory together. To Mike Brown of the Yacht Charter Asssociation for advice. To Lucy Wilson for the cover. To Willie Wilson and all at Imrays for assembling everything.

Rod Heikell
London 1997

ALSO BY ROD HEIKELL
Greek Waters Pilot
Imray Mediterranean Almanac (Editor)
Ionian
Italian Waters Pilot
Mediterranean Cruising Handbook
Mediterranean France & Corsica Pilot
Mediterranean Sailing (A&C Black Ltd)
Saronic
Turkish Waters & Cyprus Pilot
The Danube – A river guide
The Turquoise Coast of Turkey NET
Indian Ocean Handbook

I. Introduction

Going on charter

Basically you need a boat, a destination, a date and crew. Like most good ideas it sounds simple and, for the most part, it is. To make it all go smoothly you need a little preparation and you need to ask a few questions about the options available. For some the details will appear to be fixed by apparently unmovable facts – school holidays, a fixed budget, an area you just have to visit whatever anyone says, limited experience – bits of the overall equation which delimit where, when and with whom. Wherever you go remember this is a holiday you are on and it should be fun. It can be instructive, character-building, a bit scary, exciting certainly, but the one thing it must do is crease your face with a smile.

With whom?

Families

A large proportion of charterers will be chartering with the family, ergo the crew is ready made – you are stuck with it and they are stuck with you. A family holiday should be just that, a holiday for all the family and not some arduous voyage you are intent on making. Better to take sailing friends for that sort of expedition and let the family go somewhere else.

It is necessary, at the very beginning, to get some idea of what members of a family want to do on a holiday afloat. Young children will probably want to muck around in the water some of the time. Adolescents will invariably want some social life. How many members of the family actually like sailing as much as you do? Be prepared to budget for some days off along the route to prevent mutiny halfway through the holiday.

The most common mistake is to plan to cover too much ground, visit too many places, and spend as much time as possible sailing. It doesn't take long before the family mutinies and, instead of a holiday, the whole thing becomes an ordeal. If sailing is what you are after then there seems little point to me in going to a foreign country if you are not going to see anything except whitecaps and distant horizons. Any timetable made for a cruise should have lay-days built into it and a short circuit so that you can cut out part of the itinerary and get the boat back comfortably and on time.

Even if you are an experienced sailor with a yen for the freedom of the open sea, it is worthwhile considering a flotilla holiday instead of a bareboat when the family comes along. Those with younger families will find that there are usually other families on flotilla along with children of similar ages that can go off and play together. Adolescents will find other young people for a covert drink in a local bar. And parents can discuss the merits of the overhand reverse double bowline and the local beer.

If you are going on a skippered charter find out if there is enough to occupy children on board for the duration of the cruise. Most will not be happy to just lie around in the sun or sip a cool drink in the evening. As any parent knows they need activity and, on a skippered charter, chances are they will become bored very quickly unless the skipper and/or hostess are practised in the art of charming children or teenagers.

Friends

A yacht charter with friends as crew can cement friendships in a shared experience or it can destroy a life-long relationship in a very short time. It is a common assumption that friendships in the workplace or based around the home will work on board a yacht. They may not and it is worth sounding out non-sailing friends about the idea before your enthusiasm for a holiday afloat overwhelms them with descriptions of idyllic days and neglects to mention the cramped confines and lack of privacy. Non-sailing friends may wonder why you pay so much money for cramped accommodation and few facilities when you could stay in a hotel with all mod cons for less. It is difficult to explain sometimes.

Family members need time off the boat to just muck about. Budget lots of time off into the cruise so it is a relaxing affair and not one gruelling sail after another. *Photo* Martin Reidl

It is essential that friends sailing together talk about the location, the boat, the route, and tasks on board before putting a deposit on a yacht charter. Those who have not been sailing before should endeavour to see a similar boat to the one they will be living on for two weeks or so. Non-sailors should be given some time for trips ashore and, at the beginning of the cruise, start slowly so they can get accustomed to sailing and overcome any initial fear of being on the water in what appears to be a fragile plastic teacup. You may have to change an itinerary if the spectre of seasickness puts in an appearance. All these things need to be discussed beforehand so that the cruise is a shared experience and not an enforced Bligh-like voyage of endurance. You want your friends to come on further yacht charters don't you?

Pot luck

For those who cannot find friends eager and willing to go sailing with them, there are several options available. Most of the flotilla companies run pot-luck boats (also called stowaway, share-boat, share a yacht, berth sharing, or a similar name) where you will be put on a yacht with other singles or couples. The companies try to put similar sorts of people on a pot-luck boat, some even arrange for you to meet up beforehand if possible, but when finally you shake hands with your new crew-mates on the quay, it can be a sanguine time to reflect on the fact that the choice has been made. You are going to share a boat with this group of strangers for the next two weeks.

The flotilla companies require that at least one of those on board has sailing experience and he or she will then assume the role of skipper. If there is more than one would-be skipper on board then some sharing of the role is advised. Other inexperienced sharers fit into whatever role they are best suited. Most pot-luck boats work out well as long as there is no really eccentric crew or couple on board and, for some, life-long friendships result. There are a few marriages as well, but pot luck is not a dating agency so don't count on it!

If flotilla is not for you then scan the personal column of the yachting magazines for others looking for crew for a yacht charter or place an ad yourself. Most of these advertisements state a location and sometimes a boat along the lines of 'crew wanted for a sailing holiday on a 35ft Beneteau in Greece, shared expenses', and so the location, sometimes the boat, and possibly the skipper (the advertiser) are already decided upon.

Also in the personal columns you may come across advertisements for crew or single berths on owner-operated boats cruising in an area or on yacht deliveries. These can offer some exotic locations, long passages, and the company of a skilled captain and navigator who knows his boat backwards, but it will not give you much scope for command or even partial command of your own. Better to approach it as a learning experience and the chance to do some unusual sailing. Remember though that you will not have the bonding of an established company and arrange adequate insurance for the area.

Sailing schools and other institutions

For those wanting to learn to sail or to hone basic skills in yacht racing, old-timers or specific boats there are many opportunities for either single or group participation. Most sailing schools, whether offering courses for basic skills or more advanced courses, will take either singles or groups and mix-and-match as appropriate. If you are going to be on passage for a while, say on an old gaffer or square rigger, then it is worthwhile slotting into a group of a similar age and/or interests.

Like the T-shirt says: just another bloody day in paradise. Here on a Moorings catamaran in the Bahamas. *Photo* Yachting World

When?

Most areas, with a very few exceptions, have a time of the year when the charter season closes down. In the Mediterranean there are really no charters during the northern winter. In the Caribbean there are fewer charters during the hurricane season from June to October. In the Pacific islands the hurricane season likewise delimits the time of the year when charter boats operate. In somewhere like Thailand there is a two to three-month period at the height of the rainy season when it is just too hot and humid to do anything.

The charter season itself is usually chopped up into a low season either end of the high season. Naturally enough the high season is the best time to go and, consequently, the most popular. The low seasons on either end are a bit more of a lottery when it comes to wind (too much or too little) and weather, although you can have wonderful conditions with a bit of luck. Some people prefer the low season in some areas on the basis that the high season is too hot and crowded. In the Mediterranean, spring or autumn can be wonderful times to go sailing. It can also be wet and unsettled weather may keep you in harbour. In the Tropics there can be a cool drier spell in some months and there is little chance of hurricanes even if it is still officially the hurricane season.

In Part II, in World Charter Areas, the different charter seasons are given along with the sort of weather you can expect. Remember that weather is more critical for a holiday afloat as opposed to a land-based holiday so tailor the time to your experience and the expected conditions. Remember too that all weather is statistical and you can get a high-season holiday when it blows above or below average and rains a lot, even though the odds are against it. Likewise a low-season holiday may have perfect high-season conditions, but likely will not.

For many, at least those who have school-age children, the dates for a holiday afloat are locked into the school holidays. There is no escape from this and, inevitably, this is when charters cost the most. It is sometimes possible to organise a low-season yacht charter with children by running a few days over Easter or a mid-term break to fit into a one- or two-week slot. Most parents think that the experience more than makes up for the few days the children have missed at school – but check with teacher if it is OK.

Remember that in the Tropics and southern hemisphere the high season is the Christmas and New Year period. For a month either side in December and January in the Caribbean, Thailand and Australasia this is the period of peak demand. For many destinations in the Tropics the northern hemisphere summer coincides with the tropical wet season and part of the hurricane/typhoon season, so you should think about making bookings for the tropics and southern hemisphere in the northern hemisphere winter.

Those with allergies or certain medical conditions need to do some checking up on conditions at different times of the year. Hayfever sufferers should avoid seasons when pollen counts are high. Hot countries can have very high pollen counts at certain times of the year and I well remember arranging an early flight home for a hayfever sufferer from Greece in the spring. Those who suffer from heat rash should avoid the height of summer or the hottest times in the Tropics. Anyone who has a severe allergic reaction to mosquito and midge bites needs to avoid some areas at certain times. Countries like Canada, New Zealand and Scandinavia hum with the sound of mosquitoes and midges in the summer. Consult with your doctor and the charter company if you are unsure.

Where?

For most, the 'where to go' question is the most exciting one. Thumbing through brochures with all those wonderful photos of yachts tied up outside a *taverna* in Greece, in a translucent coral-fringed anchorage in the Virgin Islands, under sheer limestone cliffs covered in jungle in Thailand, in St-Tropez next to a rock star's floating home, on the waterfront in Sydney with that extravagant opera house in the background, in fact almost anywhere except where you are right now, conjures up visions of you in another world at the helm of your own yacht – at least for a while.

And why not? Even if you own a yacht the logistics of getting it to an exotic location are impossible for most and the cost prohibitive. A week or two on a charter yacht makes a lot of sense in our busy world and it also makes sense to go to paradise and have a look at it just in case there are a few things you don't like about it.

The 'where to go' question has a lot to do with your own desires and sense of where you would like to see. There are a lot of places in the world that some of us feel we must go to have a look at based on interests in the culture, history, geography, food or, in most cases, just a hazy romantic notion gleaned from things we have read and people we have talked to. Or, it can simply be, that you haven't been there before.

That is fine if you are on your own when only your own sense of adventure dictates where. If you are not, consider the others going with you. Children need things to keep them amused and will not be amused with overly long flights. Fractious children on an eight-hour flight to or from a charter destination may ruin things for the parents. Hot temperatures upset small children and can turn life aboard into a living hell looking for ways to cool off. Children may dislike the local food. Teenagers are not too impressed with geography and like to have other teenagers to mix with and places to be seen in ashore. Friends going on a charter yacht together should draw lots on where to go and reach some sort of consensus without being steam-rollered by the appointed skipper. And don't forget to tailor where you are going to your experience.

If all of these things sound obvious, in my own and others' experiences they are not. I'd beg charterers not to go to the Cyclades during the *meltemi* season when it can be windy and rough, but to no avail. Someone

The 'where' option is the exciting one. Here in Turkey. *Photo* Rod Heikell

just had to see Mikonos or Paros or Santorini. After the first day bucketing about with everyone being seasick the less obstinate would beg the skipper to take them somewhere with a lot less wind. Sorting out where to go should be a decision made for all those on board, not just one or two and certainly not just the skipper.

In the end . . .

It is the planning at the beginning which goes some way to determining whether a yacht charter is a dream come true or a nightmare not to be repeated. If there seems to be a lot of negative advice in the foregoing it is not meant to put you off yacht charter, just ensure you get the maximum enjoyment from it. In truth a very small percentage of those who go on a yacht charter would not repeat it and the majority plan to repeat it the next year and forgo the new kitchen or car. Some will choose a different company because, once having been in an area, they get to look at other boats. Some will hear from friends that XYZ Charters are a good

company to go with. Many others will stick with the company they know and often go straight back to the same area. Some get positively addicted to the whole idea and, for this group, treatment may be necessary in charter detox institutions.

Charter comes in all shapes and sizes and the first thing you have to do is figure out what is appropriate for the sort of holiday you want, the sort of holiday your family or friends want, and what is possible taking into account your experience and the size of your wallet. There are basically three types of yacht charter available and a number of other options related to yacht charter or to just getting on the water for a holiday afloat. The three basic types of charter are flotilla sailing, bareboat, and skippered charter, although there are a lot of variations on the themes.

Flotilla sailing

Also called 'sailing in company'.
- For inexperienced sailors who want to get some experience, usually in a warm climate, and have a holiday at the same time.
- For experienced sailors who want a relaxing holiday.

Flotilla sailing started in Greece around 20 years ago and has proved enduringly popular ever since. A lot of nonsense and a sort of snobbery revolves around the idea of flotilla sailing. Comments like 'it's just like ducklings following the mother duck', 'I want to get away from it all not together with other boats', and 'it's just a package holiday afloat' are often attached to Flotilla sailing by a few

When sailing in company there are lots of opportunities for a bit of impromptu racing.
Photo Yachting World

charterers or, more usually, would-be charterers to flotilla holidays. In practice none of it is like this and those who go on flotilla holidays often return again. Nor is it solely a matter of sailing experience. Often, experienced sailors who own a yacht at home choose to take the flotilla option for a variety of reasons.

On flotilla you sail in company with a group of yachts (typically 10–12) and a lead boat on which there is a skipper and hostess and sometimes an engineer. The skipper is in overall charge of the fleet and is responsible for the care and repair of boats and clients alike. He will brief the new arrivals on the ins and outs of their boats and will provide pilotage and general navigation briefings each morning. The engineer is responsible for the maintenance of the yachts, making sure the engines, plumbing, electrics and rigging are in good order. In his other capacity he usually supervises preparation of the punch served at barbecues. The hostess looks after day to day life on board and advises on facilities ashore – where to shop, restaurants, doctors and dentists, and excursions inland. She is usually a dab hand at minor first aid.

With a lead boat around in radio contact with the fleet, much of the apprehension of a new sailing area and a strange boat to cope with is removed and you can get on and enjoy the sailing and the scenery. Should you get into difficulties, members of the lead crew are there to help you. Their experience means you will have local knowledge on harbours and anchorages, a guide to the best restaurants, and immediate help to fix the loo or get the engine going.

Although yachts sail together as a fleet, this doesn't mean you have to sail in line astern behind the lead boat. In most areas you leave a harbour or anchorage in your own time, stop off for lunch in a bay somewhere if you are so inclined, and finally end up in the next bay or harbour for the evening. Depending on the area you could get anything from three to eight days independent sailing where you can go off and explore an area before rejoining the flotilla towards the end of the cruise. Flotilla options with a lot of independent sailing days are effectively a 50/50 mix of flotilla and bareboat, though with the added advantage that, when you are off sailing independently, you can always call up the lead crew should you have any problems.

Flotillas score highly for the social side of things. Evenings ashore turn into social occasions with waves getting bigger, winds increasing to way above gale force, and a few confessions of tangled kedge warps, with every glass downed. A fleet of identical boats means there are lots of opportunities for a bit of impromptu one-design racing and if you are beaten . . . well, you weren't really racing anyway. On flotilla you will make a lot of friends and some will forge life-long friendships.

The misconceptions to be found among some sailors who would never consider booking a flotilla holiday, because they are experienced sailors and don't like the idea of being in a fleet of boats, should be ignored. Often a flotilla holiday suits experienced sailors just as well with its mix of flotilla and independent days and adds a welcome social dimension.

Flotilla holidays are generally two-week affairs and typically cover anything from 100 to 200 miles in easy stages. The degree of experience needed depends on the area and the distance covered. Most flotilla companies will give you a good idea of the qualifications needed for a particular flotilla and may advise you to go on a short familiarisation course if

they feel your experience is a bit on the light side. In general, flotilla qualifications start at those with dinghy experience for the easier flotillas and work up to previous flotilla experience or small-craft owners for the more arduous flotillas.

Sailing in company may be organised by a charter company on a regular basis or it may be a one-off generated by request from a large group of charterers. The formula varies between a mini-flotilla of three to six yachts with a lead crew on one or a group of skippered yachts sailing together in an area.

Bareboat

- For semi-experienced to experienced sailors depending on the location.

Bareboat basically means you charter a boat and sail independently in a given area. Most companies require you to return the boat to the home base although many now offer a one-way cruise from one base to another. Bareboats are not bare, but come with everything you need except provisions. In fact many companies can even arrange to provision your boat should you desire it, though you can have lot of fun trying to buy peanut butter in Thailand or bacon in Turkey.

If you are going bareboat it is important that you take some time over choosing a charter company, pick your fellow companions carefully, and put some thought into planning the cruise.

When choosing a charter company check on what is included in the inventory. What safety equipment is there? What anchors, chain and warp are supplied? What navigation equipment is supplied and what charts and local pilots? Pretty soon you will get an idea of how well equipped a yacht is and some idea of how well it has been maintained. Ask about back-up should any problems occur. There is nothing worse on a bareboat charter than being stuck in a harbour for five days with a ripped sail or a blown gasket on the engine because the charter base couldn't get anyone out to you and didn't have any contacts on the island to effect repairs.

Many will go on a bareboat holiday with the family cajoled into going along as crew, cook, and deck-washer. Others will convince friends that sailing your own boat in a foreign place is the perfect antidote to work, lost loves and manic depression. Since you are all going to be not just living together in a small

On a bareboat charter you are on your own with the maximum freedom ... and maximum responsibility. *Photo* Pat Collinge

space, but also sailing the boat, navigating in strange waters, wondering if the wind and sea are going to get worse, and socialising ashore, it is important that you all get on together. This aspect is probably more important for bareboat charter over and above flotilla and skippered charter where there are opportunities to ease any tensions that may arise. On a bareboat charter you are on your own with the maximum of freedom and also the maximum responsibility for each other and the boat.

Most bareboat companies require that you have some experience handling, sailing and navigating something larger than a dinghy. The degree of experience depends on the location and likely conditions you will encounter. Most charter companies do not require an official bit of paper saying you are qualified to skipper, although if you do have a certificate of competence of some sort it will ease your way. Some companies may suggest that you take a brush-up course or even go on a flotilla holiday first. Potential charterers should not balk at such suggestions as the charter company certainly wants to sell you a holiday, but needs a minimum of experience in order that your

own safety and the boat's are not compromised. After all, boats cost a lot of money and no charter company can keep making claims for boats written off by charterers and expect the insurance company to keep paying.

All bareboat charter companies require a security deposit on the boat and gear. At the end of the holiday any gear that has been lost or damaged and any damage to the boat will be deducted from the deposit. They may also require that you have personal insurance including adequate medical insurance. If you return the boat late there are various penalties that can be invoked by the company which usually means a certain amount deducted from your security deposit for each day you are overdue. There will also be penalties for not returning the yacht to the charter base because bad weather prevented you from getting back. All of these penalties are covered by the security deposit and since the company holds on to it until satisfied the boat has been returned at the appointed time and place and in good condition, it is up to you to do so or lose all or part of the deposit. *Force majeure* applies only in exceptional circumstances to bareboat charter.

Skippered charter

- For inexperienced crew at base level.
- For anyone at skipper and crew level.

Skippered charter encompasses everything from small bareboats, where a skipper is engaged to look after the boat, up to superyachts with not only skipper but a full complement of crew. On a large yacht the crew will often outnumber the guests and this sort of charter service is expected to be the equal or better than a five-star hotel.

At the bottom level, skippered charter equals bareboat plus skipper. Charterers of a bareboat may take on a skipper if they are short on experience or occasionally because the charter company has suggested they do so. Often this will work on the basis that the charterers take a skipper for one week and then take over themselves on the second week when they feel more confident about things. At this level the skipper is responsible for the operation and maintenance of the boat although he will require help from the charterers when reefing, berthing, and anchoring. He or she will not expect to cook, clean, entertain or guide you ashore although, very likely, he will do some of these things. This sort of arrangement for bareboats will often extend up to 50–60 footers depending on the boat and how easy it is to handle.

Most skippered charter is in the mid-range, on 45–70ft yachts, which will often be run by a couple. Usually this means he is skipper and ultimately responsible for all things nautical and some things social and she is cook, crew, sometimes child-minder and the balance of things social. Many of these couples are a well-accomplished act whose service to charterers goes well beyond any job description they might have. Many people will return to the same skipper and hostess almost irrespective of their command because, in the end, it is their contribution to the charter which has the greatest impact.

At superyacht level there will be not only skipper and hostess, but usually another two to five crew depending on size and the level of luxury. This sort of operation comes at a price and it is essential that a reliable broker with a good track record is engaged or reliable personal recommendations taken up.

Whether at basic or super-luxury level, it is vital to realise that the skipper or skipper and crew are the most important ingredient in making a successful skippered charter. A sour and unhelpful skipper, however competent, can negate any amount of wonderful sailing, good food, and exciting destinations. A caring skipper and crew can overcome near disasters on a boat and make the charter a success despite any practical or logistical problems that might crop up. Many skippers and skipper/hostess couples have a following of charterers who have been with them before and who like to pick up the threads of the friendship on subsequent charters.

Motor yachts

It has to be said that most of the charter options talked about here are for sailing boats. For all the options, there are possibilities for motorboat charter although, with the exception of skippered charter, there are fewer possibilities than for sailing boats. Some motorboat flotillas operate and a few bareboat options are available in some areas. Skippered motorboat charter is the most popular option and, in most charter areas, there are numerous possibilities available, ranging from trawler-type motorboats from around 40ft up to super-yacht level.

Other options

Sailing schools and 'Learning to sail' courses

- For novices and beginners wanting to brush up on their skills.
- For sailors wanting to learn unfamiliar techniques like berthing Mediterranean-style.

The two are not quite the same thing. Sailing schools usually work towards a recognised qualification and put you through a syllabus to obtain a qualification such as the RYA Competent Crew Certificate or Yachtmaster qualification. Such courses may not teach you unfamiliar techniques found in foreign cruising areas or the skills relating to sailing there.

'Learning to sail' courses are not usually aimed at a qualification but at getting you on the water and familiarising you with techniques and procedures you will use on a charter yacht. Often they will be on the same yacht used on charter and they may be in the same country where you intend to charter. Inexperienced crew who wish to take a flotilla or bareboat yacht may be asked, in the nicest possible way, to take one of these courses by the charter company. They vary from one-day brush-up courses to three- to seven-day courses teaching you nearly everything you need to know. These courses are useful insofar as they familiarise you with techniques that might otherwise prove stressful during the first few days of a charter and allow you to get on and enjoy the sailing.

Ashore and afloat

Called variously Villa Flotilla, Stay and Sail, or Club Holidays. Usually aimed at novices or families where one half wants to go sailing and the other half wants a relaxing time ashore.

These holidays are generally two weeks split 50–50 between one week in a villa or apartment ashore and one week on board a charter yacht. The holiday ashore will have access to dinghy sailing, board-sailing, or may include a relaxed introduction course to flotilla sailing with instruction on board the same sort of boat you will be using in the second week.

Leaseback

Under this arrangement you front up with around one-quarter to one-third of the purchase price of the sort of boat used by one of the charter companies and the company leases it back from you over a period of years, usually three to five years, with the charter fees paying off the balance of the purchase price. The charter company contracts to maintain the boat and you, the future owner, get the use of the boat for certain periods of the charter season.

The arrangement has the primary advantage of paying off the balance of the boat over the agreed period of years and letting you have use of it at certain times over that period. It also means that the ongoing upkeep of the boat is out of your hands until the boat is paid off. Thus you can scheme to go off cruising in the Mediterranean or the Caribbean in your own yacht after a number of years having spent time aboard getting used to it.

If the arrangement has any pitfalls they revolve around the charter company which operates the leaseback system. In the past some companies have not maintained the boat at all well and, at the end of the lease period, the boat has been turned over to the owner in an awful state. Remember that a charter yacht gets far more use than a privately owned yacht, perhaps the equivalent wear and tear of five years' private ownership over one charter season, so it is imperative that you choose the company

operating the leaseback with care. If possible talk to others who have been involved in this sort of scheme and quiz the charter company about maintenance schedules and refits. Arrange to see what equivalent yachts that have been in charter for three or five years look like. It is all very well to have maintenance schedules on paper, but it is how they are carried out in practice that counts.

You also need to guard against the company going bust and your yacht being seized as part of the assets of the company. Most companies arrange it so that you are the owner from the time you sign the contract. Give the contract to your lawyer to check over, but even if it is watertight in the country where the contract is signed, in practice you may have difficulty extracting the yacht from the country in which it is chartered if the company goes under. It is not unheard of for yachts under leaseback schemes to be seized in the country in which they are chartered and to get one back can entail a good deal of expense and time. The best bet is to go with a company that already has a good track record in operating leaseback systems and, if possible, check out an insurance scheme to cover the risks.

Delivery cruises

• For experienced crew only

Charter companies will often move yachts between bases at the beginning or end of a charter season and may sometimes move them to a new location. These delivery cruises cover longer distances under more arduous conditions than the normal charter routes and you should not necessarily expect them to be a slightly longer version of flotilla or bareboat sailing in the season. The trips vary between slightly longer legs within an area, say from one charter area in Greece to another, or long delivery cruises with extended offshore passages, transatlantic or from the Mediterranean to somewhere like Thailand. Anyone undertaking one of these delivery cruises should be fit and experienced for the trip, something the charter company usually tries to ensure when vetting applicants.

On a more casual basis you can often pick up delivery trips from advertisements in the classified columns or by word of mouth. For some of the pitfalls encountered on this sort of trip see the section on Hitchhiking.

Sail-dive

- For keen divers

In parts of the world with good diving over coral there are yachts which combine a cruise with a circuit of the good dive sites in the area. Most of these yachts are 40ft plus and all are skippered cruises. The yacht will be equipped with all dive gear and the skipper will usually be a qualified dive instructor. This means you get to potter around an area and can stay overnight at dive sites without wasting time going back to shore-based accommodation.

Most of the areas offering sail-dive charter are in tropical or semi-tropical areas. The Red Sea, the Caribbean, the Seychelles, Maldives, Thailand, the Great Barrier Reef in Australia, and the South Pacific islands all have sail-dive charter available.

Racing

- For semi-experienced to experienced

Racing charter encompasses everything from fun events to arduous round-the-world races, and training sessions with professional racing skippers.

One design racing with Sunsail in the Solent.
Photo Pat Collinge

Most racing charter revolves around fun events like Marmaris Race Week in the Mediterranean and Antigua Race Week in the Caribbean. Fun events they may be but, as anyone knows who has been racing there, the competitive urge is only just under the skin in most of us and the racing is fiercely competitive. The parties afterwards can be just as competitive in terms of the amount of alcohol consumed.

For anyone wanting to gain experience, either for a fun week's racing or more serious stuff, there are a number of courses available with professional crew. These can vary from a one-day refresher picking up a few tips to a full week's instruction with some actual racing thrown in. These courses are not intended to be relaxing and are more akin to teaching courses than holidays. For the popular race series where charter yachts or paying berths are available see the 'box' on yacht races on page 12.

Corporate charter

Involves a company or group of people who work together under a professional association or the like, chartering a yacht or several yachts as a reward for bonuses achieved and targets met, for entertaining clients, or for the nebulous thinking that uses

The following established race series will have charter boats or berths available.

UK
- Cowes week. Yachts available for charter in various classes and berths available on some yachts (August).
- The Round-the-Island Race. A one-day affair with numbers of charter yachts racing around the Isle of Wight (June).
- West Highland Yachting Week (July-August).
- Falmouth Race Week. Features many classic yachts (August).

France
- La Niourlague. A week of racing out of St-Tropez featuring classic yachts and state-of-the-art racing machines (September-October).

Greece
- Ionian Regatta. One-day short race, involving mostly flotilla yachts, in Levkas. (September).

Turkey
- Marmaris Race Week. A week of racing involving a large number of charter yachts from Marmaris in Turkey (October-November).

Caribbean
- Grenada Sailing Festival (February).
- Red Stripe Cup (February).
- Heineken Race Week at At Martin (March).
- Rolex Cup at St Thomas USVI (April).
- BVI Spring Regatta (April).
- Antigua Race Week. A week of racing renowned for its apres- mer parties. Bare-boats and skippered charter (April-May).
- Angostura Tobago Race Week. A week of relaxed racing with bareboats and skippered charter (May).
- Martinique Regatta (June).
- Carib Cup (July).

Thailand
- Kings Cup. A week of racing from Nai Harn on Phuket. Bareboat charter available.

There are also lots of smaller race series where charter boats will be available so check race calendars and classified advertisements.

Round-the-world races are for those wanting a mainstream injection of adrenaline and are arduous affairs for the committed only. Crews are selected after a series of trials and the costs are not inconsiderable both in actual monetary terms and the time off required for the selection and training as well as the race itself. There are a number of established round-the-world races:

- Chay Blyth's Round-the-world Challenge Races. RA races going the wrong way around the world in identical steel yachts. Challenge 2000 is the latest race in new 70ft yachts. Paying berths with a professional skipper.
- Robin Knox-Johnson's Clipper Race in 60ft identical GRP yachts. Paying berths with professional skipper.
- World Cruising. Round the World Rally. Private entries with berths available on a few yachts.
- Tradewinds Rally. A two year rally around the world. Private entries with berths available on a few yachts.
- World Cruising Hong Kong Challenge. Private entries with paying berths on a few yachts.

TYPES OF CHARTER

a yacht charter for character building, group bonding, or other vaguely named matters.

Sailing for the disabled

A number of companies operate yacht charter for the disabled. Most charter is on specially modified boats to provide all the facilities needed, but it may be possible to go on a bareboat or flotilla holiday depending on the mobility and requirements of a disabled person. I once skippered a fleet which included several paraplegics and, with a little invention, it was not difficult to devise a system of putting the bosun's chair on the main halyard so that they could get on and off the boat and into the water for a swim. There will, of course, be those who need the specialist skills and equipment installed on boats specially designed for the disabled.

Adventure charters

In some of the remote parts of the world adventure charters are offered depending on experience or physical fitness. These trips operate in remote regions – like Tiera del Fuego, Antarctica, lesser-known Pacific islands, Alaska and the Arctic – and offer the opportunity to sail in parts of the world few others get to. The sailing can be arduous and life in the extreme cold testing for even experienced adventurers. The trips are always on a skippered and crewed yacht and may include other activities such as climbing mountains or sub-aqua diving on remote reefs.

Expeditions

A number of charter berths are often offered on scientific or quasi-scientific expeditions looking at anything from the migration routes of whales to the flora and fauna of out of the way places. Some of these expeditions can be arduous and you need to be committed to the project for some of the hardships you will undergo. Others are comparatively comfortable affairs with all mod cons on board and frequent visits to 'civilisation'. Expedition charter is always on a skippered and crewed basis with costs ranging from expenses for food and drink to full luxury charter rates.

Occasionally expedition cruises looking for treasure, valuable artefacts, or the lost tribe of Tokomaru will be seen advertised in the classified columns. Some care is needed over taking up these charters which usually ask for some money up front to help fund the expedition. In years past a number of fraudulent individuals have duped charterers out of not inconsiderable sums for an expedition which was never going to happen or, at best, not going to get very far.

Hitchhiking

Not really a form of charter, more a cheap way of getting on board a yacht and crewing for pleasure on a pleasurable voyage. If you turn up at popular jumping-off spots for yachts on passage it is sometimes possible to help crew a yacht from one place to another. Obviously you will have to be in the right place at the right time.

Some care is needed when hitchhiking your way around on a boat. You should carry full medical insurance for the countries you are going to and, indeed, some owners will insist on it. Most owners have pretty strict rules disallowing drugs, illegal items like firearms, and, in some cases, smoking. Some owners will also insist on you putting up a bond (usually around $500) which will be returned to you at the end of the voyage.

It pays to make thorough enquiries about the boat and skipper before you leave. If you can talk to any crew who are leaving a lot of information can be gleaned, though do not take all of it at face value. Check the boat carefully as it has to take you safely to the next port. Think about how you will get on with the skipper and other crew when cooped up in a small boat while on passage. Minor friction can grow into dangerous animosity and that is something you don't need at sea.

For the Atlantic try Gibraltar and the Canary Islands between October and January.

For the South Pacific try Florida or the Virgin Islands for passage to Panama and possibly onwards.

For the North Pacific try San Francisco, Los Angeles or San Diego in April or May.

In the South Pacific it is possible to hop through some of the Pacific islands depending on your luck. Some of the better places to pick up yachts are Tahiti, Samoa, and Fiji.

For the Indian Ocean try Darwin or Phuket.

Choosing a company

Once you have decided to book a holiday there remains the choice of which company to book with. Surveys suggest that most people pick up a yachting magazine, take a stab at likely looking advertisements, send off for the brochures, and then choose a holiday from the collection in front of them.

Some will have heard of a company by word of mouth or through recommendations from a yacht club or travel agent. Word of mouth has to be the best recommendation going. If someone you know went with company X and can recommend it then you have a first-hand unadulterated report on a company. Boat shows are another source of information and here you will probably meet some of the staff who work at the charter base or as flotilla crew and you can ask all the questions you want about the boats and the area and get answers from those who work out there. There will usually be a video of the company's boats and the area. There may also be a yacht of the type you are going to charter at the show or at least a similar sort of yacht you can look at to get an idea of the layout and amount of space inside – many brochure photos are taken with a wide-angle lens from a vantage point that suggests more room than there actually is.

Once you have the brochures in front of you, whether you have sent away for them or collected them at a boat show, it's time to choose.

Cost

Cost is an important consideration for many and one that will whittle down the choice. It is important that you establish, either from the brochure or over the phone, what additional costs there will be.

The following checklist will give you some idea of what to expect.

Flotilla

A flotilla sailing holiday is virtually an all-in package and should include the following:
- flight from the specified airport including domestic airport taxes. There may also be flights from other airports subject to supplements

- transfer to and from the destination airport to the charter base
- the yacht and a specified inventory
- fuel, gas and water for the duration of the flotilla
- paperwork with the relevant authorities when not sailing independently
- the services of the lead crew.

This is the bare minimum and many companies will offer better-equipped yachts with refrigerators and tape-decks, tempting additions to the inventory like snorkelling gear and cockpit cushions, and the shared use of equipment like sailboards.

It does not usually include:
- airport taxes and visa charges in the destination country
- security deposit or a damage/loss excess waiver fee
- food and entertainment
- harbour dues
- additional equipment like an outboard motor for the tender, gennikers or spinnakers, personal use of a sailboard
- travel insurance (though most add it on with the initial deposit)
- yacht cleaning.

Bareboat

Most bareboat holidays are not all-in packages although many companies can arrange travel and other requirements at extra cost. The holiday usually includes the following:
- the yacht and a specified inventory. The inventory is usually of a higher specification than that of a flotilla boat
- initial paperwork with the relevant authorities to get you started
- the services of the charter-base staff.

This is the bare minimum and again many companies offer much more.

It does not usually include:
- the flight or other transport to and from the charter destination
- airport taxes and visa charges in the destination country
- transfer to and from the destination airport to the charter base
- security deposit or damage/loss excess waiver fee
- fuel, gas and water for the duration of the charter
- additional equipment, such as an outboard motor for the tender, spinnaker, and sailboard (although some companies will include these free of charge with the yacht)

- paperwork with the relevant authorities and harbour dues en route
- your food and entertainment (although some companies supply a small starter pack free)
- travel insurance (though most add it on with the initial deposit)
- yacht cleaning.

Skippered and Crewed

Most crewed charters take considerable care to look after you and spare you the burdens of local paperwork, finding your way around, and choosing a restaurant. They usually include the following:

- yacht and specified inventory (on larger yachts the inventory may include toys like sailboards, jet skis, and a tender suitable for water-skiing)
- the services of a skipper and, depending on the size of the yacht or your requirements, cook and crew.

It does not include:

- the flight or other transport to and from the charter destination
- airport taxes and visa charges
- transfer to and from the charter base, although many skippers will meet you at the airport if it is not too far away
- fuel, gas and water for the duration of the charter
- harbour dues en route
- your food and entertainment (remember it is only politic to entertain your skipper and crew occasionally)
- travel insurance
- tips for the skipper and crew – a customary courtesy although considered mandatory in some areas.

A set of pricing terms have evolved over the years for large skippered and crewed yachts with the following the most common versions found.

WMT – Western Mediterranean Terms. Includes everything except food and drink, marina and harbour fees, fuel and other running charges, and any taxes.

EMT – Eastern Mediterranean Terms. Includes everything including all or a set number of meals a day, fuel for a defined period (commonly 5 hours at cruising speed), and other running charges like water, etc.

GT – Greek Terms. A variation on EMT which excludes food and drink.

CT – Caribbean Terms. Basically includes everything except tips.

Most charter companies will define what the terms are even if they do not operate under them so there is little room for confusion here. These terms are not generally used for small skippered yachts where the charter is basically a bareboat with a skipper.

Overall it is easy to see that the extra costs you have to add on increase as you move from flotilla to bareboat to skippered charter. Between flotilla and bareboat the cost can work out much the same if you shop around for flights and take a little care over costs on the water. Many of the bareboat companies can arrange flights for you and some of them do very good deals indeed. If you are not satisfied with the price of flights from a bareboat company or agent, a quick perusal of the travel columns in the papers and a few phone calls will quickly establish whether you can do better for the departure times and airport you want. Generally the bareboat company or agent has a finger on the pulse of cheap flights and you will usually find it difficult to get a better deal.

Reading a brochure

Brochures can be entirely misleading, although they do not deliberately set out to be. Having written numerous brochures in my time I know that style and content is often dictated from on high and often does not reflect the style of staff on the ground. Some brochures have started to introduce a more down-to-earth description of an area with some indication of what the reality is like rather than using brochure-speak to immerse the reader in some Arcadian cruising area that is neither a lie nor the whole truth. It will of course do all the normal things a brochure does. Photos will show an idyllic harbour, just omitting the sugar cane refinery nearby, or the limpid water of an apparently near-deserted anchorage when there are in fact 40 boats there. They will tell you they have been in operation for X number of years although you may find that the original company did not trade under the same name. And it will almost certainly claim to offer you the most personal, most caring best guaranteed holiday going.

Again the best way to sort out a brochure is to talk to someone who has been on holiday with that company. Failing that, ask for some interpretation of the brochure at a boat show or over the phone. A few questions may help you divine what a company is like although I have to say that one member of staff with an acerbic manner may dissuade you from booking with a perfectly good company. Your best guarantee with an established company is simply that it wants you to come back again – return bookings make up anything from 25 to 40 per cent of a company's bookings and to prejudice these is just not in their interests.

Company guarantees

Some companies offer various guarantees if you lose some or all of your holiday due to a breakdown. To a large extent this relies on the staff on the ground being able to carry out the promised guarantee. (You can just hear the company director: 'I don't care if it's Force 9 and the ferries aren't running, get another yacht down there yesterday'). But it does at least give you some guarantee of fulfilling the sailing part of the holiday rather than sitting around in a bar wondering when a mechanic or a new sail is going to turn up. Usually these guarantees will promise that, for sailing time lost due to no fault of your

own – typically an engine breakdown or rig or sail failure, they will do one, or several, of the following:

• provide an equivalent or larger replacement yacht
• provide a credit towards another sailing holiday with them
• make a monetary payment.

There are usually provisos to the guarantee, along the following lines:

• normally the lost time must be one day or more, although some charter companies stipulate as little as four hours lost time before they credit you with a discount or extra days
• some companies restrict the area where you can make this claim
• you must obtain written evidence of the lost time, usually from shore or flotilla staff.

You should get this guarantee in writing, including the amount of money offered towards another holiday or paid *ex gratia*. Many companies include the guarantee in their brochure. You will find that most companies want your custom again and will provide adequate compensation.

I must add here that charterers who act irresponsibly with their charge and damage craft through their own negligence – either by mooring badly, paying too little attention to their navigation and encountering underwater objects, keeping too much sail up in strong winds and damaging the rig and sails, or through not following engine checks cause damage to the engine – are themselves liable to pay the charter company or lose the whole or part of the security deposit.

Staff

The crew on flotilla, the shore-based staff of bareboat companies, and the skipper and crew on skippered charter are the backbone of any charter company. They are, in the end, the ones who can make or break your holiday.

Flotilla crew

They brief you on the boats and area at the beginning of the flotilla, repair engines, sails and toilets, and facilitate your forays ashore. Their relationship with you, and yours with them, is an important ingredient in the success of a flotilla. If you can meet them at a boat show or talk to one of them in the winter you will get some idea of the quality of

How well maintained are the boats. An old roller reefing genoa that shreds in the first bit of wind can lose you valuable sailing time.
Photo Rod Heikell

Staff are an essential part of the equation for a
successful holiday whatever option is chosen.
Here a briefing session at the Moorings
Grenada base. *Photo* Yachting World

the crew employed by a company. Most of
them will be in their twenties or early
thirties, taking a year or five off from a
conventional career, may or may not hold
qualifications, may own a yacht, and
invariably like some social life and a drink
or two in the evenings. There is really no
way to determine how you are going to get
on with the flotilla crew or how diligently
they carry out their task. If you have been
on flotilla with a crew you liked one year
then try and go with them again.

For three people to live together on a
small boat, call it home, and look after 30
to 50 new arrivals every two weeks,
requires a resilience and tolerance in the
flotilla crew that should be recognised by
new arrivals. While they are employed to
look after you, the sum total of your
holiday with them is more than just asking
them to fix things or give directions. When
I was on flotilla we allowed new arrivals
three days to wind down and turn into
human beings instead of trying to run their
holidays like their businesses or their jobs.
After three days the tolerance level for

requests to unblock a toilet before breakfast
or repair a light switch at ten at night
evaporates somewhat.

Bareboat staff

While you will see less of them than flotilla
crew, the quality of shore-based bareboat
staff is just as important to your holiday.
They are the ones who maintain your yacht,
fix any minor niggles, and get you quickly
and efficiently on your way. You need to
check the inventory with them, correct or
note any deficiencies, get some idea of the
cruising area and suggested itineraries, note
any recommended restaurants, collect the
paperwork, and get away quickly.

More importantly you need to know that,
in the event of a breakdown, they can get
someone to you to fix things or authorise
someone locally to do so. The biggest
problem on a bareboat charter is
undoubtedly a breakdown away from the
charter base and you should seek assurances
from a company that they will dispatch staff
if necessary or authorise work locally.

Skippered charter

A sympathetic skipper and crew are essential ingredients for a successful skippered charter. Someone who will look after you, discreetly amend your cruising plans using his stock of local knowledge, recommend restaurants that serve the best food and don't appear in the guide books, amuse your children and give you time to yourself – in short provide you with an exciting and relaxing holiday – without them a skippered holiday can be a disaster no matter how luxurious and well run the yacht is. Charterers often follow a skipper and hostess/crew from boat to boat, so important is this bit of the recipe, and good owners will fight not to lose a good skipper and crew.

It follows that good skippers and crew get good boats and part of their expertise is making sure the boat is in good running order. Few skippers will not be able to cope with mechanical and electrical breakdowns on the spot and most will endeavour to avoid them with preventative maintenance. If, for some reason, an unforeseen breakdown occurs then a good skipper will back you up when you claim for loss of charter or a reduction on the next charter.

Getting additional information

Finding out about charter companies is a difficult job unless you know someone whose opinion you trust who has been on the same holiday you are planning. There are a number of other options, although they all have their pitfalls.

Boat shows enable you to meet staff and ask probing questions about the company and its boats. Many of them run videos of charter holidays and some will let you have a copy if you leave a deposit for its safe return. It lets you meet staff and suss out whether their style and approach is one you like. Before you go, assemble some questions – on paper or in your head – to ask concerning the area and boat you have chosen. The honesty and willingness with which questions are answered may tell you something about the company and its operations.

Magazines, newspapers and television travel shows sometimes run features on yacht charters and, if you read between the lines a bit, you can pick up some information from these. Remember that magazines and newspapers rely on advertisers so it is unlikely an article is going to criticise a yacht charter unless it was seriously flawed.

Yacht clubs and associations sometimes have mini-lectures and slide shows on yacht charter holidays and these can be a good way to find out just what a company is like.

The Internet

There are numerous yacht forums on the Internet which provide frank discussions of areas, companies and boats. Some of the comments and criticism posted to the forums should be interpreted with the proverbial grain of salt as comments are not always representative and someone with a bee in their bonnet can post untrue and one-sided comments about a company or an area. That said, it is possible for anyone to post messages asking questions about a company, an area, a boat or whatever, and get feedback from people who have chartered in an area, with a particular company on a specific boat. The Internet promises the best way of getting the sort of details that might otherwise be unavailable by other means and should be pursued by anyone with access to it.

Most of the Internet sites belong to companies representing themselves and, as such, they are no different to a brochure. There are a lot of related sites. My last search using Sprynet turned up over 34,000 related sites on yacht charter, although many of these are peripheral and, in some cases, there are duplications by the same provider under a different title. If you are doing a search, be specific about what you want or where you want to go.

The following Internet sites provide a starting point although there are others and new sites are coming on-line all the time.

CompuServe
Has its own Sailing Forum with a main group devoted to yacht charter. This has good meaty discussions on all matters relating to yacht charter and you can post a message in the forum.

Yachting and Boating World
@http://www.ybw.com
The web-site for the IPC yachting magazines: *Yachting World, Yachting Monthly, Practical Boat Owner, Motorboat* and *Yachting*. Contains information on yacht charter including destinations and a directory of yacht charter companies.

The Yacht Charter Guide
@ http://www.guides.com
Listing of companies and areas with mostly US slant on things.

Yachting
@ http://www.yachting.co.uk
Selection of bareboat and skippered charters world-wide.

Yacht Charter Center
@ http://www.yacht-charters.com
Crewed charters only.

Bluewater Yacht Charters
@ http://yachtworld.com/
bluewateryachtcharters
Bareboat charters.

Many of the yacht charter companies like Sunsail and the Moorings also have a web site. There are many more and it is a matter of sifting through until you find a good listing or a usable forum.

Yacht charter brokers

A charter broker will rarely be used other than for skippered charter. A reputable broker will not have unsatisfactory boats on his books, will often have been to the area and should have visited the boat and crew. Various big boat shows are organised – such as the Marmaris Boat Show and Antigua Boat Show – where charter boats are on display for brokers and prospective charterers to look them over.

Finally...

To some extent, the choice of boat is determined by the choice of company although it also works in reverse in that the sort of boat you want may determine the company you choose to book with. This chapter refers only to flotilla, bareboat or skippered bareboat charter. Skippered and crewed charter on larger yachts tend to be such a mixture of craft that it is really impossible to give a general idea of the sort of boat to expect. However, the literature for crewed charters should be liberally sprinkled with photographs and descriptions of what you get and, from this, you will have to make a choice.

Choosing a boat

Type of yacht

Flotilla and bareboat yachts, up to around 35ft, are pretty much interchangeable these days. Flotilla companies do not offer craft much over 35ft and, to get on a larger craft, you will be looking at a bareboat charter. Some companies offer a 'cruising in company' formula with bigger yachts where small groups, usually of three to six yachts, cruise around together.

Most charter yachts tend to be stable forgiving craft with few vices. They are not intended to be greyhounds but they are not plodders either. When choosing a boat there will obviously be some differences in performance and characteristics although, for the most part, not a lot. If you want performance then something like a Swan or a Danish X-boat will be quicker than a standard Beneteau Oceanis or Jeanneau.

The two French boat-builders, Beneteau and Jeanneau, dominate the charter yacht market with a range of yachts which can be had as charter versions. The charter version offers more cabins than owner or racing versions and so affords more privacy for charterers. A number of other boat-builders also produce charter yacht versions, but the two French companies have the lion's share of the market and so figure prominently in charter fleets. What that means is that your chances of getting something that goes a bit faster are limited and chances are that you will get a yacht from either Beneteau or Jeanneau. A number of other boat-builders – Moody, Hunter, Feeling, GibSea, Farr, Maxi, Bavaria, Morgan, Pearson, and others – also figure prominently in charter fleets, as do a number of locally produced yachts in various countries which have been designed specifically for the charter market.

Most charter yachts provide more than enough speed and thrills from the standard range available. Most have been designed with charter in mind and have had numerous modifications made for comfort during your holiday. All these comforts – bigger watertanks, biminis, roller-reefing genoas and mainsails, three-bladed propellers and lots of other things – enhance the enjoyment of a charter far too much to worry about how performance has been degraded.

Number of berths

All charter prices are based on the boat, either directly or indirectly. For a bareboat, the price is X amount per week irrespective of how many people will be aboard. For a flotilla boat, the price is per person with a price band that decreases depending on how many will be on the boat (up to the maximum number of berths)

It is a mistake to think that everyone will be able to live comfortably on board if the maximum number of berths are utilised. There will be little privacy, insufficient stowage space, queues for the heads, insufficient water capacity and an overcrowded cockpit when sailing. If cost is the prime concern, and you just can't afford not to fill every berth, then that is the way it has to be. If you can manage it, restricting the number on board will go a long way towards increasing the enjoyment of the holiday for all on board.

It is important to remember that, in hot climates, ventilation is important. Two friendly souls in a small forepeak will be comfortable if there is a windscoop to funnel air down below. In a restricted quarter-berth cabin which does service as a double there will be limited airflow and it can get very close and sticky in hot weather. Small hatches do not let enough air circulate and, the bigger the hatches and the more of them there are in a cabin, the more comfortable your sleeping arrangements will be.

If it is possible to sleep in the cockpit or on deck this can provide some relief from the heat, it can even feel cold at times and, for those who enjoy sleeping under the stars, this is a wonderful option. Check to see if the cockpit berths are long enough or that there is a comfortable space on deck. If there are full-sized cockpit cushions use these or purloin a berth cushion from below.

Equipment

Charter yachts are now much better equipped than in the early days of charter. Most of the refinements and additions to equipment cater to the comfort of those on board, especially in a hot climate. On most flotilla and bareboat yachts you can expect to find the following as standard equipment over and above the standard trim of the yacht:

- roller-reefing genoa
- fold-down swimming ladder on the transom
- windscoop for the front hatch
- basic instrumentation and basic navigation equipment to include charts and a yachtsman's pilot
- VHF radio
- fridge
- masks and snorkels.

Many of the yachts also have the following as standard depending on size:

- roller-reefing mainsail
- bimini
- manual or electric anchor winch
- autopilot
- GPS
- mobile phone
- more extensive instrumentation
- cassette/CD player and radio
- pressurised water system
- transom shower
- transom barbecue
- outboard motor.

Most of the charter companies offer extras at an additional cost. These extras are commonly items that are frequently damaged on charter, such as outboards which get dunked in the sea after a heavy session ashore and cruising chutes or spinnakers which are left up a little too long in a rising wind and come down on the deck shredded. Other extras – like mobile phones, an autopilot and a GPS – are additional to standard equipment on the basic bareboat and are considered to be a 'luxury' of sorts. Some of the larger yachts in some fleets will have some of these extras as standard.

In the charter area in which a yacht operates there must be a certain standard of safety equipment and, depending on the country and the licence, this will include life-jackets, horseshoe buoy(s), a life-float or life raft, fire extinguishers, a first aid kit and flares. It may also include safety harnesses, a Dan-buoy, a more extensive medical kit and additional flares.

For all equipment it is important to realise that the maintenance of gear is crucial given the hard use it gets on charter. There is little point in choosing a boat with an electric anchor winch, roller-reefing mainsail and extensive instrumentation all thrown in at the basic price if none of it works properly. Here,

Moorings Beneteau 405 in the Bahamas.
Photo Yachting World

word of mouth from other charterers who have been with a company before can steer you towards a more basic boat where, at least, everything works properly.

A few questions

When considering what sort of boat to charter it is useful to ask a few questions.

What is the age of the boat?

Some companies now operate a policy whereby boats are banded by age with older boats costing less to charter than newer, better-equipped boats.

What are the maintenance schedules?

A new boat has a hard life on charter and it is important that maintenance of the equipment is carried out every year. In this context an older boat that has been constantly maintained can be a better bet than a one or two year-old boat that has not been properly maintained in the off season. Constant maintenance during the charter season is important if basic things like the engine and batteries are going to be reliable. Unless regular oil changes are made to an engine through the season and a full winterisation programme carried out it will give trouble. Sails should be properly valeted and repaired in the off-season.

Does the company operate a compensation policy for gear that is missing or not working?

A little working around the edges of these questions with a charter company should give you some clues as to how thorough maintenance schedules and practice are.

What spares are available?

Good charter companies should have a fairly extensive store with items that constantly give trouble readily available. Some companies carry a complete spare engine ready to pop into a yacht should there be terminal problems with an existing engine. Spare sails should be stocked. Some stock a spare mast. If there are problems not of your own making can another yacht be made available and what is the company's policy on that?

Is there a company engineer available on call-out?

Some flotillas have an engineer on board the lead boat and other flotilla companies and bareboat operators usually have a shore-based engineer available to deal with any problems. If there is not and local skills are relied upon, try to get some opinions on how well the company has coped with problems in the past.

The yachts

The following are fairly typical of the sort of yachts operated by charter companies on flotilla and bareboat charters. Most of them have been built with charter in mind and most have been extensively modified for charter conditions.

Jeanneau Sun Odyssey 31

A typical small charter boat with two separate double cabins ex saloon. Ideal for one couple and two children or two couples. More than four adults on board pushes the stowage capacity and personal space although there could be room for up to six good friends on board.

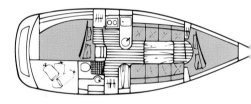

Beneteau Oceanis 350

A popular mid-range boat with three double cabins ex saloon. Good for three couples or two couples and two or three children. Although it can sleep seven to eight it is really only suitable for six adults without becoming unduly cramped.

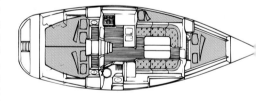

Gib Sea 414

A spacious boat with three double cabins ex saloon. Easily accommodates six adults and could be pushed to eight adults without compromising stowage too much. Good performance boat.

Beneteau Oceanis 440

Has four double cabins ex saloon squeezed in with just about enough stowage for four couples. Wonderful for two couples and two or three children.

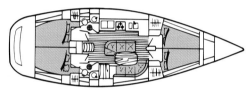

Jeanneau Sun Odyssey 51

Has four double cabins ex saloon and crew's quarters forward. One of the double cabins has two single bunks. Wonderful for three couples and spacious enough for eight adults. Often used as a skippered yacht.

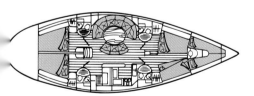

Lagoon 42

One of the more popular catamarans offering shallow draught for coral cruising and spacious accommodation. Four separate double cabins, a spacious saloon and vast cockpit area.

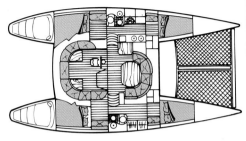

Sunseeker 38

A popular mid-range motor cruiser with two double cabins ex saloon. Has a good-sized saloon with a fold-down double and a good cockpit area.

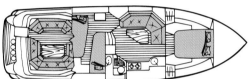

the track record of a charter company says more about it than its *modus operandi* and how it looks on paper or in a brochure, and you should bear this in mind when booking a holiday.

How charter companies work

Things are not always what they seem. The charter company that sells you a sailing holiday can operate in several different ways. Basically, these are as follows.

Owns and operates boats Most of the larger companies own and operate the boats they are selling to you. Most flotilla holidays and some bareboat operators work in this way.

Manages boats The company either leases or contracts to operate the boats for a set period. Although the boats are not owned by the company they will usually employ the staff who run the charter fleet.

Sole agent The company has the exclusive rights to charter the boat for the owner. A large number of companies selling bareboat holidays and also many crewed charter yachts are sold this way.

Agent or broker One of several agents who can sell a flotilla, bareboat or crewed yacht holiday. A broker is pretty much like an insurance broker and will source hard-to-get charters or review charter options. A broker may also be a sole agent.

Small owner-operators Usually advertise in the classified columns and own and operate the boat with friends or family organising the booking of the boat.

Although it all seems very neat dividing the companies up into categories like this, in practice many companies, including some of the large charter companies, are a mixture of several of these categories. The reason for making mention of these categories is that it is useful to know how much control or otherwise a company booking the yacht has over its maintenance and upkeep and how much control over the running of the yacht in the season. It also affects the question of bonding.

It is important to know that an agent, because he or she does not own or manage a yacht, is not necessarily a worse bet than an owner-operator. There are many good agents around who have only the best-run and maintained boats on their books and whose integrity is impeccable. As in all these things,

Bonding

The bonding of a company will influence some choices. In years past the demise of travel companies has left large numbers of people stranded at foreign airports, unable to return home unless they paid for a flight out of their own pocket. The size of a company seems to have little influence on whether it will go under or not, with large companies seemingly as vulnerable as small. Yacht charter companies have hardly been touched by this phenomenon and only a few small companies have gone under leaving clients stranded abroad. Yacht charter companies may have ceased trading or been voluntarily dissolved, but this has rarely had any effect on charterers except to deprive them of a company they enjoyed going on charter with. (It is usually the suppliers to yacht charter companies that have been stung.)

The matter of bonding is a minefield, with outright deception in a few cases and half truths in others. There are a number of bonding schemes which go some way towards guaranteeing a holiday.

ATOL (Air Travel Organisers Licence) Operators who provide flights as part of a package must by law hold an ATOL which means their accounts have been carefully scrutinised and they have placed a bond for their 'licensable' turnover with the Civil Aviation Authority. The ATOL covers any moneys paid to the ATOL holder, whose number must always be shown in any advertising and on invoices, for the flight, together with accommodation, (yacht and/or hotel), and any other items. A 'flight only' must also be covered by an ATOL. It is important that a 'Confirmation Invoice' is received from the ATOL holder within a few days of paying over any money. The

'Confirmation Invoice' is proof of payment and will have to be produced to the Civil Aviation Authority in the event of a claim as a result of the financial failure of the ATOL holder. In such a case the bond money is used to refund you before your holiday, or to repatriate you if the company collapses while you are on holiday. If the bond is insufficient the CAA uses a reserve fund to make up the difference. Holidays which do not include a flight are not covered by an ATOL (see ABTA, AITO, YCA) and come under what is rather misleadingly called 'non-licensable' holidays.

ABTA (Association of British Travel Agents). Is the largest of the travel associations whose members are both tour operators and travel agents. Tour operators providing holidays which do not include a flight e.g. ferry and yacht; yacht and hotel; or yacht only, must provide a bond for this 'non-licensable' turnover. The rules regarding receipt of a 'Confirmation Invoice' as proof of payment for all items are the same as for an ATOL holder, and, as with the ATOL, the bond money is used to refund or repatriate clients in the event of the collapse of the tour operator. ABTA also has a reserve fund in the event of a shortfall.

AITO (Association of Independent Tour Operators). Is an association for the smaller and specialist tour operators. Some tour operators are members of both AITO and ABTA and can choose whether they bond their 'non-licensable' turnover through ABTA or the AITO Trust. The same rules and cover apply to AITO members as for ABTA. Both ABTA and AITO run independent arbitration schemes in the event of a dispute.

ABSC (Association of Bonded Sailing Companies). Includes the bulk of the larger established charter companies representing about 80% of the overseas charter market. The ABSC insists that all its members are ATOL holders and cover their 'non-licensable' turnover with an ABTA, AITO or ABTOT bond. Thus all ABSC members

offer fully bonded holidays in their own right. **YCA** (Yacht Charter Association). Provides a bond for the yacht charter element only for bareboat operators in the UK and for British-based companies selling charter holidays overseas. For flights and 'non-licensable' arrangements other than a yacht YCA members ensure that you are contracted directly with operators covered by the appropriate bonding. The YCA operates a replacement scheme whereby if one member defaults on a boat then another member will step in with a replacement. It also has a code of practice and regulations governing safety equipment on members' yachts.

Other financial protection. The Department of Trade and Industry (DTI) has approved other bonding schemes for 'non-licensable' holidays such as ABTOT, (Association of Bonded Travel Organisers' Trust). Other schemes approved are third party Trust Holding arrangements. These Trust Holding arrangements are the most open to abuse and it is reported that the DTI is considering abolishing them.

How best to protect yourself? If arranging an overseas charter with or without flights, an ABSC member, by the nature of his membership, will automatically cover you for everything without having to worry about the complexities of the licensing system.

For UK and overseas yacht charters a YCA member protects you against failure for the yacht charter. If booking other elements ensure they are properly covered by the 'Confirmation Invoice(s)' you receive. The problem with part bonding, when more than just a yacht is involved, is that it can be open to abuse. There are, however, operators who legitimately act as 'agents' for ATOL holders under a CAA approved agreement, in which case they must clearly state for whom they are agents and issue a receipt for the money received for the flights showing the contact details and number of the ATOL holder. In the event of the failure of either the agent or ATOL holder your money is protected. This receipt will only cover the flight and not the yacht or hotel accommodation, so you have to make sure that the other parts of your holiday are protected too. The key is to look at the 'Confirmation Invoice(s)' you receive to determine with whom you are contracted and what is covered in the event of financial failure. There will always be rogues in the business who illegally purport to use other legitimate tour operators' licences without their knowledge. If in doubt contact the following bodies for clarification:

Civil Aviation Authority
Air Travel Organisers' Licensing
CAA House
45–49 Kingsway
London WC2B 6TE
☎ 0171 832 5260

Association of British Travel Agents
55–57 Newman Street
London WIP 4AH
☎ 0171 637 2444

Association of Independent Tour Operators
133a St Margaret's Road
Twickenham TW1 1RG
☎ 0181 744 9280

In the end your best protection is to go with a company that has a good track record. This is little comfort to the first-time charterer who may have little in the way of personal recommendations or other avenues of checking out how good a company is. Once you have been on charter in an area, it is more than likely that you will encounter yachts from other charter companies and, on this basis, by talking to other charterers and looking over the competitors' yachts, some assessment can be made of how one charter company stacks up against another. If you go with a company that lives up to its promises, and the majority do, stick with it. Most companies rely on repeat bookings and so have every incentive to make sure you book with them again.

Payment and cancellation charges

Payment for a yacht charter holiday is usually along the following lines:

- 25 per cent deposit to secure a booking
- 25 per cent or the balance 90 days prior to departure
- balance if 25 per cent stipulated at 90 days
- travel insurance is taken out from the first booking date.

There are many variations on this but what it basically means is that you pay most of the holiday cost well before departure. While this may seem unreasonable to some, in fact charter companies need to operate like this as it is next to impossible to dispose of

unwanted boats during the season. Unlike land-based holidays where accommodation can be disposed of relatively easily, expensive yachts usually just lie idle if they are not booked.

Cancellation fees are also fairly stiff and it is for this reason that most charter companies insist on travel insurance being taken out when the deposit is paid so you will be covered for cancellation fee losses if they fall within the remit of the insurance policy. The cancellation penalties are usually something like this:

- 90 days prior to departure you lose your deposit, or a smaller cancellation fee may be levied
- 45 days prior to departure you lose 50 per cent of the total holiday cost, or a smaller cancellation fee may be levied
- 15 days prior to departure you lose 75 per cent of the total holiday cost
- less than 15 days, 100 per cent of the holiday cost is forfeit.

Again there are many variations on this and there is some leeway if you are a regular client with the company or if you intend to book again the following year. Some charter companies will waive all penalty payments if you re-book within 30 days of cancellation. Most charter companies go out of their way to accommodate changes in dates and the number of people going without charging swingeing penalties. If they do not try to help you out then think about going to another company. That said, there needs to be reason exercised by both sides and you should not expect to incur no penalty at all for cancellation close to the departure date

Paying by credit card

Paying for your holiday with a credit card means that the credit card company (Visa or MasterCard) is responsible for the debt if a holiday company does not satisfactorily fulfil its contract to you or goes bankrupt and cannot provide for its contracted services at all. Under the Consumer Credit Act you can claim compensation for amounts over £100 from both the charter company and the credit card company. You will not get two settlements but what will happen is that the credit card company will put pressure on the charter company or the insurance company to settle your claim quickly. In the absence of a quick settlement it may make a temporary credit to your account until it is settled by other means or it will front up with the money itself. This does not apply to charge cards like American Express or Diners Club.

To claim from a credit card company:

- write a letter of complaint to the company or make a claim to the insurance company. Send a copy of the letter to the credit card company with a covering letter telling it you are holding it jointly liable with the charter or insurance company
- if no action is forthcoming from the charter or insurance company, write asking for a settlement from the credit card company
- keep copies of all correspondence and, in the last instance, take the charter company to arbitration and complain to the banking ombudsman about the credit card company. In most instances the credit card company will act responsibly.

Given the additional protection under the Consumer Credit Act that paying by credit card gives it is well worth paying for your whole holiday in this way.

Booking flights

Most companies booking a bareboat or skippered charter for you can also book flights. Most of the companies know where to get the best deals on flights at the time of year you are going but, in case they do not, take some time to look around yourself.

Basically there are three avenues open to you when booking flights.

Full-fare flights These can be booked at any travel agent or by phone and offer the most flexibility. Dates can be changed with a small re-booking charge.

APEX fares These are basically the same seats as full-fare economy-class but must be booked at least two weeks prior to departure. They offer significant savings (often 50 per cent or more) over the full fare economy ticket but are totally inflexible. You must travel on the specified flight at the specified time. They are low-risk tickets and, as long as the ticket issuer is a member of ABTA, they are guaranteed (with the sole exception of the airline itself going out of business). The latter is unlikely for most established airlines.

Charter flights. These are the cheapest flights going and can often be 60–70 per cent cheaper than the standard full fare. They are non-refundable and cannot be changed. They are covered by the ATOL bond as long as you buy them from a company that has an ATOL number and, as such, are comparatively low-risk.

Buying tickets at cut-rate prices from bucket shops used to carry some risk but, these days, most of that risk has been eliminated by the bonding requirements. For APEX tickets you are covered when buying from ABTA members. For charter flights you are covered by ATOL members.

Sourcing these tickets is a matter of wandering along the local high street to a travel agent, browsing the columns of the papers – particularly the Sunday papers – or using Teletext or the Internet. A few phone calls will soon sort out what the base price is. Obviously, at busy times of the year, it pays to book well in advance. In the low season you can leave it nearer to the departure date in the hope of picking up a cheaper flight, although this runs the risk of missing the connection with the yacht. It is all really a matter of gauging availability of flights and figuring out how close to the departure date you can afford to leave it before booking.

Insurance

Many of the larger yacht charter companies make it mandatory for customers to take out travel insurance when you put a deposit on a yacht charter package which includes flights and a charter yacht. These policies normally cover you for the usual range of things including the following.

Medical expenses At least £250,000–£500,000 in Europe and at least £1–1·5 million elsewhere.

Air ambulance cost Around £500,000 in Europe and £1 million in the USA

Personal liability (third-party) cover of £1–1.5 million except for the USA where it should be £2–3 million.

Baggage loss Normally £1000–£2000. Check on the upper limit for individual items which is usually £150–200. For more valuable items like cameras, camcorders and jewellery you may have to pay an additional fee. Excess of £50–75.

Money Usually around £500–750 with a limit of £200–300 for cash. Excess of £50–75.

Cancellation Up to £3000 for cancellation because of illness, death, quarantine, or redundancy. Excess of £50–100.

Travel delay £10–30 for each 10–12 hour period normal. Maximum of £200–300.

Missed departure Normally £500–750 when caused by failure of connecting transport (car breakdown, cancelled trains, etc).

Personal accident Up to £25,000–50,000 for loss of limb, eye, etc. Payouts normally limited by a formula – e.g. eye, around £1,500–2,000; death £5,000–75,000, depending on insurer.

Legal expenses Up to £25,000–30,000.

Most insurers have exemptions for sports like sub-aqua diving, hang-gliding, water-skiing and similar although not for sailing as long as you are not racing. An additional premium will cover you for some of these.

For those over 70 years old there may be additional premiums and some restrictions on cover.

Some credit card holders (usually gold card holders) get travel insurance automatically when they use the card to pay for the holiday, but this is generally not comprehensive cover and may not cover loss of baggage, money, cameras, etc. while on the charter or may provide only limited cover.

It makes good sense to have this policy right from the beginning when you put a deposit on the holiday so that you can reclaim cancellation charges made by the charter company should the reasons for cancellation fall within the insurer's clauses. It is also essential to have alternative comprehensive travel insurance should any misfortune overtake you during the holiday.

Security deposits

All charter companies ask for a security deposit. The amount varies depending on the size and value of the yacht, the equipment on board, and the duration of the charter. The actual amounts and method of payment vary as follows:

- a security deposit in cash or traveller's cheques deposited at the charter base where you pick up the boat. Commonly varies from around £500 ($750) to as much as £1500 ($2000–2500).
- a security deposit in either cash, traveller's cheques or a blank credit card or charge card slip signed by the charterer and deposited with the charter company with which you booked the boat.
- a non-refundable insurance premium paid to the charter company with which you booked the boat.

By far the best option is to pay the non-refundable insurance premium. This covers every contingency including major damage or total loss of yacht equipment which can easily exceed the total of a cash or other security deposit. It is also one less thing to worry about at the end of your holiday.

Security deposits in cash, traveller's cheques or a blank credit or charge card form will normally be redeemed at the end of the yacht charter once the yacht and inventory have been inspected by the charter base staff. Most companies do not make deductions for minor breakages or losses such as cutlery and crockery, the odd fender, a winch handle, boat hook or similar. Deductions will be made for damage to the hull, stanchions and lifelines, sails, shaft and propeller, and for major losses like the dinghy, outboard motor, life raft, anchor(s) and chain, warps, sun awning, etc.

Problems arise mostly from assessments of damage by the charter base staff. Damage to yachts, even when it appears minor, costs a good deal more to repair than most customers think. This is especially so in some overseas destinations where the materials for a repair, gel coat, sail repair materials, spare parts, must be imported to carry out the repair. Gel coat repairs take a lot of time and effort to make as anyone who has ever carried them out knows. What may appear to be a minor scrape to a customer can be a headache to repair in time for the next charter. A bent stanchion may have cracked the gel coat around the stanchion base. A rope around a propeller can bend the shaft and damage engine mounts. A torn sail may be unusable again.

Most charter companies are fair about assessments for damage to a yacht. However there are cowboys around who have kept the whole security deposit without good cause. The problem for the charterer is how to get his/her money back. If it is lodged at a charter base overseas there are really no avenues open to you. Talk to the company with which you booked the charter. Take photographs and make a report on the damage before you leave the boat. Try to get an independent assessment of the cost of repairing the damage before you leave the boat. In the end it really boils down to your word against that of the person from the charter base who made the assessment.

If you have a security deposit lodged with a charter company in the country in which you live then take your evidence there if a deduction is made which you believe to be unreasonable. If you think your case is strong enough and you get no satisfaction from the company then you can start proceedings against them. This really is a last resort as it is not only costly but, even if you have a judgement against a company, you still have to extract the money from them.

The moral is clear. Paying an insurance premium instead of putting up cash or some other deposit is by far the preferable method of making a security deposit. Failing that, leave the security deposit with the company in your own country. The last option is to leave it with the charter base where you pick up the yacht. In truth, a very small number of problems arise over security deposits given the number of people who go on yacht charters.

While the charter company must act in a responsible manner when it comes to security deposits, so must the charterer. If it decides that a charterer has acted in a wilful manner to damage a yacht, the company can take the customer to court for the full amount of damages whether the security deposit is in the form of an insurance premium or by cash, cheque, or credit card deposit. If the damage has been caused while the charterer was under the influence of alcohol or drugs it is likely that action will be taken to redeem monies for the damage.

Complaints

Most of the larger companies have an established complaints procedure should you feel that there were problems with the boat or the organisation of the charter. If you have a complaint, the following advice will help you to get redress:

- before you leave make a written report of problems with the boat or the conduct of staff. For boat problems take photographs if possible
- get an independent assessment on the spot if possible
- give a copy of the report to the charter base staff and inform them you are going to make a complaint
- as soon as you arrive back from your holiday, send a copy of the report to the charter company.

Most of the large charter companies arrange for an independent arbitration body to look at your complaint if they decide not to settle outright.

Some smaller yacht charter companies who belong to ABTA or AITO will similarly arrange for independent arbitration. If the charter company is a member of YCA you have recourse to a mediation service provided by the YCA. If the arbitration process fails you still have recourse to the law and can take the company to court. The latter should be avoided if possible as it is a lengthy and costly exercise.

Compensation

What do you do when you arrive if the boat is not available or is unsafe or unusable? What do you do if the boat becomes unusable during the charter for reasons which have nothing to do with you?

Most of the established companies now spell out unequivocally in their brochures and booking terms what your redress is should a boat be unavailable, in unsafe condition or should it be out of commission for a certain period during the charter. The fact that companies are prepared to make these promises effectively means that they will do their utmost to avoid getting into this situation. Most compensation clauses are along the following lines.

- The company will find an equivalent or larger yacht for your charter holiday should the exact yacht you booked be unavailable.
- Should a yacht be out of commission for more than a day the company will credit you with extra sailing days, give you a credit for another sailing holiday with them, or make a cash refund to you. The details vary from company to company and in some cases compensation will be made for the yacht being out of commission for as little as four hours. Some companies will give you two free sailing days for each day you lose while others award compensation on a day for day basis. All of these compensation clauses will be clearly‚ stated in the brochure.

There are also exception clauses which will rule out compensation. Compensation will not be paid for those not sailing in the defined charter area, or anchoring where they have specifically been told not to by the charter base staff, and those not taking due care with the charter yacht under their command.

Should a yacht be considered unseaworthy by a charterer then the procedure outlined under 'Complaints' above should be followed if it cannot be sorted out at the charter base. If you can sort it out, this is by far the best thing to do as getting redress can be difficult afterwards.

For companies that do not spell out compensation clauses in their brochures or booking conditions, you will have to negotiate on the ground, or when you get back, over compensation for unsuitable substitute yachts or a yacht being out of commission for reasons beyond your control. Make sure you obtain any promises in writing from the charter staff or the company itself. If you get no satisfaction then make a complaint with adequate documentation as outlined above.

Most companies want to avoid any unpleasantness and many of them go way beyond the call of duty to arrange a substitute yacht or effect repairs to a yacht out of commission. Remember that it can be difficult in some out-of-the-way cruising areas to find the spares or skills to make repairs and there should be consideration on both sides. If the charter base staff are doing all in their power to get you on your way again then be reasonable about compensation claims.

There are also some difficult souls in this world who believe they should get compensation for just about anything they care to open their mouths about. Because there were not the number of sunshine hours stated in the brochure. Because they were kept in port with an unseasonable summer gale. Because a reef they hit was not adequately marked on the chart they had been provided with. Needless to say these sort of claims can be safely ignored by a charter company.

Legal considerations

The legal status of charter varies from country to country and, in a good number of countries, no distinction is made under law between yacht charter and big ship charter. This is an entirely different matter to your agreement with the charter company. It is impossible to untangle the ramifications of the legalities involved with yacht charter in different countries in a few paragraphs, but in general, the following points should be borne in mind. Most of the following applies to bareboat charter and not to skippered charter where the skipper/owner is responsible for the boat. Flotilla sailing can be assumed to fall under the bareboat category for these legal points as well.

The charterer is considered to be responsible for the operation and safety of the vessel and its crew and other people on board. This means that others in the party or an insurer can sue the charterer of the vessel for injury, material loss, and so on.

The charterer must ensure that the vessel remains fit and safe under the regulations of the country chartered in. He/she will be liable for any damage or the loss of the craft if it is illegally modified in any way. An example of this may be over-tightening the standing rigging causing loss of the mast or vessel.

The skipper/master may be held accountable for the safe operation of the vessel and will be responsible for any damage or death caused by failure to operate safely. This usually means third-party actions.

A charterer may not use the vessel for illegal purposes such as carrying drugs, contraband, or aliens within a country.

In a number of countries, the charter agreement specifically names those in the charter party and this may not be added to on an ad hoc basis.

The skipper/master will be at all times governed by the maritime law of the country and is responsible for enforcing it. One example is that the skipper is responsible for illegal spills and discharges (for example from toilets, holding tanks, diesel tanks etc) and any penalties must be paid by him or her. Another example is damage or injury caused by leaving port in weather considered by the port captain or other authorities to be unsuitable for the vessel.

A bareboat can be seized by the authorities and will be forfeit for illegal activities even though it is chartered and the owner is not on board.

In practice, this muddled area of legal points will not affect the majority of yacht charterers, but it needs to be mentioned. It is also worthwhile to check up on how much legal cover your insurance provides for.

Planning a cruise

Talking to the others

It is important when you sit down with those who are going on charter with you that you consult them about their needs, wants, preferences and dislikes and it is important that these are built into an itinerary and not over-ruled by you. Remember what happened to Bligh.

The following suggestions for involving family and/or friends will enhance not only the enjoyment of those who go with you, but your own enjoyment as well. The pleasure principle is all-important here.

If possible, some other member of the crew should know the rudiments of how to sail and handle a boat under power. Like teaching a person to drive a car, this tuition is best administered by someone else. There are numerous one-day or weekend courses run

by sailing schools to teach the rudiments of sailing and boat-handling and some of the larger companies offer courses specifically aimed at new flotilla or bareboat charterers, often on the same sort of boat that will be chartered on the holiday. Sending your wife or friend off on a course may appear indulgent, but the likelihood is that they will learn more, with less stress, without you around on one of these courses, and they will receive a boost to their self-confidence as well. There is also the safety angle to be considered in all this. It is important that one other person on the boat knows the rudiments of how to sail and how to start the engine and handle the boat in case you, the skipper, fall overboard or are incapacitated in some way.

Everyone going on the charter should, if possible, be involved in the planning of a cruise. Buy a chart that covers the area, pilot or travel guides, and let everyone put something into the cruise. Planning routes and stops is half the fun and in the end you – with your Captain Bligh hat on – can intercede with sage advice on unsafe anchorages and sticky navigation problems that mitigate against some of the choices made.

Now if we head on 185° that should clear Deadman's Reef and then....
Photo Yachting World

When planning the cruise, ensure that there are sufficient lay-days so that you and the crew can lie around doing not a lot except swimming, reading, sitting in bars or whatever. This is especially important if young children are part of the party as they will get a good deal of their enjoyment from messing about swimming, snorkelling, playing on the beach and in the dinghy, fishing and collecting marine fauna and flora when the boat is at anchor or berthed in a harbour. Lay-days should also be built in for visits to interesting sites or for the simple joys of shopping for curios and trinkets.

On a bareboat charter make sure that you allot plenty of time to getting the boat back to the charter base. Lots of bareboat holidays are ruined by the last couple of days because too little time has been left to cover a lot of distance and the boat must be thrashed back against the prevailing winds. Talk to staff at the charter base and consult the pilot guides when working out a cruise. The last thing you want at the end of a relaxing cruise is to get stressed out by a tight timetable.

Charts and guides

Although charter companies provide all the charts you need on board, it is still worthwhile buying a chart or perhaps two of the area you will be chartering in so that you can more easily plan the cruise. It will also acquaint you with the area so it is not all frighteningly new when you arrive. Charts for all the areas are fairly easily found at any large chandlers or in many cases the charter company you book with will be able to suggest a source or may even supply the charts themselves.

For most the popular charter areas there are sailing pilots or guidebooks available. Again the charter company will be able to help you out or refer to the relevant world charter area section of this book where a list of the popular guides will be found. Admiralty pilots to areas not covered by yachtsman's pilots are pretty hard going for cruise planning purposes and it is best to ask the charter company if they have any material you can use for that purpose.

It is also worth buying a general guide book for your charter destination so that some planning for land-based trips can be

'I think its around the tree and into the hole ...'
Photo Pat Collinge

PLANNING A CRUISE

carried out. There are general guidebooks to all charter destinations with very few exceptions. Try the Rough Guides, Lonely Planet series, Footprint Handbooks, or Collins Independent Traveller series. These or other popular series are not necessarily the best guides, but give you a head start in the absence of detailed knowledge of the literature covering a country.

Children

At what age children go on a yacht charter is a question for parents to decide as they are the ones who must look after their needs. For popular destinations like the Mediterranean and the Caribbean, babies of less than a year old have been taken on charter and appear none the worse for the experience. In rough weather they seem to cope better than their parents. To some extent it depends on the destination as to whether very young children should be part of the party. Does it make sense to take a young child to an exotic destination when it hardly knows if you are in the Mediterranean or the Caribbean? In the Tropics the heat and humidity, not to mention the mosquitoes and tummy upsets can make a small child's life intolerable. Really it is up to the parents to decide if the enjoyment they get out of an exotic destination is worth the aggro of having unhappy children around them.

Older children may also find that going on a yacht charter holiday with their parents is more of a chore than the exciting adventure their parents have told them about. I find that parents too easily deceive themselves about the enjoyment their children are having on a yacht. Talk to the parents and they will tell you the children are loving every minute of it, even when Jamie was sick and little Laura covered in a heat rash. Talk to the children away from the parents and they may tell you it's the pits and they would rather be at home playing computer games. If a decision is made to take them time must be built into the holiday for them to do their own thing. Methods of keeping them occupied and happy should be devised beforehand and any props for keeping them that way taken with you. Don't expect them to like doing the things you like doing on holiday and make sure plenty of time is allotted to stopping over in places they enjoy.

For children who like sailing, swimming, fishing, indeed anything to do with the water, a yacht charter holiday can be one of the most exciting things they experience. Think about a flotilla holiday even if your heart is set on bareboat. It is likely that there will be other children around of similar age or disposition and some flotilla leaders are wonderful at organising activities to keep them happy. On some of the shore-based watersports holidays trained staff are employed to look after children and keep them busy while parents are off in yachts, dinghies, sail-boards or just sitting around spinning yarns. Some companies split the children into groups, with different activities for different age groups, and it is worth thinking about this sort of watersports holiday if you are taking children along. Often it is possible to split a sailing holiday 50/50 between a land-based watersports holiday and a sailing yacht and, in this way, parents and children get equal enjoyment from the overall holiday.

Documents and money

Whatever documents you need should be planned well in advance. Anyone in the group who doesn't have a passport, or whose passport is due to expire soon, should get a valid passport. Children may need to be added to your passport or to get one of their own. Any visas you need should not be left until the last minute. For some countries it may take up to two weeks to get a visa after application and, at busy times, it can take longer. If you have convictions for a number of offences (including any that are drugs-related) you may find that it either takes longer to get a visa or, in some cases, you may be refused one outright. In the World Charter Areas in Part II there is a section dealing with documentation, including visas. EU nationals should remember that, although they can travel freely through EU countries, they are still required to have either a passport or identity card for all other countries.

Additional documentation, such as a certificate of competence showing you can skipper a yacht or that you are a competent crew, is needed in some countries and if you are going on a course then get it all over and done with well before departure. Most charter companies will furnish you with a certificate of some description to support your competence to handle a yacht, if they are satisfied you are competent, and these certificates are often rather more impressive than the 'real thing'.

Most charter companies can give you some idea of how much money you will need on the holiday although your spending habits may be more or less than the norm. Also in the world charter areas section, there is some advice on the relative cost of destinations, although this information is subject to variations from year to year depending on the economy of the country you are going to and the sort of places you visit. If you insist on being in a marina or harbour every night and eating out ashore in the best restaurants with lots of imported alcoholic beverages then the amount of money you need will escalate dramatically. If you anchor in a bay for some of the time and cook on board and drink the local hooch then costs plummet.

The form in which you should take your money depends on the destination. There are few countries now where you cannot get cash out of an ATM (hole-in-the-wall machine) with a credit card (Visa or MasterCard) and few countries where at least some of the restaurants and shops will not take a credit card in payment. For this reason, at least one member of the group should have a credit card in case it is needed. One of the advantages of using a credit card to get cash is that you will be billed at the rate of exchange several days later in the country where your credit card was issued. A service charge is made by the credit card supplier, usually around 1·5 per cent, but overall this method of obtaining money is as cheap as any other and has the advantage of flexibility. Take at least some cash and traveller's cheques with you. American dollars are universal currency and are the best form of cash to take. Similarly take traveller's cheques in American dollars as these will be popular in most countries. For Mediterranean countries cash or traveller's cheques in British pounds (£GBP) or German Deutschmarks (DM) are quite OK and will be accepted everywhere.

What to pack

Clothes

Most people take too much and the old maxim for back-packing applies equally to sailing: pack your bag with the bare minimum and then take it all out and halve it. It saves you taking all sorts of useless clothes you will never wear and cuts down the risk of ending up with a hernia from lugging it all about. For most destinations, like the Mediterranean and the Caribbean, you will be wearing very little most of the time. When sailing, a swimsuit is the normal attire or, at most, shorts and T-shirt. You will want a few shore-going clothes but not a change of outfit for every occasion. Among the things you should pack are the following:

- a swimsuit or two, towel(s), several T-shirts, several pairs of shorts, a couple of sweatshirts or light pullovers and light cotton underwear. Remember you are more than likely to buy a couple of souvenir T-shirts while you are on holiday and quite often some other light clothes of one description or another
- a wide-brimmed hat or two – with ties. The peaked visors that tennis players used to wear are also useful as they do not restrict peripheral vision as much as a hat
- a neck scarf to keep the sun off your neck
- a light cotton long-sleeved shirt and light cotton long trousers for protection from the sun in the first few days
- a light anorak or wet-weather jacket for hot climates and heavier wet-weather gear for less temperate destinations. Few charter destinations require anything like full wet-weather gear and, if they do, the charter company will advise you on the matter
- sailing shoes and some tough form of footwear for walking around rocks and coral
- loose clothing for the flight to and from the charter destination.

Everything should be packed into soft sailing bags that can be easily stowed once you have unpacked on board. There is no room to stow suitcases on board a yacht and no rigid bags should be taken.

Jewellery and valuables

Jewellery – such as rings, gold chains and bracelets, expensive watches, and any other bodily adornments – should be left at home. This is not because you are likely to be mugged, but because they are dangerous on a yacht and liable to be lost. If a rope or part of the boat gets entangled with items of personal jewellery it can be dangerous. Fingers have been lost because a ring snagged on the anchor chain, or injured because the ring hooked on to wood trim. Likewise hands and necks can be injured if a chain gets snagged by a rope or a bit of the boat. These are not hypothetical examples.

Apart from doing damage to yourself, there is always the possibility of losing jewellery overboard. Watches get flicked off by anchor chains and sheets, rings get misplaced and disappear into the bilges, chains are whipped off by winch handles, all irretrievably to the depths of the sea or the bilges. Other valuables just disappear when the dinghy inadvertently capsizes on the way back from the barbecue. Unless you can see where the item has come to rest, the chances of working out where it has landed on a sandy, weedy, mottled and variegated bottom, in crystal-clear water, even if you can free-dive that far down, is very low.

Most items will be covered by the insurance you have taken out, but the insurance doesn't cover the attachment to personal jewellery that was given to you by a husband, wife or lover. Better to leave those bits of sentiment at home where you can safely reclaim them when you get back.

Protection from sun and sea

In Australia the catchy 'slip, slop, slap' – slip on a shirt, slop on sun protection cream, and slap on a hat – cannot be bettered for encapsulating what you need for protection from the sun. Out on the water the reflected sunshine greatly increases the risk of sunburn and sun-damaged skin. Make sure hats, sun-block cream of at least factor 15, 20 or 30 (the systems seem to vary), and light shirts are taken for everyone in the group. Do not rely solely on sun block cream which, while it cuts down on harmful rays reaching the skin, does not eliminate them and, even with waterproof varieties, still gets washed off to some extent. If you are snorkelling make sure you wear a T-shirt, at least part of the time, as it is easy to underestimate the amount of

When snorkeling it is a good idea to wear a
T-shirt so your back doesn't get burnt. Pack a few
extra or buy some when you get to the charter
destination. *Photo* Yachting World

WHAT TO PACK

sun reaching your body when it is partially
cooled by the sea. If you have very fair skin,
take a pair of loose long trousers to keep the
sun off. And don't forget to take lots of
moisturising cream for apres-sun application.

Wind and sea can also take their toll. Fair-
skinned souls should take along a scarf or
bandana to stop wind-burn when beating to
windward. Spray and wind can soon set your
cheeks burning and cause tender lips to chap.
Take along lots of lip salve to keep those lips
tender and moisturising cream for glowing
cheeks.

In most of the warmer charter areas no
waterproof gear is required for short day-
sailing legs or, at most, just a light anorak or
jacket. However, if you are going to be sailing
at night, it is surprising how cool it can be –
even in the Mediterranean or the Caribbean
– once a bit of spray has come aboard. The
further away you are from the equator, the
more likely it will be that wet-weather gear is
required. Check with the charter company
and consult the temperature tables in the
relevant world charter areas section, always
remembering that these are averages.

Navigator's kit

While flotilla and bareboat yachts will be
equipped to a certain level, it can be useful to
bring along a few items of your own.

As I have mentioned previously, it is useful
to buy a chart or two and a yachtsman's pilot
so that you can familiarise yourself with an
area. Bring these along as, while charts are
always provided, they can sometimes be a bit
scrappy and may not be of the type you are
used to. Yachtsman's pilots on board can be
old editions or they may be sheets cobbled
together by a company.

If you have useful portable items – a
portable GPS is probably the most useful –
then bring them as well. Most flotilla and
smaller bareboat yachts do not yet have GPS
fitted and really do not need them. Even if a
GPS is fitted you will be familiar with the
operating system on your own portable GPS
and this will save time and effort getting to
grips with some other operating system. With
a bit of planning you can have a number of
useful waypoints plugged in beforehand for
use on the holiday. Remember that chart

datums can vary and, importantly, that the accuracy of charts varies greatly in different areas. A lot of modern metricated charts are still, in truth, old 19th-century surveys.

A hand-bearing compass can be useful to have along as some of those provided by charter companies are not the best units around. Other useful items you might think about bringing are a pair of binoculars and silly little things like a couple of pencils and a rubber. The latter always seem to go missing from chart tables.

One item which you may think does not strictly fall into the category of an aid to navigation is a good pair of *Polaroid* sunglasses, and I mean *Polaroid* not UV-resistant, photochromatic or whatever else manufacturers of sunglasses like to call them. Polaroid lenses allow light through on one plane only and, by cutting down on the reflected light off the water, allow you to pick up shallow patches, rocks, coral reefs or anything under the water with a good deal more clarity than other sunglasses. It can be one of the most important aids to navigation you have when eye-balling through a tricky channel or close to dangers to navigation.

Camera and camcorders

On any charter boat it is unusual if there is not one camera around – chances are that there will be several. If you have a full-blown 35mm SLR camera and a bag full of lenses then my advice is to leave it at home. Unless you are a dedicated amateur, the bother of lugging a bulging camera bag around will wear thin after a while. Better to purchase a compact 35mm camera that fits into your pocket and is not obtrusive. If you are thinking about purchasing a camera then there are numerous small compacts on the market which produce excellent results.

Weatherproof, waterproof cameras are somewhat more expensive than the basic camera they are derived from. On holiday you rarely need anything more than a weatherproof camera if you are going to be out taking pictures with spray coming on board or for beach shots. Waterproof cameras usually offer only a wide-angle lens, which is limiting for anything other than on-board shots and, of course, underwater pictures. If you really want to take some underwater pictures I think you are better off buying one or two throwaway cameras which now come in waterproof versions, usable down to 3–4 metres. For above-water

pictures, stick to a normal compact or, at most, a weatherproof version.

Camcorders are a bit of a bother to take on holiday, mostly because they are bulky affairs compared to most cameras especially when you add in the power supply, spare batteries and tapes. You will need at least one spare battery with you and however many tapes you think you are going to need. The main problem you will have is recharging the batteries. Ask the charter company if there is a cigarette-lighter plug on the boat (some charter companies fit them so that clients can recharge portable phones, camcorder batteries, laptops and the like) and, if there is, buy or borrow an adapter for charging batteries this way. Failing that, buy an adapter plug so that you can inveigle someone ashore to charge the batteries for you. If you eat ashore at a restaurant, for example, ask one of the staff if you can plug in the charger and remember to leave a good tip for their benevolence in letting you do so. A couple of fully charged batteries will give you a pretty good run until you find somewhere to recharge them but, once a battery is flat, take the first offer to recharge it that comes along.

Camcorders are particularly susceptible to a salty atmosphere and especially to salt-water damage. You need to be careful about when you use them and keep them out of the way of any spray coming on board. You could try wrapping the camera in a clear plastic bag with a rubber band around the lens or investigate one of the ready-made plastic weatherproof camcorder bags sold in some camera shops and chandlers. Take some care over how and where you film. I recall one client who stepped backwards off the transom while filming and ended up with a wonderful sequence of the sky arcing overhead followed by bubbles and watery shots. The camcorder didn't care for the experience and ground to a corroded halt not long after its immersion.

Music

Many charter yachts are now equipped with cassette players and, in some cases, CD players. Take a small selection of your favourite music to accompany ghosting along, beating hard to windward, romping downwind and sitting quietly at anchor.

If there is one thing you don't need to do, it is to inflict on your neighbours, or the natives, your own taste in music at volume.

While it may enhance the quality of your enjoyment to listen to Verdi or heavy metal at 100 decibels, it will certainly not enhance the enjoyment of anyone else around you. Noise pollution is to be avoided as much as any other sort of pollution. Take your personal stereo (Walkman) if you want to hear that deafening crescendo at full volume while you watch the sun go down – but don't spoil the sunset for others.

Essential treats

In most parts of the world you can find, if not the exact 'can't live without' nibbles, spreads, sauces or breakfast cereal, then at least a passable substitute. If you really feel you have to take along a certain brand of sauce, a certain textured cereal or only brand X peanut butter, do so. My advice is that you should not need to take anything if you exercise a little flexibility when shopping. Moreover you will discover all sorts of wonderful home-grown treats in the country in which you are travelling. Part of the joy of going to another country is discovering its food. Charcoal-grilled sweetcorn in Greece, dried fruit and nuts in Turkey, fresh pineapple in Thailand, Italian ice cream, *pomplemousse* in Tahiti, melon and rum punch in the Caribbean . . . all sound better to me than crisps and a can of cola. If they don't sound good to you, pack what you need.

The exception to this is foodstuffs for those with special dietary needs. Diabetics, those with a wide range of allergies and anyone on a strict diet regime for whatever reason should bring along a small selection of foodstuffs that they can dip into if necessary. Vegetarians will have few problems in most countries. Vegans should not find things too difficult in hot climates where few dairy products are used, but neither should they expect their dietary needs to be commonly understood.

In the alcoholic beverage line you should need little other than a bottle of your own choice of duty-free. Nearly everywhere, you will find mixers for your own particular potion and, besides, there is the local hooch. In Greece there is *ouzo*, in the Caribbean rum, in France excellent wines at bargain prices, in Thailand local whisky which is passable with soda or another mixer. In most countries there will be a lager-type beer which is always quaffable and often very good. Experiment with the local beverages and you may be surprised at how well they slip down, even if you are none the wiser in the morning.

Miscellaneous checklist

Spectacles and contact lenses If you wear spectacles take a spare pair. There is nothing worse than being blind for part of a holiday because you misplaced your specs, sat on them in the cockpit or dropped them overboard. To avoid the latter, get a spectacle chain or, in the spirit of the holiday, one of those brightly coloured stretch bands that slip over the ends to hold them securely on your head. Contact lenses have a magical way of disappearing during high-spirited barbecues so take spares and all the kit you need for cleaning them.

Fishing equipment If you like to go fishing don't bother to take a rod. It is bulky and awkward to carry and, for trolling, you won't really need it. Take just the reel if you are keen plus a couple of stainless jubilee clips to attach it to the pushpit rail. Otherwise a hand-line is sufficient. *Rapallo* lures, made in Finland, are the favoured brand for trolling, but if you are into fishing you will no doubt have your own favourite. In tropical waters take a stainless wire trace or bigger fish will just bite the lure off.

Linen Most charter companies will supply everything you need in the way of linen, duvets or sleeping bags and pillows. For some home-waters charter, a few small operators will want you to supply these. Check with the charter company to see if this is so.

Miscellaneous A small flashlight of the *Mag-Lite* variety is useful for getting back to the boat at night, as is a boat penknife or bosun's kit if you want to feel nautical.

Safety equipment

All charter companies must have a certain level of safety equipment on board according to the regulations of the country in which they operate. In most countries this level of equipment varies according to the stated use of the boat: usually how many miles it is permitted to go from the coast, the number of berths, and the type of charter (with some exceptions made for small flotilla yachts over bareboat and skippered charter).

Most charter yachts will have the bare minimum, as follows. (The maximum number of people on board a yacht is usually determined by reference to the number of berths on the yacht, though not in every case.)

Life-jackets for the maximum number on board. Some countries stipulate an additional one or two life-jackets. Children's life-jackets may or may not be part of the regulations, but most charter companies will supply them anyway. Check with the charter company and take along your own if unsure. This may be a good idea anyway if you have a life-jacket with integral harness for a toddler.

Life harness Varies from country to country and often the specification is for two or three harnesses on a yacht, depending on its size. There will often be insufficient harness points around the yacht and jackstays are not common. In truth there are few destinations where you will need a harness, but check with the charter company and take along your own if worried.

Safety flares All countries specify a minimum number of in-date authorised safety flares.

Life-buoy All countries specify a life-buoy and, in some cases, two. A lifebuoy light is also usually specified. Dan-buoys are specified only in some countries.

Certified life raft Most countries specify a life raft for the maximum number on board. In some countries a life-float capable of supporting the maximum number of people on board may be specified for yachts under 30ft or so which have a limited range from the coast.

VHF radio Just about all countries specify a VHF radio and, even if not specified, it is more than likely one will be fitted.

Certified fire extinguishers depending on the size of the boat.

Safety harnesses should be part of the yacht's inventory. It's rare but you may need one as here in New Zealand. *Photo* Yachting World

In all charter destinations there are fairly rigid safety-equipment specifications and an annual check on equipment, plus spot checks in some countries. On the whole, charter companies are concerned about safety on board and this is reflected in the small number of accidents that have occurred in the last 30 years. Many that have occurred have been through negligence on the part of the charterer and not through safety-equipment failure.

Most accidents on charter boats have involved fire. Anyone who has attempted to use a fire extinguisher on a fire will know just how pathetic they are. If possible try to smother a fire on board either with a fire blanket if provided or with anything like a blanket, duvet or coat – whatever can be grabbed quickly. Depriving a fire of oxygen is the best way of putting it out. Check if your charter yacht has a fire blanket and, if not, suggest to the company that, for a modest investment, it can save lives. Safety precautions over gas and petrol stowage should be rigorous. Keep cigarettes out of range when changing gas bottles or filling an outboard and always turn the gas off at the regulator when you have finished using it. Do remember that the number of incidents of fire is relatively low and probably no higher than for privately owned yachts.

A number of incidents on charter holidays have occurred while someone is swimming or snorkelling. Always keep an eye on anyone, particularly children, in the water – not just in case they get into difficulties, but also to ensure that morons on waterbikes or dinghies with outboards do not stray too close to them. A waterbike can knock out a person and outboard propellers cause horrendous injuries; in some instances death has resulted from the injuries inflicted. There always seems to be an element of the macho involved with waterbikes and inflatables with outboards, and macho is no use unless others can see it. Hence the need for these benighted souls to rush around yachts at anchor displaying their macho egos and not only inflicting noise pollution on others, but also endangering those swimming in the water.

Vaccinations

For many charter destinations, no vaccinations are required over and above ensuring that tetanus and polio jabs are up to date. Tetanus and polio vaccinations last ten years, so you need to be within this period until the end of your holiday. For other areas, particularly tropical environments – such as some of the Pacific islands, Thailand and parts of the Caribbean – some additional vaccinations may be necessary.

Hepatitis A is only a moderate risk but Hepatitis B is on the increase. The latter is only transmitted by sexual contact or contaminated blood. For Hepatitis A, gammaglobulin is not now widely used and the only effective vaccination is the new Hepatitis A (Havrix) vaccine. Havrix can be given in conjunction with other vaccinations.

Japanese encephalitis is on the increase in a few tropical areas. Effective vaccines are available.

Typhoid is a risk only in a few areas. Injectable or oral vaccines last for just three years so check with your doctor or Medical Advisory Services for Travellers Abroad (MASTA).

Cholera is a low risk in most areas. As the vaccine is only 60 per cent effective and lasts for only three to six months, it is not normally recommended. If there has recently been a cholera outbreak in an area you will be visiting, your doctor or MASTA will be able to advise you if vaccination is useful.

Rabies Vaccination is not normally recommended as the incidence is extremely low.

TB Children should be immunised at any age.

Advice on vaccinations can be obtained from your doctor, the charter company, or MASTA. MASTA is most likely to have the latest information and can be telephoned (in the UK) on 0891 224100. Calls are charged at 0891 rates and you must give answers to a recorded answerphone system with a fairly tedious system of pressing digits in response to questions. You will be sent a print-out detailing health risks and recommended vaccinations as well as the latest health warnings from the countries you have specified.

Malaria

The risk of malaria is nil or low in most charter destinations with just a few exceptions. In some of the Pacific islands, Thailand and a few other places there is a possible risk in some areas although not usually in the coastal regions. Check with

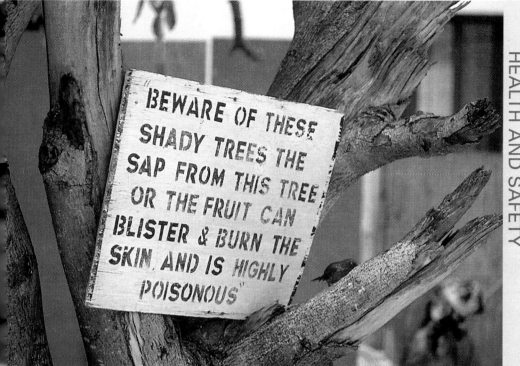

There are some unexpected health hazards in places as here in the Caribbean.
Photo Pat Collinge

your doctor or MASTA for up-to-the-minute details since malarial areas can shift and the risk of malaria can recur in areas which were once free of it.

It is important to know that, while malaria is transmitted by mosquito bites, it is only transmitted by the *anopheles* mosquito. Mosquitoes are common in most parts of the world, but the majority of species do not transmit malaria. The fact that there are mosquitoes around does not mean you are necessarily at risk and, in fact, *anopheles* normally only come out in the evening and at dawn.

Choice of treatment is between the old-fashioned prophylactic regime of two proguanil (commonly Paludrine) a day and two chloroquine a week (commonly Nivaquine or Avloclor) or one mefloquine (commonly Lariam) a week. While the weekly regime may seem more attractive, it does produce side effects in a certain percentage of people (thought to be as high as 10 per cent – although only 0.7 per cent experience serious effects). These side effects can include dizziness and, for a small

minority, rapid mood changes or depression. The latter side effects can be long-term for the 0.7 per cent so affected. If you have any history of dramatic mood changes or depression it is suggested that you do not use mefloquine. The possibility of depression on a small yacht invites some worrying scenarios.

The best protection against malaria is to prevent mosquito bites. Some boats have mosquito screens fitted but, unless you are going to stay below on balmy evenings, this is not much of a help. In the following section on dealing with unwanted visitors there are suggestions for keeping mosquitoes (and other aerial visitors) at bay.

Unwanted visitors

It is unfortunate that the warmer parts of the globe we like to visit when chartering are also the parts that flying insects like to inhabit.

By day there can be unwanted visitors like flies, wasps, bees, flying ants and an assortment of other creatures, depending on where you are. Wasps and bees are the only ones that are dangerous and this is really only because you will be wearing fewer clothes than normal and are, therefore, more likely to be stung. Wasps and bees are attracted by the odour of food and drink and, if these are removed, they will soon disappear. They particularly like sweet drinks such as cola and other fizzy pop, the mixers in your evening tipple, jam and chutney, and meats like ham and salami. It is best not to try and swat them or they may get angry and sting. One tip is never to drink out of a can, whatever the beverage inside. I know of two incidents where a wasp crawled unseen into the can and stung the recipient in the throat while travelling down the oesophagus. The subsequent swelling in the throat obstructed the windpipe and nearly caused death in one case. Always tip canned drinks into a glass. Take antihistamine cream to treat stings or something like aerosol *Waspeze* which contains a mild local anaesthetic as well as antihistamine.

In the evening and early morning, mosquitoes and midges are a problem in many charter areas. Midges come in different varieties including the tiny ones called variously 'no-no's' or 'noseeum'. In the Caribbean, Australia, some Pacific islands, Thailand and places like Alaska, Scandinavia and Scotland, midges can be a real problem. They are not disease carriers but can inflict an irritating bite out of all proportion to their size. In most areas, mosquitoes are not malaria carriers, but the bite is irritating and some poor souls have an allergic reaction to the anticoagulant the mosquito injects, which is what causes the irritation. If you know that mosquitoes or midge bites cause you an allergic reaction take whatever medication is necessary.

In the evenings cover yourself up with a long-sleeved shirt and long baggy trousers. Use a reliable mosquito repellent. Those that contain DEET are the most effective although, in some people, they too cause an irritable reaction on the skin and will also dissolve some plastics, including watch straps and the like. There are various other repellents of varying effectiveness. Use vapour coils if these do not suffocate you and if the boat has a cigarette lighter adapter it is possible to purchase 12-volt tablet 'cookers' for anti-mosquito tablets which plug into lighter adapters (similar to those that plug into 220V mains sockets).

AIDS

The worldwide incidence of AIDS continues to increase dramatically and nowhere more so than in popular tourist destinations. The *TravelSafe Code* from the Department of Health, reproduced below, should be followed at all times.

- Avoid unnecessary medical or dental treatment and situations which may make this necessary.
- Avoid having casual relationships but, if you have sex with someone new, always use a condom.
- Don't inject drugs or share needles and syringes.
- Remember that alcohol and drugs affect your judgement.
- Avoid having a tattoo, acupuncture or your ears pierced unless sterile equipment is used.

Marine perils

This doesn't mean sharks or conger eels, which you will rarely encounter, but the more common perils of jellyfish, sea urchins and coral cuts.

Jellyfish stings are the most common injury encountered in the marine world. All jellyfish sting – it's the way they immobilise their prey and is also their defence against predators. They will only sting if you bump into them or inadvertently become entangled in their trailing tentacles. Some jellyfish, the Portuguese man-o-war, New Zealand bluebottle, and Australian sea wasp, are vicious stingers and the latter causes a number of fatalities in Australia every year. Other jellyfish, like the more common *Aurelia aurita* and *Pelagia noctiluca*, are stingers but never fatal.

Different people have different reactions to jellyfish stings. For some there is a violent allergic reaction with loss of breath and increased heart rate while for others the symptoms are just a mild irritation of the skin. There are various treatments although none are 100 per cent effective. Those likely to have a violent reaction should use antihistamine creams and, again, something like *Waspeze*. Other treatments include dilute ammonium hydroxide, neat alcohol, vinegar, lemon rubbed on the sting, and even meat tenderiser which is said to break down the protein base of the venom. One tip is to wear gloves when hauling up an anchor as jellyfish tentacles can become wrapped around it and will still sting you even if detached from the body of the jellyfish!

Sea urchins are a problem when wandering around rocky areas if you tread on one and get the spines embedded in your foot. Always wear shoes or sandals when walking in shallow water around rocky areas and watch where you put your feet. The spines themselves are not venomous but are difficult to remove and may cause an infection.

Coral cuts are common when you go swimming or walking around reefs and, for some reason, they take an age to heal. Coral does sting mildly, but this is not the cause of cuts taking a long time to heal. Any cuts should be washed with an antiseptic solution and then kept dry. If necessary, put a plastic bag on the foot with a rubber band around the ankle when going ashore in a dinghy or anywhere else the foot is likely to get wet.

Ciguatera is not a well-known disease but it does claim a number of victims every year. It causes nausea, diarrhoea, stomach cramps and dizziness. It occasionally leads to respiratory failure. Though it is seldom fatal its effects can be long term. It is caused by eating certain types of fish, usually reef fish although others have been implicated, which for some reason become infected and pass the infection on to humans when eaten. The problem is that the disease affects fish which are normally edible and there is no way of knowing whether a fish is infected or not. It only affects tropical fish and has been associated with fish living around coral that has been damaged in some way. Fish caught on a line trolled behind a boat are seldom affected. Local fishermen normally know if ciguatera is around and, consequently, will not deliver certain types of fish to market at certain times of year. If you have been fishing around a reef ask the locals if the fish is OK to eat.

There are other things lurking in the sea that can cause injury, but in truth you are unlikely to come across them. If you have some sort of morbid interest in the subject then get hold of *Dangerous Marine Animals* by Halstead, Auerbach and Campbell or *Cruising in Tropical Waters and Coral* by Alan Lucas.

Potions, lotions and pills

There are a few basic items you need to take with you. Most important are sun-block creams of factor 15–30 to protect delicate skin from sun damage. Get a waterproof type as it tends to rub off less easily out of the water as well as in it. It doesn't really matter which brand you use as long as it offers maximum protection. Take some other suntan cream with a lower factor and lots of moisturising cream as well.

As already mentioned above, remember to take adequate supplies of a good insect repellent and antihistamine or other creams to treat insect bites. If you have severe allergies to insect bites take antihistamine tablets or whatever medication your doctor suggests.

A small first-aid kit with basics like aspirin, anti-acid tablets, a few waterproof sticking plasters, mild medication (such as *Dio-calm*) for tummy upsets and heavier treatment (like *Lomotil* or *Enterosan*) for more serious diarrhoea. All charter yachts will carry basic first-aid kits and many provide telephone numbers for doctors and hospitals along the way. On flotilla the lead boat will carry a more comprehensive medical kit and crewed charter yachts also carry full medical kits.

Stock up on any special medication you are on (for high blood pressure, angina, diabetes, etc) to see you through the duration of the trip. Asthma sufferers should ensure that they take adequate refills for inhalers and any other necessary medication. They usually find that the sea air helps their breathing but in some cases the humidity in some areas can aggravate their condition. Hayfever sufferers should take whatever medication they need. It is unwise for them to assume that, because they are going to a warmer climate in the summer when pollen counts should be low, they will not have a strong reaction to the different sorts of pollen they may encounter there.

Seasickness

Most people suffer at some time or other from seasickness, some more chronically than others. If you know you are susceptible, take your preferred remedy with you. In most charter areas the relatively short day passages in sheltered waters and the warm weather can have remarkable curative effects on even long-term sufferers. If you are new to the water a number of remedies are listed below.

Tablets There are a number of anti-seasickness remedies on the market, including: *Avomine, Dramamine, Marzine RF*, and *Stugeron*. Of these, *Stugeron* is widely accepted as the most effective. They all cause drowsiness to some extent, though *Stugeron* is reported to do so to a lesser extent than the others. The course of tablets should be started prior to going sailing, sometimes as much as four hours beforehand. Other tablets, such as *Phenergan*, *Kwells* and *Sereen* contain hyoscine hydrobromide which has a sedative effect and leaves the sufferer drowsy.

Patches A small elastoplast patch is stuck on the body, usually behind the ear, and releases the sedative slowly into the bloodstream. This has the advantage of a small continuous dosage as opposed to the instant dosage in tablet form and thus is less likely to cause drowsiness. Patches commonly contain hyoscine hydrobromide. Young children cannot use this system and it does have side effects on some people, usually drowsiness although a few people have experienced mild hallucinations.

Homeopathic cures A number of homeopathic treatments are available, including: *Nux Vomica*, *Cocculus Indicus*, and *Ipecac*. Other natural remedies include crystallised ginger, glucose and vitamin B12. Ginger appears to come out favourite.

Sea bands Elasticated bands with a small knob sewn into them. When slipped over the wrist, the knob is supposed to press on the *nei-kuan* pressure point that reduces nausea. The problem is hitting exactly the right spot – something an acupuncturist spends years learning to do.

In general, someone who is seasick should be kept warm, but should stay in the cockpit if possible. Watching the horizon seems to have a curative effect and giving sufferers something to do, like steering if they are able, seems to take their minds off the nausea. Any odours from diesel, gas, cooking smells and the like will aggravate nausea. When seasick try to eat something like crackers or dry bread and drink plenty of water as vomiting causes dehydration.

Water

Water is a tricky issue and staying clear of waterborne diseases or complications cannot be achieved by drinking bottled water. In any of the charter destinations you go to you will come into contact with water by virtue of eating ashore. Salad vegetables and fruit will be washed in it, local ice and ice-cream will be made from it, cooking and other utensils will be washed and rinsed in it, and you will wash and clean your teeth in it. Even the

most fastidious will not be able to avoid contact with it in one way or another.

In most places the water is safe to drink although it may contain local micro-organisms which are not dangerous in themselves, but may cause minor stomach upsets until your digestive system adapts to them. If there are problems with water supplies in an area, your charter base should advise you. Otherwise my advice is that you might as well drink the local water as you will inevitably come across it in one way or another.

Infants and children are another matter. It is probably best to use bottled water for their needs as the micro-organisms which initially cause an upset tummy in adults can cause babies and small children a good deal more distress. An additional measure for infants is to use water-purifying tablets in the boat's water tanks or keep a jerry can of water that has been purified for the use of infants. Ashore there is not a lot you can do except to get the kids to drink bottled water.

One last plea. Dispose of used water bottles in garbage containers. There are too many plastic water bottles littering the seas and beaches of the world and none of us should add to this very visual form of pollution.

Finding the boat

Not as silly as it sounds. You may think that, because you have booked a Beneteau 35 called *Crazy Horse*, finding it in Kalamaki Marina will be a cinch. By the time you have walked around looking at 600 boats in the dark, including at least 20 charter white Beneteau 35s, none of which are called *Crazy Horse*, you finally locate someone from the charter base who tells you the boat is now in Poros and you need to get a ferry there, except the ferries don't run until the morning. One of the things that can make or break a charter holiday is how efficiently transfers are carried out and how caring charter base staff are after you have had a delayed flight, a baby who cried for most of it in the row behind you, and an argument with the taxi driver over just how much he was entitled to overcharge you.

For flotilla holidays and bareboat charters from companies who arrange transfers, a lot of hassle is taken out of getting the sailing holiday off to a good start. You will be met at the airport, shepherded on to the coach, have snippets of information fed to you en route about what to expect when you arrive, and be able to get answers from the representative on just where you can change money tomorrow and how much the local beer costs. Couriers on these transfers are the unsung heroes and heroines of the piece who have often been up all night getting the last charter party off before returning with the new group and who, quite possibly, are part of the charter base staff who are expected to go straight to work with new arrivals. They deserve medals.

Many bareboat companies and most skippered and crewed charters will arrange for a member of the crew or charter base staff to meet you at the airport and arrange transport to the boat. If this is an option take it, or at least arrange for the company to have a trusted taxi driver to meet you at the airport. Although the scenario outlined at the beginning is not common, it does happen and leaves you tired and emotional before you even get on the boat.

If you are going to find the boat on your own get explicit instructions from the charter company on how to get to the marina or

Figure out how you are going to get to the boat.
Photo Rod Heikell

harbour, what the going rate is for whatever transportation is available, where exactly the boat is located, and a local contact telephone number. Give the charter company a ring just before you leave home to see if there have been any last minute changes. Get the name, address and telephone number of a hotel nearby – just in case you need it.

To be fair, most charter companies, whether large or small, are old hands at arranging transfers and getting you on to the boat. They know you will be frazzled after your flight and possibly close to breaking point after last-minute panics at work and home.

Stowing gear

Boats are small environments compared to houses and it is essential that things be stowed away properly. When you arrive everyone should have a locker (or two) allotted to them and some space in the hanging locker. You also need to allot space for a booze cabinet (teetotallers excepted) and for bits and pieces like sun-protection creams, sunglasses and the novel you picked up at the airport. Then you can pack away your sailing bags in a locker under one of the berths. It's too late to figure out where you are going to put that suitcase I suggested you would have trouble stowing earlier on.

It is essential that gear is stowed away, not just because boats are small places, but also so things don't fall about when you get out on the water. For novices and even some hardened salts there is nothing more irritating than things crashing out of shelves and on to the cabin sole when you hit the first couple of waves. It can also be dangerous if bottles or glasses fall and break on the sole when anyone venturing down below could tread on shards of glass – or any sharp object for that matter. And when bottles of peanut butter, jam, chutney or similar squidgy things break they make an appalling mess. Everything should have its place on a boat and everything should be in that place when you set off.

Inventory and boat checks

Once you are settled in on board, the inventory of boat gear and other items on board must be checked. The company will supply you with a checklist sheet and this should be ticked off against the items on board. It is inadvisable to assume from a quick glance around that all the items are there. The inventory should be meticulously checked or you may have to pay for missing

items overlooked by the charter base staff from the last charter group. The inventory is usually divided into categories along the following lines.

On deck Includes life buoy and life raft, sails, anchors, chain and warps, fenders, awning and bimini, transom barbecue, boathook and other sundry items. Check that the life raft has a valid in-date certificate. Check the sails are in good condition, with no tears or badly chafed seams. Check warps to ensure there are no badly chafed spots. Make sure fenders are of an adequate size and that there are at least six of them. Make a note of any missing equipment and note any wear and tear or damage, especially to sails.

Cockpit and lockers Dinghy (if not rigid or already inflated), outboard, dinghy pump and oars, water and fuel jerry cans, winch handle(s), warps, gas bottles, funnels, masks and snorkels, cockpit cushions and other sundry items. Check the dinghy for wear and tear as it gets a hard life on charter. Make

Get to know how the gear works on board. A simple thing like an anchor winch may have its own quirks and can cause injury if used without care. *Photo* Yachting World

sure the outboard works and the fuel can is full. Check the gas bottles are full and get any empties filled before you leave. List any missing equipment – winch handles are a favourite.

Galley Cutlery, crockery, glasses, pots and pans, tea towels, fire extinguisher and fire blanket, cleaning materials. Check all burners on the stove work. Check the fridge works. Check there is a bottle opener and a corkscrew. Make sure there are sufficient cleaning materials.

Chart table Instruments, VHF, charts and yachtsman's pilot, basic navigator's kit, hand-bearing compass, torch, and binoculars. Check the instruments work and see if there are manuals for them, particularly for GPS and Loran which may have different operating systems to the instruments you are used to. Check the VHF and, if necessary, make a test call to another boat or the charter base. Check that the charts and pilot book are up-to-date and in good condition. Make sure there is a pencil sharpener and eraser in the navigator's kit.

Cabin lockers Life jackets (including children's), safety harnesses, fire extinguisher(s), tool and spares kit, cassette/CD player, flares and first-aid kit. Check the fire extinguishers are in-date. Check the tool kit and the first-aid kit to be sure everything is there.

Other Linen, pillows, duvets or blankets and windscoop. Duvets and blankets may need airing but this is something you do for yourself as the salty environment always means that things feel a bit damp.

Hull Check to see that any gouges and scratches are known to the charter base staff and make a note of them on the inventory.

Checking over the inventory in this sort of pedantic fashion is useful for two reasons. First of all you familiarise yourself with where things are stowed. Often a member of the charter base will go over the inventory with you and this speeds up the process of finding out where things are. It also means that he will be able to give you an on-the-spot answer to questions and make his own list of anything that needs replacing or mending before you leave. Second, it eliminates any problems at the end of the cruise about losses or damage when the boat is checked in. This is especially important if you have lodged a security deposit in cash with the charter base office.

Familiarisation

Nearly all companies have a member of staff from the charter base run a familiarisation check on the boat. On flotillas this is carried out by the skipper who will run through all procedures with the group. Don't be afraid to ask questions later if you are not too sure of something. The familiarisation check should include the following.

Sails A quick demo on the roller-reefing genoa and mainsail. Mainsails are usually slab-reefing or roller-reefing into the mast or boom and it is worthwhile putting a reef in on slab-reefing systems just to make sure they are set up properly. This demo also allows you to look at the sails, point out any problems and make a note of any damage. Sails are one of those contentious issues when it comes to recovering security deposits.

Engine starting and operation Find out the whereabouts of the oil dipstick and enquire about any other checks you need to make before starting the engine. The engine should be started and engaged briefly in forward and astern to check the operation of the gear and throttle lever. Check the instruments and ask about cruising revs. A rough guide to fuel consumption should be given although most modern diesels are now so fuel efficient that you can just about motor everywhere and still come back with fuel in the tanks. Check the whereabouts of the fuel-stop lever as boat manufacturers often hide them away in all sorts of places. Ask what happens should the engine break down en route.

Outboard motor Check where the choke, fuel cock and stop button are. Start the motor and run it for 15 seconds or so. Check what the petrol/oil ratio is and that there is two-stroke oil on board.

Gas procedures If there is a gas sniffer or similar on board, get the lowdown on how it works. Ensure that everyone on board knows where the gas bottles are and that the regulator must be turned off after the cooker has been used.

Water and fuel Check where the fillers are for water and diesel. One of the most common disasters on board is to confuse the two and put diesel in the water tank and vice versa. Cleaning out the diesel tank and flushing the engine fuel system is a messy job that can easily lose you a day. Likewise, cleaning out the water tank will take repeated flushing. Ensure that everyone knows which is which.

Batteries Find out where the battery switch is to switch between batteries for domestic and engine starting. Get an idea of consumption for the fridge and other power-hungry equipment like electric anchor winches.

Have a chat with the charter base staff member about your itinerary. He or she can help you out with all sorts of local knowledge on good anchorages, lively nightlife, unsafe harbours, possible lunch stops, dangers to navigation, what the prevailing winds are likely to be – all manner of useful information that can enhance your holiday. Remember that charter base staff have been around the area for a while and, if they advise you that including Hangman's Reef or the prettiest harbour in Greece (so the guidebook says) in your itinerary could result in damage to the boat or at best a very uncomfortable night, listen to them and be prepared to change your plans.

Essential supplies coming aboard.
Photo Yachting World

Boat papers

In most countries there is a fair amount of paperwork involved with getting a charter party on to a boat and away. The charter base will organise all this paperwork for the charter, but you will be required to sign various agreements and forms and you may be required to accompany one of the staff members to the harbourmaster, customs or coastguard to finalise it all. This paperwork is a necessary part of the charter and the papers you carry on board may be asked for at any of the harbours along the way. In places like the Caribbean, where you will be going from one country to another, it is up to you to clear yourself in and out with the relevant authorities.

While you may find this tedious and a blot on your holiday, do not neglect to do it or you may find the holiday is quickly curtailed for illegal entry into a country. The charter base staff will advise you on all this and on any possible pitfalls or fees to be paid.

It is useful to keep all the boat and charter papers together, along with any relevant certificates and the passports of all those on board. A plastic zip-up folder is useful for keeping papers and passports dry when going ashore from an anchorage.

Provisioning

Most bareboat companies will provision up the boat if requested beforehand. The charter company you book with will usually supply a checklist and many companies give you a suggested list, from basic starter pack to super-luxury provisioning. If you want to get off quickly then checking off items on a list is the way to do it. The provisions will either be on board when you arrive or will be delivered the same day.

Most flotilla companies provide a basic starter pack with things like oil, sugar, salt and pepper, a few tea bags and a packet of biscuits, just so there is something to keep you going as soon as you arrive. There will be time to do the shopping before you set off.

The hostess will be able to direct you to the best shopping places and advise you on what days you will be able to stock up again.

For some of us, going shopping in a foreign place is part of the fun of being there. If this is the case, order a basic starter pack so you can least make a hot drink when you arrive or gulp down a can of fizzy something or other and then, when the boat has been stowed, some of the crew can go off to do the shopping. In every country there are all sorts of goodies to try, whether you are shopping in a supermarket or wandering around a local market with funny looking dried fish and meat and poultry on the hoof or claw.

Water and fuel

Before you leave, top up with water and fuel – including any reserve supplies in jerry cans.

For anyone new to a boat it is necessary to inculcate the need to be careful with water and not waste it. In our homes we just turn on the tap for an unlimited supply, never realising how precious the stuff is. On a boat it is a finite quantity and, if it is used up before the next place you can fill up at, that's it. Ablutions invariably use the most water so educate any new crew about the dire consequences they will face if they take lengthy showers, leave pressure taps running while they wash and clean their teeth, and are generally not conscious of rationing water. In some small harbours you may have to lug water from the shore by jerry can and this task can have a sobering effect on dissolute water wasters.

Fuel is less of a problem, as the charter base staff will be able to tell you where you can refuel en route. Most diesels are fairly economical these days and it is unlikely you will need to refuel more than once on a two-week itinerary. Bareboats must be returned to the charter base with full tanks, but this is easily arranged once you get back to base and you are simply charged for however much was needed to top up the tanks.

Living on board

For those not used to being on a boat it all seems so small and cramped at first – unless you are on a superyacht where the space resembles that of a small apartment. There is less room to put things away, no room to leave things lying about, and not a lot of privacy. Everyone on board should respect the space of the others and endeavour to stow things away and not hog all the space in the cockpit or saloon. Noise travels without let or hindrance from one end of the boat to another so keep your singing in the shower to a modest level as well as any other noises you might manufacture.

Those not used to moving around a boat should familiarise themselves with the deck layout when in harbour. Wander around it and get the feel of where things are, especially handholds, before you are beating into a healthy breeze and need to go forward to retrieve a fender someone forgot about. Boats move in a fairly rhythmical fashion when under way and it is just a matter of moving about in synch with that movement. Try to fight the movement of a boat and it will catch you out. Moving with a boat rather than fighting against it is important not only for your safety, but also because it enhances your enjoyment of being at one with the boat and helps you understand how it is working with the wind and waves. If this sounds like romantic slush, it is not. Observe the way different people move around on a boat and you will see that some of them expend little energy to move around on deck and get things done while others are constantly being thrown off balance and fighting to hold on, let alone pull down a reef in the mainsail.

Under power

It is essential that someone else on board knows how to start the engine and get going under power. This is for the simple reason that, if the only person who knows how to start the engine and get under way falls

Coming into harbour the last thing you need is panic on board as crew haul down sails, look for fenders and ropes and generally tidy up the boat. Get it all done well in advance.
Photo Yachting World

overboard, no-one else will know how to get back to the unfortunate soul. It is also useful to be able to hand over to someone else when the skipper has other things he wants to do.

Before you leave harbour at the beginning of the charter, instruct one other member of the crew in the basics of starting and operating the engine. Then, when you have left harbour, let the chosen one helm under power for a bit to get the feel of the boat and, later, let them have a bit of a potter around in calm water. Remember that someone may have to manoeuvre the boat back to pick you up out of the sea.

Before you start the engine, run through a number of basic checks. The charter base will advise you on these and they will be likely to include: check the oil, check the fresh-water coolant level, check you are on the engine-starting battery, and check the gear lever is disengaged and on throttle only for starting. Once the engine is started, check there is water coming out of the exhaust and check the oil pressure gauge. Always let a diesel warm up for a few minutes before getting under way. At the same time make sure there are no warps trailing in the water which might get wrapped around the propeller.

If there is one thing that irritates charter companies it is charterers who insist on gunning up the engine to maximum revs when under power. Most yachts will get up to cruising speed at around half of maximum revs or just over. If there is a rev counter, the charter base staff will advise you on cruising revs. Using maximum revs will increase your speed by only a small amount, it will dramatically increase your fuel consumption, and will probably lay a film of unburnt diesel on the water from the exhaust. It is a silly macho habit and environmentally unfriendly.

Organising the skipper and crew

On a new boat and in strange waters it is essential that the crew members know what to do when coming into an anchorage or a harbour. This does not mean that everyone has to jump to it navy-style, rather that they know who is doing what and in what order. Before coming into harbour it pays to have things prepared well in advance and to detail specific jobs to those on board. Thus someone ties on fenders, someone coils ropes ready for heaving ashore, someone gets the anchor ready to let go, and someone keeps an

eye out for a suitable berth or anchoring spot. There is nothing worse than the chaos seen on some charter yachts where lack of preparation has engendered last-minute panic bordering on hysteria as the skipper screams to his crew to get fenders out, find some damn mooring lines, and get the anchor (what anchor) down, all within 50ft of the quay. Preparation is all and it dramatically decreases divorces and tiffs caused when berthing or anchoring.

It is also distressing to see yachts coming into anchor or berth with the male standing impassively at the helm directing his (usually) female partner to get the anchor ready and drop it, or leap 10ft to the quay with a couple of mooring lines, when it might be more appropriate for him to be handling the anchor or taking lines ashore. In my experience the female of the species is commonly better than the male at helming the boat, with a more delicate touch on helm and throttle.

When leaving harbour it is also necessary that everyone knows their allotted tasks. The boat will need to be stowed so that things don't fall about, towels should be retrieved from drying on the lifelines, fenders and lines put away, the anchor must be secured, and someone needs to keep an eye out up forward for swimmers, sailboards and ferries charging into the harbour at speed.

Etiquette

While you are on holiday to relax and have fun it should be remembered that you have a responsibility to be polite to those whose country you are visiting and especially polite to those on the water.

When you go into a harbour do not take berths obviously occupied by fishing boats or local boats of any description. After all it is their harbour and they are working on the water for a living. Think about what it would be like to get back home and find someone parked in your front drive. It's not worth the aggro in any case as the locals will give you an earful when they get back to find you in their spot and you'd better believe that, whatever language they use, it isn't polite.

Likewise in harbour take care of other people's yachts. Some cruising yachts may look a bit scruffy to you, but to the proud owners they are old friends that have transported them safely across thousands of miles. Ensure you have sufficient fenders out to avoid damage to other yachts and that

your lines do not chafe on theirs or on their boat. And, if you befriend them, there may well be some interesting salty yarns in return for a drink or two.

All-night parties are fine if that is what you're after but, to others in an anchorage, it may be just plain irritating when they are trying to get some sleep. Sounds carry wonderfully well across a quiet anchorage as I've discovered on not a few occasions when alcohol-inspired conversations have been louder than intended and have been repeated word for word in the morning from yachts a considerable distance away. Keep the noise down . . . or invite everyone in the anchorage over.

In some anchorages, particularly in the Caribbean, boat boys will row or motor out to yachts to assist when anchoring and taking a line ashore, tout for restaurants or sell you fresh fruit and vegetables and souvenirs. There is a strict protocol to follow in the Caribbean which applies equally well elsewhere. The first boat boy who gets to you should be engaged (after ascertaining the price), asked to keep the others clear and wait until you are ready for his services. If you don't do this, mayhem will result, with a cluster of boats impeding your way and a lot of arguments over who should be employed. The charter base can give you a pretty exact idea of the going rates for services so you will not be out of pocket when engaging the first to arrive. Other boat boys who arrive later to sell you anything and everything and to tout for restaurants should be addressed politely and a polite refusal made if you are not interested. Do not ignore them in the hope that they will go away. A short, polite conversation is the way to get on with these nautical salesmen and avoid offending them.

In other parts of the world, on-land touts will offer you all sorts of products and services. If you are not interested, decline politely and, if they persist, just walk on by having made a first refusal. Touting in many countries is a way of life and, even when touts are persistent, don't get upset at them.

When double- or triple-banked outside other yachts on a quay, ask permission to walk across the inside boats to reach it. Do not put your shoes on until you have reached the quay and try to tread gently, especially when returning at night. Anyone trying to

Opposite Boat boys plying for business in Grenada. *Photo* Yachting World

sleep will not be amused by you banging across their deck in the wee small hours with little regard for the amount of noise you are making. And try to avoid peeking down hatches and through the main hatchway – it's called being a peeping tom in most parts of the world and you can be arrested for it on land.

Boats with generators should not run them at night when people are trying to get to sleep. In harbour, be careful of where the generator exhaust is squirting its cooling water – I've seen morons on some boats with a high exhaust apparently happy to squirt oily water and fumes straight into the cockpit of a nearby yacht. In an anchorage, generators should be run sparingly . . . if at all. It is ironic that, in some of the most beautiful and the quietest anchorages, one boat running its generator can totally destroy the ambience and peace of the place. My question would be why go there at all if you can only hear the puttering of an exhaust and see an oily sheen on the water of your own making.

If you have toys like sailboards and waterbikes on board, stay clear of anyone swimming in an anchorage. A sailboard or waterbike can cause severe injury to a swimmer if you hit them and it doesn't take long for someone who has been knocked out to drown. Waterbikes in particular should keep well away from swimming areas and yachts at anchor, if only to reduce noise pollution. You don't need an audience if you are really good on a sailboard or waterbike.

Cardinal sins

Anchoring Careless anchoring causes a lot of damage to the sea bottom. The damage is not great on sand and mud but, over coral, it is long-lasting and can be catastrophic. There is a global effort under way to establish a code of anchoring in coral reef areas which suggests the following: never anchor on coral reefs themselves; reconnoitre an area and drop your anchor in sand; if mooring buoys are available use them; even if you have to anchor in comparatively deep water to be free of coral, do it. Living coral has a relatively thin and delicate tissue covering the hard skeleton and is easily damaged by anchors and chain which can cause a coral colony, hundreds of years old, to die.

Garbage Always dispose of your garbage in the proper areas. Most places will have some form of receptacle for garbage and, even if it looks as if it is never emptied, smells, and is overflowing with nasty bits of detritus, garbage is better in there than in the sea. No inorganic rubbish should be thrown into the sea and even organic rubbish should be sparingly dumped overboard when at least three miles off the coast.

Holding tanks Never pump out the holding tank in a harbour or anchorage. In many places heavy fines will be levied for the smallest infringement. Apart from that it is just not nice to see human waste floating around a harbour and it is even worse to bump into it when swimming in an anchorage. Most authorities recommend you be at least three miles off the coast before pumping out holding tanks although regulations vary and the charter company will be able to inform you as to the specific regulations in force.

Sailing at night Most charter companies have restrictions on sailing at night. These restrictions apply mostly because a lot of charter areas are comparatively poorly lit and buoyed compared to Europe or the US. Moreover local boats may not be carrying lights or may have incorrect navigation lights which can cause confusion and a possible accident. Sneaking in at twilight is one thing, but sailing back to a charter base at night to make up time will most probably invalidate your own insurance and you may be liable for the cost of replacing the boat should anything happen to it. Talk it over with the charter company as conditions vary between companies and charter areas.

Returning the boat

It all has to come to an end, usually much too quickly after you have settled into the pace of cruising around harbours and anchorages and got used to handling the boat. Still the advantage of chartering is that you can return to exactly the same location next year or extend your horizons and head off somewhere else. For the time being there is the nitty gritty of returning the boat and heading home.

I know I've already said this, several times, but allow plenty of time to get the boat back to the charter base. If you are flying out on, say, a midday or early-afternoon flight then you need to be back the night before. Leave an easy leg for the last day so you do not arrive back exhausted and stressed out. After all, your holiday is about leaving your normal

hectic and cluttered lifestyle behind for two weeks, so make the final few days a relaxed affair.

Once back at the charter base the inventory will have to be checked off (that careful checking on arrival will now pay off), fuel tanks filled, and your safety deposit retrieved if it was lodged with the charter base office. It is common practice to donate any left-over provisions and booze to the charter base staff.

In some countries, particularly the US and Caribbean, it is normal to tip skippers and crew. The usual going rate is between 2–5 per cent of the charter fee. For staff at the bareboat base the going rate is less.

If you're planning some sailing in the sun, whether it be the Caribbean,
Thailand, or perhaps somewhere cooler like Greenland,
Yachting World will help you choose the charter destination of your dreams.

For a subscription to the world's most authoritative yachting magazine call + 44 (0) 1444 445555 or + 44 (0) 1622 778778, the subscription credit card line quoting code 24Y.

Our Charter World section brings news of charter bases and practical information for yachtsmen visiting overseas. If you want a flotilla in Greece or a bareboat in St. Lucia, Yachting World will bring you a tantalising choice of yachts and destinations.

Every month we carry a special charter advertisement section bringing details and prices of sailing holidays available in the UK and abroad.

YACHTING WORLD

II. World charter areas

The information in this section is all pretty straightforward. Areas in which there is a good deal of charter or which have several popular charter areas are allotted more space than areas which have only a small amount of charter. Some unusual areas get just a mention at the end of the section.

When putting together a guide like this it is inevitable that some information will be dated by the time you read it. A large charter company may pull out of the charter base mentioned here and move elsewhere while the book is at the printers. Political considerations ranging from squabbling over borders to a government imposing punitive taxes on yachts and yacht equipment may cause charter companies to pull out of a country altogether or relocate to another area. Smaller charter bases come and go depending on all sorts of factors, usually whether they attracted enough charterers to the area.

The suggested itineraries for some areas are just that: a suggestion. You should consult the charter company and the staff on the ground for up-to-the-minute details and plan your route using their local knowledge. Before you go consult charts and pilot guides as part of the fun of yacht charter is reading up and planning your own cruise before you set off.

Included for many of the charter areas are climate tables for the charter season. Most of the data, average maximum and minimum temperatures, highest recorded temperature, and sea temperature can be interpreted directly to give a clue as to how comfortable or inviting an area will be. Other data in the tables will need a bit more interpretation.

The number of days of rain with x amount falling should be interpreted with care. In the tropics there will often be a downpour for an hour or less in the afternoon and that is the rain over and done with. In other areas that rain may be a grey drizzle falling all day.

The relative humidity of an area needs to be linked to average maximum temperatures and the graph opposite shows a 'comfort index' for maximum temperatures and relative humidity. Basically, an area's maximum temperatures do not tell the whole story and, unless linked to the relative humidity, will not give you an idea of how comfortable the heat is. With high humidity clothes do not dry out and body perspiration cannot evaporate easily, leaving you feeling sticky and hot. For example, at 30°C (86°F) and 20 per cent humidity, a few people will feel uncomfortable but, for most, it is quite bearable. At 30°C and 60 per cent humidity, everyone feels distinctly uncomfortable. There are some modifying factors, of which the most important is wind speed and, fortunately, on the sea there is usually a bit of breeze.

Note On the maps the symbol below indicates a charter base.

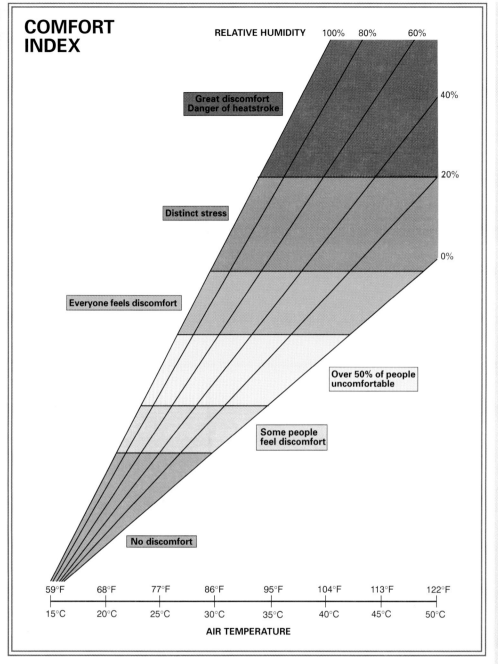

COMFORT INDEX

RELATIVE HUMIDITY   100%   80%   60%

40%

20%

0%

**Great discomfort
Danger of heatstroke**

Distinct stress

Everyone feels discomfort

**Over 50% of people
uncomfortable**

**Some people
feel discomfort**

No discomfort

| 59°F | 68°F | 77°F | 86°F | 95°F | 104°F | 113°F | 122°F |
| 15°C | 20°C | 25°C | 30°C | 35°C | 40°C | 45°C | 50°C |

AIR TEMPERATURE

United Kingdom

FOR

- Easy international access and good infrastructure
- Long sailing tradition with lots of interesting boats around and maritime heritage sights ashore
- Wide range of charter options, including many sailing schools and specialist skills like racing and learning to sail old timers
- Magnificent scenery and peace and quiet in Scotland
- English pubs

AGAINST

- Unpredictable summer season
- Some areas, like the south coast, crowded in the summer

Types of charter

- Sailing in company
- Bareboat
- Skippered
- Luxury
- Sailing schools and advanced teaching courses

Note Much of this chapter will be redundant for many readers and is aimed at non-UK residents interested in chartering here.

There is more yacht charter in Britain than most people realise, despite the vagaries of the weather. There are also a lot of variations on the basic yacht chartering you get in many other parts of the world, with a strong emphasis on learning sailing skills rather than just sitting back and enjoying a sailing holiday. As well as mini-flotillas, bareboat and skippered charter, there are all sorts of learning-to-sail programmes including: Royal Yachting Association (RYA) courses and short courses for those going on flotilla holidays elsewhere; competitive sailing, including match racing and entering some of the big races such as the Round the Island Race; sailing older traditional craft; corporate and team sailing; and day charters on large classic yachts and ocean racing yachts. Chartering a yacht in Britain is a bit of a lottery because of the weather and you can expect to spend a few days weather-bound even in summer. In recompense there are good hostelries ashore.

When to go

In Great Britain the season normally starts around May and runs through to October. In the early and late season (spring and autumn) there is a good chance that weather will hold you up for around 25 per cent of the time.

Early season (April to June) Day temperatures are typically 15°–18°C in the south and 14°–16°C in Scotland, but drop to 6°–11°C at night. Wind patterns are not regular, with depressions coming in from the Atlantic determining much of what happens. The sky is frequently overcast and there are numerous days of rain.

High season (June to September) Day temperatures are typically 19°C in the south and 17°C in Scotland in July and August. The sea breeze is well established in the summer, blowing onto the coast except when a depression coming in from the Atlantic disturbs the normal wind pattern.

Late season (October) Temperatures and wind patterns are much as for the early season. Sometimes at the end of October there is a period of settled weather and higher temperatures.

At Plymouth

	Av. max °C	Av. min °C	Highest recorded	Relative humidity	Days 0·25mm rain
Apr	12	6	22	69%	12
May	15	8	26	71%	12
Jun	18	11	28	73%	12
Jul	19	13	29	74%	14
Aug	19	13	31	75%	14
Sep	18	12	27	75%	15
Oct	15	9	23	77%	16

At Edinburgh

	Av. max °C	Av. min °C	Highest recorded	Relative humidity	Days 0·25mm rain
Apr	12	6	22	69%	12
May	14	6	24	76%	14
Jun	17	9	28	75%	15
Jul	18	11	28	78%	17
Aug	18	11	28	80%	16
Sep	16	9	25	89%	16
Oct	12	7	20	82%	17

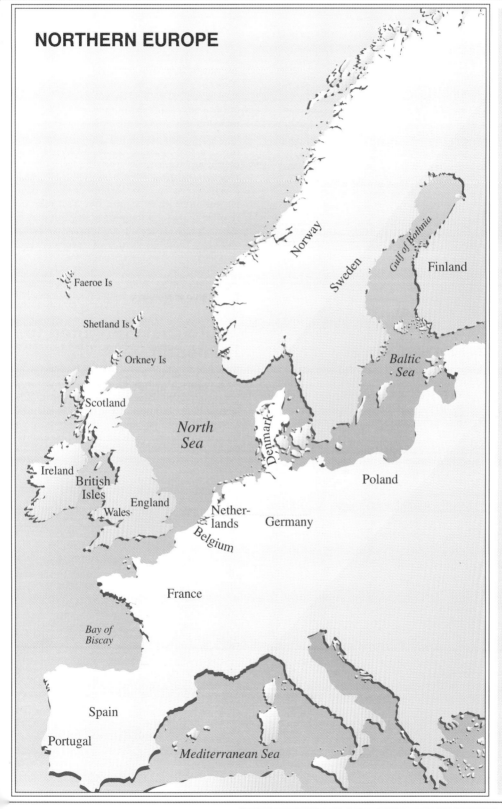

NORTHERN EUROPE

Faeroe Is

Shetland Is

Orkney Is

Scotland

North Sea

Norway

Sweden

Gulf of Bothnia

Finland

Baltic Sea

Denmark

Ireland

British Isles

England

Wales

Nether-lands

Belgium

Germany

Poland

France

Bay of Biscay

Spain

Portugal

Mediterranean Sea

Sailing guides and charts

There are a large number of sailing guides to different parts of the country. Have a look in chandlers or nautical bookshops. The following may be useful.

The Shell Channel Pilot Tom Cunliffe. Imray. Covers all south-coast harbours

South Coast Cruising Mark Fishwick. Yachting Monthly. Good coverage of most of south coast including the Solent

West Country Cruising Mark Fishwick. Yachting Monthly. Covers Devon and Cornwall

A Cruising Guide to Northwest England and Wales. George Griffiths. Imray

The East Coast. Derek Bowskill. Imray

The Western Isles/Skye & Northwest Scotland Martin Lawrence. Imray. Covers west coast of Scotland

West Highland Shores Maldwin Drummond

Macmillan Nautical Almanac Annual publication

Admiralty and Imray charts cover the British coastline in great detail.

Essential information

Time zone UT DST (+1) Apr–Sep

Telecommunications Automatic dialling. Country code 44. Good pubc telephone service with phonecards. Telephone and fax services from stationers and other shops.

Dinghy sailing in the Solent. A bit of learning, a bit of racing and a lot of fun. *Photo* Pat Collinge

Mobile phones with GSM card supported.

Health Reciprocal medical care is available for EU nationals with *Form E111*. It is advisable to take out medical insurance if you are not from an EU country.

Money The unit of currency is the pound sterling (£). Banks are open 0900–1500/1600 Monday to Friday. All major credit cards and charge cards widely accepted. Eurocheques, postcheques and traveller's cheques accepted. ATM machines commonplace.

Documentation Members of the EU must carry their passport or identity card. All other visitors must carry a passport. You may not require a visa for a temporary stay but may be asked for evidence of an onward ticket or sufficient funds. A licence to operate VHF is required.

Charter areas

South coast (Brighton to Falmouth)

This is the sailing and charter hub of England with charter companies large and small operating from bases along the coast. The largest concentration of yachts in England is around the Solent which, naturally enough, has the largest concentration of charter yachts.

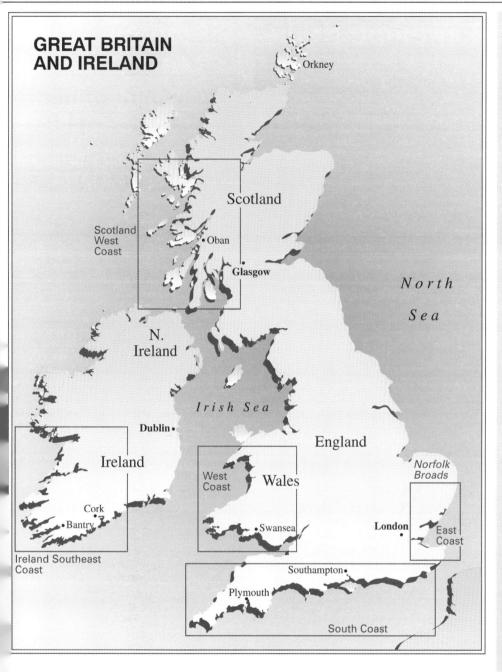

GREAT BRITAIN AND IRELAND

Orkney

Scotland

Scotland
West
Coast

Oban

Glasgow

North

Sea

N.
Ireland

Irish Sea

Dublin

Ireland

England

West
Coast

Wales

*Norfolk
Broads*

Cork

Bantry

Swansea

London

East
Coast

Ireland Southeast
Coast

Southampton

Plymouth

South Coast

Wind and sea

Winds are much dependent on the Atlantic and the passage of depressions in from the west. In the summer, when a high is stationary over Britain, there is some sea breeze effect and along the south coast it can last for a week or more if you are lucky. During these periods in summer there are wonderful sunny days with sufficient sea breeze for a good sail. Winds in the English channel are channelled into a westerly or easterly direction when light, but with stronger winds the pressure differences are the major determinant of direction. Weather forecasts are widely available, either in marinas, by telephone or fax, or on BBC Radio 4 (198kHz 92·4/92·6MHz) at 0033,

NORTHERN EUROPE

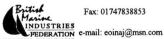

NORTHERN EUROPE

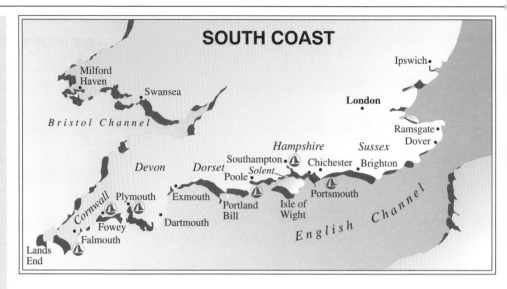

SOUTH COAST

Milford Haven
Swansea
Bristol Channel
Ipswich•
London•
Ramsgate•
Dover•
Hampshire   *Sussex*
Southampton•⚓
Chichester Brighton
Devon   *Dorset*
Solent
Poole•
Portsmouth
Cornwall Plymouth
Exmouth
Portland Bill
Isle of Wight
English Channel
Fowey
Dartmouth
Falmouth
Lands End ⚓

0555, 1355 and 1750 local time. Pilots for the area carry all necessary details.

The seas along the south coast are generally moderate except, of course, in strong winds generated by depressions passing over. Where there are strong tidal currents there can be dangerous overfalls with wind against tide.

Tides

Tides along the south coast are not extreme but do give rise to problems where there are complex streams and eddies. Around the major headlands there is often a tidal race and, when wind is against tide (and sometimes even when it is not), there can be

severe overfalls. It is prudent to keep well off the headlands so afflicted which are well known and mentioned in the relevant pilots.

All tidal data is referenced to Dover. The tidal range at springs varies from around 5·3m (17ft+) at Falmouth, 4·9m (16ft) at Torquay, 4·7m (15ft+) at Portsmouth, to 6·5m (21ft+) at Brighton. The tidal streams generated in the Channel and in areas like the Solent are complex and reference must be made to a tidal-stream atlas.

Suitable for...

The area is for beginners, intermediate and experienced sailors. There are sufficient harbours within a close distance along the coast for plans to be changed in the event of deteriorating weather conditions when it may be necessary to seek shelter. For sailing schools and learning-to-sail charters the skipper/instructor will of course be on hand, although the conditions can be trying at times, especially in early or late season.

Harbours and anchorages

There is a mix of everything – from yacht marinas, commercial ports, fishing harbours, river and estuary anchorages to a few

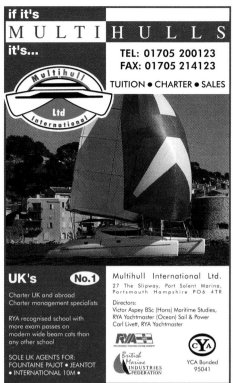

NGA   GREECE   TURKEY   BALEARICS   BRITTANY   CÔTE D'AZUR   UNITED KINGDOM

Sailing area

The sailing area is basically along the coast
from your chosen charter base. Most
charterers will want to potter around the
coast locally whether it be the west country or
the Solent. Some charter companies will
arrange cross-Channel passages for
experienced bareboat charterers or provide a
skipper for charters to France and the
Channel Islands. Effectively it all depends on
your experience and the vagaries of the
weather. A number of charter companies can
arrange for you to pick up the boat at one
base and leave it at another for an additional
fee.

Scotland

The west coast of Scotland is dramatic, with
hundreds of miles of coast sheltered by
islands and cut by lochs extending miles
inland. The scenery is superlative and, for
peace and tranquillity, there are few places to
equal it. It has a few drawbacks, which
include midges in the summer and
changeable weather. On a yacht the midges
are less of a problem than ashore and the
changeable weather at least includes heat

sheltered bays. Many harbours and most
estuaries and rivers have a bar or shifting
sand-banks at the entrance and can only be
entered a number of hours either side of high
water. Many of these are dangerous to enter
with strong onshore winds and the pilot
should be consulted or local knowledge
sought. Once you have discussed your
itinerary with the charter company it will be
able to advise on tricky entrances and
possible safe alternatives.

Berthing in marinas is generally on finger
pontoons. Berthing in commercial and
fishing harbours will generally be alongside
and, in summer, there can be as many as five
or more boats deep, requiring some planning
for boats on the inside to get out. Anchorages
frequently have moorings and many harbour
authorities provide visitors' moorings. Some
of these will have either a maximum tonnage
or LOA on them or will be colour coded for
LOA or tonnage and this must be adhered to.

Main charter bases

The main charter bases are concentrated
around the Solent in the Hamble,
Southampton, Portsmouth, Chichester and
Lymington. Smaller concentrations of yachts
will be found at Poole, Plymouth and
Falmouth. After that there are small numbers
of charter boats dotted around in just about
all the major yacht harbours in between.
Boats can frequently be delivered to a
convenient harbour along the coast for a fee
and depending on the weather. It is essential
to get a forecast for each day and, when
planning the cruise, to ensure that there are
options and free days built in.

SCOTLAND WEST COAST

NORTHERN EUROPE

waves as well as Arctic-like winds. Bring both the sun-tan cream and your wet-weather gear!

Wind and sea

Winds around the Scottish coast are dependent on the Atlantic influence – as for the south coast, except more so. The prevailing winds in the summer are westerlies between NW and SW, but winds are channelled and funnelled locally to give significant variations on the breeze out to sea. Winds can change quickly and one day there may be a balmy westerly and the next a cold Arctic blast funnelling down the mountains and lochs. In the summer you can strike it lucky with a week or more of balmy breezes without interruption but, in the early and late season, this is less than likely. It is essential to anticipate how the weather may change in one day and from day to day. Weather forecasts are as for the south coast on the BBC and inshore forecasts are also given on VHF Ch 67 every four hours by the coastguard. Times are: Oban 0240, 0640, 1040, 1440, 1840, 2240; Clyde 0020, 0420, 0820, 1220, 1620, 2020 (all local time).

Seas around the Scottish coast vary from the large Atlantic swell rolling in on exposed coast to calmer waters behind the islands and in the lochs. However, strong breezes funnelled into the lochs and passages between the islands mean it can be wet and bumpy with strong breezes even in sheltered waters. The strong tides in the channels and around headlands can give rise to overfalls, even whirlpools, and it is essential to consult a yachtsman's pilot for dangerous areas during the flood and ebb.

Tides

The tides around the west coast are not extreme and range from around 1·5–2m (4·9–6·5ft) in the outer islands to 5m (16ft+) or so along the mainland coast at springs. What complicates the picture is the narrow channels the water is forced through which give rise to fierce races, overfalls and, in places, whirlpools. The whirlpool at Corryvreckan between Jura and Scara is reckoned to be the second biggest in the northern hemisphere and the tide through Dorus Mor can reach 8 knots at springs. It hardly needs to be said that it is essential to plan passages with tide tables and a tidal atlas to hand.

Suitable for...

The area is for intermediate and experienced sailors. This is no place for the novice without an experienced skipper and, even for intermediate sailors, some care is necessary to plan a cruise within the capabilities of the crew. The changeable conditions and climate mean that pre-cruise planning is essential.

Harbours and anchorages

There are a few purpose-built yacht marinas and yacht pontoons at some harbours, but mostly there are endless anchorages in bays and bights in the lochs or between islands and islets. Some of the anchorages will have visitors' moorings laid either by the Highlands and Islands Enterprise Board or by local hotels and restaurants eager to increase trade. In popular spots in the summer there may be more than one yacht on a laid mooring. Anchorages in many of the bays have a weedy bottom which can be difficult for the anchor to get through and dig in, so care is needed.

Main charter bases

There are no large concentrations of charter bases along the coast, rather a scattered collection of bases including those around the Clyde, Ardfern, Oban and Skye amongst others. The Scottish Tourist Board issues a free brochure on watersports which includes most yacht charter companies large and small. Scottish Tourist Board 3 Princes St, Edinburgh EH2 2QP ☎ 0891 775700, 0131 557 1700 or 0171 930 8661 *Fax* 0131 557 5118.

Sailing area

Nearly all of the charter companies restrict the sailing area to within the islands and adjacent coast, the exact definition varying somewhat between companies. It is possible to extend this area for experienced charterers and an additional fee is usually payable for this extension. In truth the best part of the area is within the islands and coast, the offshore area often being rough and uncomfortable with few places to visit anyway.

Wales and the west coast of England

Along the west coast of England and Wales there are a number of small charter bases offering bareboat and skippered charter. The cruising area is restricted by the paucity of good harbours within easy reach of one another and an exposed coast with strong tidal races and overfalls. Charter companies operate from Swansea Marina and a few other places where owner operators base their boats.

The area is for experienced skipper and crew combinations and some care must be taken when planning a cruise. Cruising is mostly around the Swansea area or the Welsh coast to the west or it may be possible to arrange a cruise to Ireland.

East coast

There are few charter companies around the east coast of England with two exceptions. The Norfolk Broads is an area that has long been involved with yacht charter and there are numerous charter companies operating there. The east coast is also home to numbers of traditional craft which are available for charter around different parts of the coast, mostly between Ipswich and Burnham-on-Crouch.

Sailing on the Broads is about as English as you can get. It has a pedigree stretching back to the beginning of the century and is an experience that should not be missed and which, for some, is addictive. The skills required for sailing through the channels in the Broads are particular to the area and essential to getting the best out of the yachts that operate here, although the sheltered waters mean that beginners can get under way after a short period of tuition. Many of the craft are gaff or gunter rigged and masts are counter-balanced so the mast can come down to go under bridges. The sailing is not demanding but the tides do run at an appreciable rate. Fortunately there are lots of places to stop, whether for a night near a convivial hostelry or just parked up by the bank. Motorboats are also available for charter on the Broads.

The shallow muddy waters of the east coast have bred boats adapted to the area and, in many circles, it is considered the home of traditional sail, a mecca for lovers of gaff riggers as well as a few others like the spritsail and lug. Many of these craft are available for charter, including a number of Thames barges, and traditional-boat enthusiasts can find a wide variety of different shapes and sizes and sail plans available for skippered charter.

Ireland

FOR
- Outstanding hospitality and the best pubs anywhere
- Wonderful scenery and idyllic anchorages

AGAINST
- Weather unpredictable

Types of charter
- Bareboat
- Skippered

Ireland has long been a favourite with cruising yachts but, until recently, there have been relatively few charter yachts available. There are now charter yachts, bareboat or skippered, available for charter on the west, south and southeast coast of Ireland. However, with considerable tides, challenging navigation and the possibility of depressions coming across the Atlantic and causing delays, the area is no place for beginners to take a bareboat. There is also the possibility of 'soft' weather, the rain that keeps Ireland green. Ireland has a long racing tradition and the oldest yacht club in the world is at Cork.

When to go

Early season (April to May) In May there is a high probability of unsettled weather. June is a better bet when there can be periods of wonderful sunny weather, though it is still chilly at night.

At Cork

	Av max °C	Av min °C	Highest recorded	Relative humidity	Days 1mm rain
Apr	13	5	22	81%	11
May	16	7	26	78%	11
Jun	19	10	29	79%	10
Jul	20	12	28	80%	11
Aug	20	12	29	83%	11
Sep	18	10	26	86%	12
Oct	14	7	21	90%	12
Nov	11	4	21	90%	14

High season (July to August) This is the most settled period when depressions from across the Atlantic are least likely to hold you up. There can be periods when the weather will be hot at times. Evenings are balmy and sometimes cool.

Late season (September to October) Can be warm but turns chillier at night.

Getting there

There are daily scheduled flights to Dublin, Cork and Shannon from the UK and ferry services to Dublin and Rosslare from the UK and France. Internal flights and buses, train and hire car. Taking your own car across on a ferry is also an option.

Sailing guides and charts

Sailing Directions for the South and West Coasts of Ireland Irish Cruising Club Publications
Sailing Directions for the East and North Coasts of Ireland Irish Cruising Club Publications
Admiralty and Imray charts cover the coast adequately.

Essential information

Time zone UT DST (+1) Apr–Sep
Telecommunications Automatic dialling. Code 353. Public telephones with phonecards. Fax services possible from marinas and agents. Mobile phones with GSM card supported.
Health Reciprocal medical care is available for EU nationals with *Form E111*. It is advisable to take out private medical insurance for the trip as medical costs are medium to high. Travel insurance should also be arranged.
Money The unit of currency is the Irish pound (punt). There is no problem changing most European currencies or US dollars. Banks are open 1000-1600 Monday to Friday. Eurocheques, postcheques and traveller's cheques widely exchanged. Major credit cards and charge cards accepted in cities, towns and tourist areas. ATM machines will take major credit cards (*Visa* and *MasterCard*).
Documentation Members of the EU must carry their passports or identity cards. Most non-EU countries do not require visas.

No documentation is required to charter a yacht.

Charter areas

Most charter companies in Ireland are concentrated around the southwest corner between Cork and the Shannon River. There are a few small companies elsewhere, mostly concentrating on skippered charter.

Wind and sea

The weather around Ireland, especially on the west coast, is variable depending on the general synoptic situation for areas of high or low pressure in the vicinity. Depressions travelling across the Atlantic disrupt any prevailing weather caused by a high sitting over Ireland and the UK and weather forecasts need to be constantly monitored. The shipping forecast on the BBC gives useful long-range information and the Irish Meteorological Service issues detailed weather reports on RTE Radio 1 at 0633, 1253, 1823 and 2355 hours. (Getting up in the morning for the 0633 forecast is an integral part of sailing in Ireland.)

Any seas generated by depressions in the Atlantic travel across to hit fair and square on the west coast. This can make some harbours and bays with a bar dangerous to enter. In the summer there is less swell, but still large watery dales and valleys to sail 'up and down'. There are a number of sheltered estuaries in which to sail should it be too uncomfortable outside.

Tides

The tidal range varies between 4m (13ft) at Dublin, 4m (14·6 ft) at Cork and 3·8m (12·3ft) at Dingle. Tides are mostly 1-2 knots but over shallow entrances they will be stronger and around prominent headlands there can be overfalls. In some estuaries, like the Shannon, tidal streams can be very strong and it is essential to work the tides to get up or down. Around headlands it is wise to stay 2–3 miles off to avoid overfalls, especially when the wind is against tide.

Suitable for...

Experienced and intermediate sailors. Intermediate sailors should take a skipper for a few days because of the numerous hazards to navigation around the coast and the strong tidal streams. Anyone sailing around this area needs to pay constant attention to navigation and should monitor the weather forecasts assiduously.

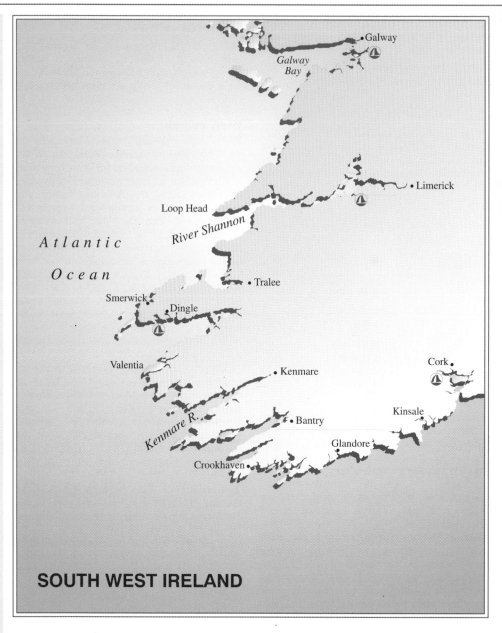

SOUTH WEST IRELAND

Harbours and anchorages

There are a few marinas, but for the most part you will be tying up next to a trawler on the town pier or anchoring along the indented coastline. There are mooring buoys in some bays. When anchoring, care is needed to cope with the thick kelp which grows in places and makes it difficult for the anchor to get through to the bottom and dig in.

Main charter bases

Bareboat and skippered charter is largely out of Kinsale near Cork. There are also boats near Dublin and at Dingle. One way charters between Cork and Dingle may be possible. There are a few other companies like the one operating a traditional Galway Hooker out of, naturally enough, Galway.

Sailing area

If starting from Cork it makes sense to shape a cruise around the southwest corner of

Ireland. Between Cork and Galway there are so many places to visit along the indented coast that you would need more than a month to visit half of them. From Cork there are places like Crosshaven, Kinsale, Castlehaven, Baltimore Haven, Bantry Bay, Castletown, Kilmakilloge in the Kenmare, and Portmagee that will leave you with a taste for Ireland. It is a wild spectacular coast with deserted anchorages and small fishing harbours. There are pubs everywhere as anyone who has been to Ireland knows. From the Shannon a cruise can be planned north or south depending on inclination. Because the weather can deteriorate quickly cruising plans must remain flexible, with a few days earmarked for getting back to the charter base.

In the event of unsettled weather, the Cork Estuary, Dingle Bay and the Shannon provide fairly sheltered waters.

Land excursions

Some time should be allotted for looking around Cork and if you are transiting through Dublin, around that fair city as well. The pubs (and the music), the dramatic scenery and the people are the best thing going, but there are castles and monasteries aplenty if you decide to escape the local pub and do some sightseeing.

Northern France

FOR
- Much indented coastline with wonderful harbours and anchorages
- French food and wine
- Easy to get to from Europe

AGAINST
- Weather can be unsettled at times and especially so in spring and autumn
- Strong tidal streams
- Crowded in July and August

Types of charter
- Sailing in company
- Bareboat
- Skippered

In northern France there is really only one charter area of consequence and that is Brittany. On both the channel and Atlantic coasts there are a number of charter bases offering bareboat and skippered charter.

When to go

The season runs from May to September or October at a pinch. At the beginning and end of the season there is some likelihood of depressions crossing the Atlantic and causing periods of unsettled weather, sometimes for several days.

Early season (May to June) Day temperatures are warm at around 15–18°C and when the sun is out it gets pleasantly balmy. Nights are still chilly enough to require a pullover. Wind patterns are irregular in May with the westerly sea breeze becoming more dominant in June. There is a probability of depressions passing over and bringing a period of unsettled weather.

High season (July to August) Day temperatures are warm or hot at around 19–20°C and on sunny days, when temperatures can get up to the high 20s and low 30s on occasion, you may need to retreat into the shade. The weather is predominantly settled with a westerly sea breeze, usually Force 4, with the chance of a land breeze at night which can sometimes be strong.

Late season (September to October) Temperatures are mostly warm at 10–13°C but it can be chilly at times. Care is needed of passing depressions which can bring long periods of unsettled weather.

At Cherbourg

	Av max °C	Av min °C	Highest recorded	Relative humidity	Days 1mm rain	Sea temp °C
Apr	12	7	24	73%	12	13
May	15	9	30	73%	11	14
Jun	18	12	31	74%	10	15
Jul	19	14	32	74%	12	17
Aug	20	14	33	75%	12	18
Sep	19	13	30	74%	15	18
Oct	15	10	26	73%	16	17
Nov	12	8	19	77%	17	16

Getting there

International flights to Paris. There are daily scheduled flights to St-Malo, Lorient, Nantes and La Rochelle from Paris. The TGV high-speed train takes around three hours to Nantes, Vannes and Auray from Paris. From across the channel there are car ferries to Cherbourg and St-Malo. Driving to Brittany is a feasible option from neighbouring countries as the autoroutes in France are fast and well maintained.

For general information, see Mediterranean France section.

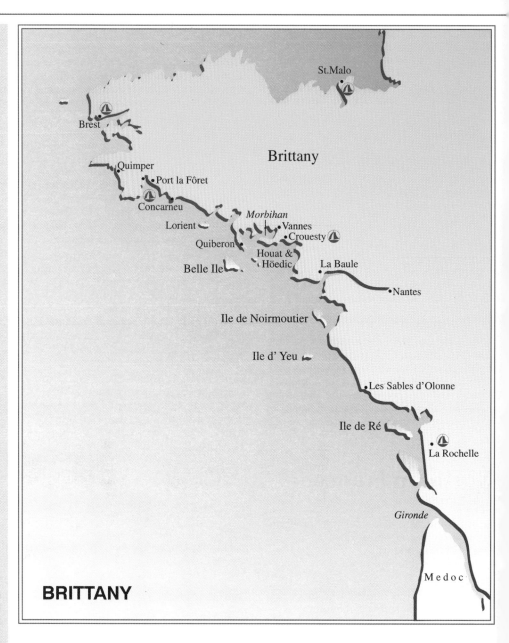

BRITTANY

Sailing guides and charts

North Brittany RCC Pilotage Foundation.
   Nick Heath. Imray. Covers St-Malo to
   Ushant in detail
North Brittany and Channel Islands Cruising
   Peter Cumberlidge
North Biscay RCC Pilotage Foundation.
   Nick Heath. Imray. Covers Brest to the
   Gironde in detail
Admiralty, SHOM (French Hydrographic
Service), Navicarte and Imray charts cover

the coast in detail. They are readily available
in most places, including large centres in
Brittany.

Opposite St Malo on the northern Brittany coast.
Photo Yachting World

Charter areas

Atlantic coast

The main charter area extends along the western Atlantic coast of Brittany from Brest to La Rochelle. There is some charter on the north coast, but the bulk of it is concentrated on the western coast. This western coast is much indented and there are enough offshore islands to make up an interesting cruising area. It is a rugged, rocky coast, supremely beautiful in places, though not somewhere to be trapped on a lee shore. Charter here is mostly bareboat with some skippered charter as well. The Bretons are passionate about their traditional sailing craft and there are a number of these available for skippered charter. The area can be crowded in July and August when the French are on holiday so it may pay to go just before or just after the high season if possible.

Wind and sea

The prevailing wind is a sea breeze blowing on to the land anywhere between NW and SW. It generally blows around Force 3–5. At night there may be a land breeze from an easterly direction which can, at times, get up to Force 5 or so, though generally less. The main disruption to the normal sea breeze is from depressions passing across or north or south of the area. These are not infrequent and in early and late season you should listen carefully to weather forecasts. Fortunately weather forecasts in the area are good with adequate broadcast radio and VHF services, forecasts posted daily in the marinas, and a telephone forecast service.

Seas are generally moderate in the summer except when a disturbance out in the Atlantic sends in a large swell. This will not necessarily be accompanied by wind and, by the time the swell has reached the coast, the wave period is long and it is pretty much like sailing up a gentle dale and down into a valley. With a depression around heavy seas set on to the coast and it is wise to be tucked up in harbour or in a safe anchorage during these periods. With wind against tide there are severe overfalls and rips in some areas and care is needed.

Tides

The tidal range in the area is high at around 7·5m (24ft+) at springs in the Chenal du Four and 6·2m (20ft) at La Rochelle. The consequence of these tides over some comparatively shallow parts of the coast are extremely strong tidal flows with around 9 knots in the entrance to Morbihan at springs. Care and attention to tides is required over the whole area if you are not to spend fruitless hours stemming the strong tidal flows. The strong tides also require you to plan anchorages and visits to drying harbours with due care if you are not to be left high and dry until the next tide. Many of the harbours are either dredged or have a lock at the entrance, so care is needed to arrive near high tide to get into some harbours depending on depths either side of high tide.

Suitable for...

The area is for intermediate and experienced sailors. Intermediate sailors can stick around Morbihan and the immediate coast where there are plenty of places to visit and still enough challenges to keep you occupied.

Harbours and anchorages

There is pretty much an even mix of marinas, harbours used by yachts, and anchorages. In this respect the area offers a little of everything and you can mix and match marinas, old harbours in the middle of a small town and peaceful anchorages. In the inland sea of Morbihan it is usually possible to find somewhere to anchor away from it all, even in high season. In the high season (July and August) you may find that you are rafted out up to five or six deep in popular harbours. In marinas, berthing is typically on finger pontoons while, in many of the harbours you will be rafted out from the quay. In a number of the outer harbours there are fore-and-aft moorings for yachts and, again in summer, there may be up to six or seven yachts rafted up together between just one pair of mooring buoys. This can cause some problems if the wind blows into the harbour as well as from the wash of ferries and fishing boats entering or leaving. In some anchorages there are mooring buoys to pick up, but check whether they belong to a local boat first.

Main charter bases

The main charter bases from north to south are at St-Malo, Port la Fôret, Port de Crouesty and La Rochelle. Getting to any of these is relatively easy by air, train within France or – probably the easiest option – car and ferry.

Sailing area

Depending on the charter base, yachts cruise pretty much north or south along the coast. There are sufficient indentations and offshore islands for you to vary the itinerary when returning to the charter base. Most charter companies on the west coast will restrict your cruising area to between Brest and La Rochelle. Yachts from St-Malo will often go to the Channel Islands or, in inclement weather, can lock into the Rance estuary.

Land excursions

To some extent, in the Morbihan and the Loire river, you can get some distance inland by boat. Many will have driven to the charter base and it is not a bad idea to allot a couple of days to a leisurely drive back home so that you can dally along the way. On some of the islands bicycles are available for hire and it is well worthwhile getting off the boat for half a day and exploring the island by bicycle. In much of the area there are peaceful walks to be had, whether to get to the local village bar a few miles away or to explore the rugged coastline and get some exercise.

Most of the old towns and cities in the area are worth an excursion ashore, as much just to wander around and look in the shops and boutiques as to come to grips with the architecture and 'must-see' monuments. On several of the islands there are the remains of fortresses built to defend the coast and at St Nazaire there are the remains of the old U-boat docks.

Other charter areas

The Channel Islands

The Channel Islands are Crown Dependencies sitting in the sea area above NW France. They are a popular holiday destination and a popular spot for those seeking low taxation for large sums of money they have acquired. The two main islands of Guernsey and Jersey have a number of sheltered yacht harbours between them and there are numerous anchorages around the group.

The Channel Islands sit in a sea area peppered with rocks and subject to a tidal range at springs of 6−9 metres (19–29ft) which gives rise to exceptional tidal streams. Rates in the Alderney Race can reach 10 knots with severe overfalls when the wind is against tide. This combination means the area is suitable for intermediate and experienced charterers only and even experienced skippers should exercise caution in the area and listen carefully to local knowledge.

There is limited bareboat and skippered charter available. Look in the yachting magazines or try a charter broker.

Sailing guides

The Channel Islands Pilot Nick Heath RCC Pilotage Foundation. Imray.
North Brittany and Channel Islands Cruising P Cumberlidge. Yachting Monthly.

The Netherlands

A number of charter companies operate in The Netherlands offering bareboat and skippered charter. There are numerous opportunities to charter traditional Dutch sailing yachts such as the *botter* complete with leeboards and lots of bits of string to pull on the gaff rig. The Dutch are passionate about their sailing and spend a lot of time on the water in both traditional craft and more high-tech yachts.

Nearly all of the sailing in The Netherlands goes on in the protected inland stretches of water, especially the IJsselmeer. The outer 'sea' coast is beset by shifting sandbanks and has few harbours that are not actually in the inner enclosed areas. It is also one long lee shore to the prevailing winds. It should not be assumed that the inner areas are tame stretches of water as, in strong winds, they get very rough and are not at all pleasant places in which to be out and about.

The authorities in The Netherlands are very strict about certification and you will need to have a certificate of competence such as the RYA Helmsman's certificate and a VHF licence.

Sailing guides

Cruising Guide to The Netherlands Brian Navin. Imray. Covers all Netherlands
IJsselmeer Harbours Hilary Keating. Covers 36 harbours around the IJsselmeer
Vetus Marina Guide to The Netherlands Aerial photos and plans for The Netherlands. Brief text

Germany and Poland

The 'German and Polish coasts are interesting areas, but demanding on navigation and seamanship. There are numerous shifting sandbanks, tricky currents in places, and few harbours with all-weather access. It is also a comparatively flat and uninspiring coast although, ashore, there is much of interest to do and see.

Germany's yachting history is well known, but its neighbour Poland also has a long yachting tradition. For both countries there is little charter around apart from local skippered charter which is the recommended way to go along this coast.

Sailing guide

Cruising Guide to Germany and Denmark Brian Navin. Imray

Baltic States

At present there is little in the way of yacht charter in the old Baltic states of Latvia, Lithuania, and Estonia, but in the future it is likely that skippered charter will expand here as these states, along with Russia, have a long seafaring and yachting tradition.

Sailing guide

The Baltic Sea B Sheffield and O Robinson. RCC Pilotage Foundation. Imray

Scandinavia

Denmark, Sweden, Norway and Finland

FOR
- Wonderful cruising areas and friendly locals
- Warmer in the high summer than you might think
- No tides in the Baltic

AGAINST
- All Scandinavian countries are expensive
- Short season

Types of charter
- Bareboat
- Skippered

Despite the long indented coastline of Scandinavia there are no large charter companies operating here and only pockets of charter by small companies in a few places. The principal reason for this is the short summer season. Nonetheless sailing in Scandinavia is well developed with large numbers of yachts registered in each country and extensive facilities for yachtsmen. Those who do charter here are universal in their praise for the area and it should not be struck off the list of possible destinations because it does not have the tropical allure of some other areas.

There is yacht charter in Denmark, Sweden and Finland and more limited opportunities in Norway. In the summer months the weather is reasonably settled and it can be surprisingly hot, although evenings are always cool.

When to go

The yachting season in Scandinavia lasts from mid-May to mid-September, with June–July being the high season. Effectively the low temperatures in May mean that June, July and August are the best months. The long summer days, especially in the north, give you the opportunity to easily get between anchorages and harbours. Around Denmark and southern Sweden and Norway the season can be longer, but in the north it can get very cold at night. The temperatures in the tables are averages and, this far north, they mask the dramatic swings between high day temperatures and low night temperatures. Remember to take adequate clothing and good wet-weather gear.

At Copenhagen

	Av max °C	Av min °C	Highest recorded	Relative humidity	Days 0·1mm rain	Sea temp °C
Apr	10	3	22	68%	13	5
May	16	8	28	59%	11	9
Jun	19	11	33	60%	13	14
Jul	22	14	31	62%	14	16
Aug	21	14	31	64%	14	16
Sep	18	11	27	69%	15	14
Oct	12	7	20	76%	16	12

At Stockholm

	Av max °C	Av min °C	Highest recorded	Relative humidity	Days 0·1mm rain	Sea temp °C
Apr	8	1	20	60%	11	2
May	14	6	28	53%	11	5
Jun	19	11	32	55%	13	10
Jul	22	14	35	59%	13	15
Aug	20	13	31	64%	14	15
Sep	15	9	26	69%	14	13
Oct	9	5	17	69%	14	10

NORTHERN EUROPE

At Helsinki

	Av max °C	Av min °C	Highest recorded	Relative humidity	Days 0.1mm rain
May	14	4	26	58%	12
Jun	19	9	31	59%	13
Jul	22	13	33	63%	14
Aug	20	12	30	67%	15
Sep	15	8	24	72%	15

Getting there

There are regular scheduled flights to the capitals (Copenhagen, Stockholm, Oslo and Helsinki). There are also flights to Arhus in Denmark, Gothenburg in Sweden, and Stavanger and Bergen in Norway. There are few charter flights and, for the most part, you must rely on scheduled flights.

From northern Europe it is possible to drive to Scandinavia, but the distances are considerable and the actual size of the countries is disguised by the bunching together of latitude on the Mercator projection as you get towards the north pole. There are also train, coach and ferry connections, but it is generally best to fly to destinations in Sweden, Norway and Finland.

Eating and drinking

Food in Scandinavia is good with that very Scandinavian affair, the *smorgasbord* widely available. Food is typically fresh, features seafood and, for those who like clean uncluttered flavours, it is a delight. It is also very expensive. Fish – including the ubiquitous herring, salmon, whitefish and crustaceans – is prepared in all sorts of scrumptious ways. There are ethnic restaurants – Chinese, Lebanese, Turkish and so on – where prices are cheaper. Vegetarians will have a hard time in Scandinavia where restaurants are not really geared up for them.

Alcohol has long been a state monopoly in the Scandinavian countries and the cost is quite simply exorbitant. Beer is mostly of the lager type and wine is imported from southern Europe. *Aquavit* is worth trying once or twice by the resilient.

Provisioning

There are supermarkets in the major centres of population and smaller shops elsewhere. There will be no problem finding what you want although it is expensive. Some of the pressed and processed meats are worth sampling as are fishy things like rollmops. If you are sailing off the beaten route in Norway or Finland remember that the population is scattered thinly in places and provision accordingly.

Costs

The overall cost of living is high and for eating out and provisioning it can be two or three times the EU average. Denmark is the least expensive country, followed by Sweden, then Norway and finally Finland where eating out is astronomical. On a boat you at least have the advantage of being able to cook on board and unless you intend to splash out very large amounts of money every evening, this gives you the chance to trim costs. Prices in supermarkets are, likewise, high and you need to shop carefully if you are on a budget.

Typical costs for eating out range from around £25–£35 a head in Denmark and £30–£40 in Sweden, Norway and Finland. This is for a restaurant meal with a bottle of wine and maybe a small beer. Ethnic restaurants and local eating houses are cheaper. The cost of wine with a meal can send the bill sky high, with the cheapest house wine costing around £13 in Denmark and £20 in Norway. In Denmark a small beer will cost £1.60–£2 and in Sweden a small beer is £4.50–£5.

Buying beer or wine in a supermarket or state-controlled shop is a lot cheaper, but still two or three times the EU average. Whether this will change in the new EU countries of Sweden and Finland remains to be seen. When you arrive in any of these countries be sure to take full advantage of your duty-free allowance. Even if you don't drink it, any alcohol will be a prized gift for anyone here.

Car and taxi hire throughout Scandinavia is uniformly much higher than the EU average. Taxi fares commonly have a minimum charge of around £3–£4 when you step inside and rates per kilometre are high. Car hire is typically £400 a week in Sweden with unlimited mileage, but you may be able to arrange special deals before you leave.

Crime and personal safety

Scandinavia is one of the safest places in Europe with very low rates of violent crime and theft and most of these concentrated in the cities. Invariably the people are helpful and polite and, with a few normal precautions, it is unlikely you will be troubled by anything anywhere.

Sailing guides and charts

Cruising Guide to Germany and Denmark
Brian Navin. Imray. Covers North Sea
and Baltic coasts
The Baltic Sea B Sheffield and O Robinson.
RCC Pilotage Foundation. Imray
Norwegian Cruising Guide J Armitage and
Mark Brackenbury
Den Norske Los (NSKV) Sailing Directions
Norwegian Hydrographic Office. Nine
volumes with harbour and anchorage
plans covering the Norwegian coast
Admiralty charts cover the coasts well.
NSKV charts cover the Norwegian coast.
Netherlands Hydrographic Office (NV)
charts cover the Baltic in a convenient A2
format. NSKV and NV charts available from
Imrays.

Essential information

Time zone Denmark, Sweden & Norway
UT +1. Finland UT +2. From late
September the time is put back one hour for
one month
Language
Danish/Swedish/Norwegian/Finnish.
Swedish widely spoken in southern Finland.
English widely spoken
Telecommunications Automatic dialling.
Codes: Denmark 45; Sweden 46; Norway
47; Finland 358. Good service with coin and
card phones throughout Scandinavia. Fax
services available in numerous places. Mobile
phones with GSM card supported
throughout Scandinavia.
Health Reciprocal medical care is available
for EU nationals with *Form E111* in
Denmark, Sweden and Finland and there is a
reciprocal agreement between many
countries with Norway. Health insurance is
advisable as health care is expensive. There
are few health risks and no vaccinations are
necessary except standard tetanus. The only
pests in the summer are mosquitoes,
especially in the north. They are everywhere
ferocious little beasties so take a good supply
of insect repellent.
Money The units of currency are the *kroner*
(Denmark and Norway), the *kronor*
(Sweden) – all abbreviated to *kr* here – and
the *markka* (Finland). Although the
exchange rates for Denmark, Sweden and
Norway are within a similar band against
other currencies, they are not
interchangeable between the different
Scandinavian countries. The Finnish *markka*
is worth slightly more than the *kr* against

other currencies. All currencies are easily
changed in the adjacent countries.
Banks are open from around
0900–1500/1630 Mon–Fri. In Norway,
banks are open 0800–1530 Mon–Fri.
Exchange offices and post offices also
provide exchange services. Traveller's
cheques, Eurocheques, postcheques and cash
are easily changed. Many of the banks and
other exchange offices charge a hefty fee for
changing currency, some by the number of
cheques and some by the total amount. It is
usually worth changing larger amounts rather
than dribs and drabs. Major credit and
charge cards can be used in most centres of
population. ATM machines are common and
work with most credit cards for cash
advances.
Documentation Members of the EU must
carry their passport or identity card.
Although access is not restricted there are
frequent checks at airports and ports of entry.
Most non-EU countries do not require visas.

In some cases proof of competence to
handle a yacht may be asked for, but this is
rare. The charter company will advise you on
documentation and provide the relevant
papers for the boat at the charter base.

Charter areas

Denmark

All charter is within the Kattegat around the
islands of Fyn (Funen) and Sjaelland. Yachts
potter around the indented coast and
between the smaller islands with a good
choice of marinas, yacht harbours and
anchorages available. Actual charter bases
may change but are usually around Fyn and
Copenhagen.

Tides in this area, a sort of halfway house
between the Baltic and the North Sea, are
not great, but in confined channels can reach
appreciable rates – tides up to 5 knots have
been recorded in the channel between
Helsingor and Helsingborg. Most of the
currents are north-going with the water from
the Baltic escaping into the North Sea, but
there can be curious reversals of currents
depending on the conditions, particularly if
there is a depression around.

Winds are variable depending on the
passage of pressure zones across the area. In
the summer there will often be westerlies
influenced by the continental land mass.

The area is suitable for those with a little experience up to more experienced crews.

Sweden

Most charter is out of Stockholm where the much-indented natural harbour allows for plenty of exploration, along with an indented coastline to the north and south. The Stockholm archipelago in the approaches to Stockholm proper provides a myriad choice of anchorages and routes amongst the many islands and islets. There are also yachts in Gothenburg. There are yacht marinas and yacht harbours here and numerous anchorages everywhere. The coastline is so indented that you can easily find your own little patch. Many of the small islands have holiday homes on them with private jetties and, if you enquire, you may be able to use a jetty to tie up alongside overnight. You may even get invited ashore, but do not ramble ashore without permission as many of the islands/islets are privately owned.

Winds here are mostly sea and land breezes, with the predominant sea breeze blowing from the SE. Tides in the Baltic are next to non-existent although there may be surface-drift currents set up by the wind blowing constantly from one direction.

Norway

Most charter is out of Oslo with some adventure charter operating further north. There are a few yacht marinas and numerous harbours which a yacht can use. There are enough anchorages in magnificent surroundings to satisfy anyone.

Most bareboat or small skippered yachts will cruise around the coast near Oslo. However some adventure cruises now go much further north past the Arctic circle and here the sailing, while hard, takes you to areas that are well off traditional cruising routes and where the surroundings are spectacular. The Gulf Stream running up the side of Norway keeps things warmer than you might think, although temperatures can suddenly plummet. The midnight sun (late May to late July) throws body clocks out of synch but is a phenomenon well worth experiencing and the Norwegians just seem to forget about sleeping altogether.

Finland

Most charter is out of Turku near the Aland Islands although there is some charter from Helsinki. There are also some charter bases through the islands themselves. The Aland Islands form a huge archipelago lying off the SW corner of Finland stretching pretty well right across to Sweden. The area is well charted but navigation amongst the islands and islets needs constant attention to rocks and reefs in the channels which, thankfully, are well marked. There are a number of marinas and yacht harbours and the possibility of mooring at private jetties on some of the islands. As far as the latter goes it is always necessary to obtain permission although, having done so, you may find that the owner of the jetty provides additional hospitality for nothing more than a bit of conversation. Most of the islands are partly or wholly privately owned and are used only in the summer, although there are permanent settlements as well.

The most popular sailing period is July and August although the months either side are warm enough. The prevailing wind is a sea breeze blowing from the NE on the eastern side going to east and SE on the Swedish side. As elsewhere in the Baltic, tides are virtually non-existent.

Anchoring Scandinavian-style

Around much of Scandinavia the depths drop off quickly and, when anchoring, it is common practice to drop anchor and take a line ashore. It is also necessary to do this in tight inlets where there is insufficient room to swing on anchor. In many places you can get the yacht nearly right up to the shore. It takes a bit of practice and co-ordination between the helmsman, the person on the anchor and whoever is delegated to row the line ashore but, after the first or second time, it becomes a relatively easy process.

Gibraltar

FOR
- Access to Costa del Sol and Morocco

AGAINST
- Often strong winds and significant tides in the Strait of Gibraltar

There is a small charter company and sailing school based here. Yachts head off for either Spain or Morocco.

When to go
The season runs from around mid-May to mid-September.

Getting there
There are scheduled flights from Britain and some charter flights in the summer to Gibraltar. Transfer time to the harbour is around 10 minutes.

Sailing guides and charts
Imray Mediterranean Almanac ed. Rod Heikell. Imray. Covers Gibraltar and the Strait of Gibraltar
Costa del Sol and Blanca Robin Brandon. Imray. Covers Gibraltar
Admiralty charts cover Gibraltar and approaches.

Essential information
Time zone UT +1 DST Apr–Sep
Language English
Telecommunications Automatic dialling. Code 350.
Documentation Members of the EU must carry their passport. Gibraltar is not a full EU member but most EU nationals and most non-EU nationals do not require visas.

Sailing area
Charter yachts based in Gibraltar usually cruise along the Spanish Mediterranean coast or cross to Morocco. The Strait of Gibraltar is a windy area and one of the few places in the Mediterranean subject to significant tides. Charters here will usually be skippered charter or the skipper must be experienced for bareboat charter. It is not an area for beginners.

Spain

Balearics

FOR
- Good mix of marinas, harbours and anchorages around the coast
- Picturesque rocky coastline
- Good food and bars ashore
- Settled summer weather patterns
- Cruising programme can be extended from Majorca to Ibiza or Menorca to fit in more sailing

AGAINST
- Possibility of strong winds in spring and autumn
- Many of the *calas* have been turned into marinas restricting the number of anchorages

Types of charter
- Sailing in company
- Bareboat
- Skippered
- Luxury

Spain, despite its long coastline, has little charter except around the Balearics. Probably more than 90 per cent of yacht charter in Spain is based around Mallorca, Ibiza and Menorca. Between these islands there is a good mix of marinas, harbours and anchorages within convenient sailing distances.

When to go
The season in Spain runs from around mid-May to mid-September, although weather patterns do not settle down properly until June.

Early season Mid-May to June. Day temperatures are warm, 22–30°C in the day, and evenings are balmy. Sea temperatures have not yet warmed up at around 15–17°C. The sea breeze, the *brisa de mar*, blows intermittently. There is a good chance of a *tramontana* or *mestrale* blowing up to Force 7–8 (28–40 knots) from the NW–N–NE. There are, on average, 3–5 days of rain per month.

High season June to mid-September. Day temperatures are hot, often around 29–32°C, and evenings are pleasantly warm. Sea temperatures are around 23–24°C. Wind

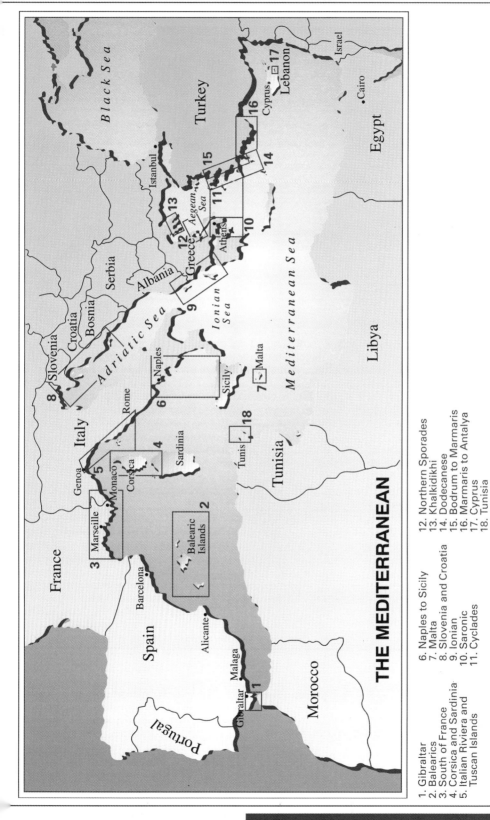

THE MEDITERRANEAN

THE MEDITERRANEAN

1. Gibraltar
2. Balearics
3. South of France
4. Corsica and Sardinia
5. Italian Riviera and Tuscan Islands
6. Naples to Sicily
7. Malta
8. Slovenia and Croatia
9. Ionian
10. Saronic
11. Cyclades
12. Northern Sporades
13. Khalkidikhi
14. Dodecanese
15. Bodrum to Marmaris
16. Marmaris to Antalya
17. Cyprus
18. Tunisia

patterns have settled down and the *brisa de mar*, blowing from the NE–SE along the coast and the E–SE over the Balearics is the prevailing wind. There is still a chance of a *tramontana* blowing, though usually at less than gale force.

Late season To the end of September. Air temperatures are around 27–29°C and sea temperatures remain as for the high season. There is the likelihood of a *tramontana* blowing at gale force.

At Palma (Mallorca)

	Av max °C	Av min °C	Highest recorded	Relative humidity	Days 0.1mm rain	Sea temp °C
Apr	19	10	26	66%	6	13
May	22	13	31	67%	5	14
Jun	26	17	37	65%	3	17
Jul	29	20	39	65%	1	21
Aug	29	20	37	65%	3	24
Sep	27	18	35	69%	5	23
Oct	23	14	31	71%	9	22
Nov	18	10	26	47%	8	19

Getting there

There are daily scheduled flights from many European destinations, charter flights and internal flights to Barcelona and Palma. There are some charter flights and internal flights to Ibiza. Most international flights go to Madrid where it is possible to get an internal flight to Barcelona or Palma. There are good deals on the numerous charter flights to Palma in the summer.

There are regular ferry services from Barcelona to Palma and Menorca and also ferries and hydrofoils from Alicante and Valencia. It is possible to drive from nearby European countries and put the car on the ferry from Barcelona to Palma, but this is not a cheap option and you are better off flying. Barcelona is connected by good rail services.

Getting to the charter base will usually involve a taxi or bus. If the charter company offers a transfer service this should be taken as it is much the easiest way of getting from the airport to the charter base.

Eating and drinking

Spanish food is varied fare which, unfortunately, has been swamped in some of the more popular resorts by the ubiquitous steak and chips so loved by the English. My advice is to stay away from these places and seek out local restaurants which will have an interesting variety of stews, grilled meat and fish, and *tapas*. The latter are small dishes – of anything from roast meats, vegetables in a vinaigrette, salads, olives of all types, and

fried seafood – which you order individually and they give you the chance to sample all sorts of things you might not otherwise have tried as a plateful. *Paella* is of course everywhere, but remember that a good *paella* takes time to cook and, if you see it arriving instantly at another table as soon as it is ordered, try it elsewhere.

Most restaurants offer a *menu del día* (set menu) which will usually have three courses for a set price. These are generally good value. Don't be afraid to investigate local dishes. Stay away from 'English pubs' and anywhere offering 'English food' and you will find interesting and tasty food.

Spanish wine is good, relatively cheap, and has some excellent varieties which are little known outside Spain. Local wine can often be bought by the carafe in restaurants. Spanish beer is of the lager type and eminently thirst quenching. Spirits are cheap and Spanish brandy is not at all bad.

Provisioning

All provisions are easily found in the larger towns and resorts and most supermarkets will have some recognisable names on their shelves, clearly priced. At Palma there are several supermarkets which will supply and deliver to yachts. In the larger towns there are good fish markets, bakeries and groceries-cum-delicatessens which have good cured meats, salamis and a mind-boggling range of olives.

Costs

The overall cost of living is medium-plus according to EU averages. Typical costs for eating out are £7–£10 a head and upwards depending on the class of restaurant. Local wine is around £3·50–£5 a bottle and beer is around 80 pence in a bar. Provisioning is on a par with other EU countries and wine and beer is cheap in the supermarkets.

Public transport is relatively cheap and bus and rail services are good. Taxis are moderate and hire cars average around £25 a day. Motorbikes can be rented in a number of places.

Crime and personal safety

Mugging and petty theft occur with increasing frequency in Spain but, for those cruising in the Balearics, the chances of anything happening are very low. Afloat, you are unlikely to have any problems although the yacht should always be locked when you leave it to go ashore and loose items on deck should be locked to the boat or removed. When wandering around ashore, few precautions are in order except in the larger resorts and cities. Do not ostentatiously display items like cameras and camcorders or expensive jewellery and you are unlikely to be troubled.

Sailing guides and charts

There are several useful guides to Mediterranean Spain. British-produced guides are best purchased before you go or you may have difficulty tracking them down. The following may be useful:

East Spain Pilot (two volumes: *Costas del Sol and Blanca* and *Costas del Azahar, Dorada and Brava*) Robin Brandon. Imray. Cover the Mediterranean Spanish coast in detail

Islas Baleares RCC Pilotage Foundation / Anne Hammick. Imray.

The Yachtsman's Directory edited by Richard Ashton. PubliNautic. Annual publication in English and Spanish covering marinas around the Spanish coast. Available in Palma

Admiralty charts cover all areas adequately. Imray produces a set of three small-scale charts covering the areas in the Brandon pilots. Spanish charts give excellent coverage.

Essential information

Time zone UT +1 DST Apr–Sep

Language Castilian Spanish. Catalan. Some English and French

Telecommunications Automatic dialling. Code 34. Good public telephone system. Fax service from agencies. Mobile phones with a GSM card work everywhere.

Health Medical services range from good to excellent. Reciprocal medical care for EU nationals with *Form E111*. You are advised to take out private medical insurance for the trip as medical costs are high. Most charter operators will be able to organise something and flotilla operators and some bareboat operators make travel insurance mandatory.

Money The unit of currency is the *peseta* and rates have been generally stable over the last five years with only minor fluctuations. You can obtain *pesetas* before you go, but there is little advantage over obtaining them in Spain.

Banks are open 0900–1400 Mon–Fri and 0900–1300 Sat. Exchange offices and travel agents operate outside these hours. All major credit cards, charge cards, Eurocheques and traveller's cheques accepted. ATM machines are common and work with most major credit cards.

Documentation Members of the EU must carry their passport or identity card although there are no real controls on internal EU borders. Most non-EU countries do not require visas.

In some cases proof of competence to handle a boat will be asked for, although this is rare. If you are worried consult the charter company. All other boat documentation will be provided by the company although it will rarely be asked for.

Charter areas

Balearics

The Balearics account for more than 90 per cent of charter in Spain with most charter bases at Palma on Mallorca. The three major islands provide a large cruising area with numerous marinas, harbours and anchorages in the *calas* around their coasts. All charter here is either skippered or bareboat although at times there are 'cruises in company' with between three and five boats. The climate is hot in the summer with temperatures frequently around 30–32°C, although the breezes blowing over the islands make it feel cooler.

Wind and sea

The prevailing summer wind is the *brisa del mar* blowing from the E–SE over the islands. It typically gets up at midday, blows at Force 3–6 and dies in the evening. At times the *tramontana* will blow down from the Golfe du Lion and this can blow up to Force 8 (35–40 knots) at times, especially in the spring and autumn. In the summer the *tramontana* is rare and does not blow as strongly.

Seas around the Balearics are generally higher than in the more enclosed areas of the Mediterranean. Even when it is calm there may be a ground swell from wind blowing elsewhere in the sea area around the Balearics. With the *tramontana* a steep high sea is set up from the N–NE and care is needed. Some harbours can be difficult to enter with a heavy *tramontana* blowing.

Suitable for...

The Balearics are suitable for intermediate to experienced sailors. A number of companies have tried to run flotillas around Mallorca but, for various reasons, these have failed. There is, however, no reason why a group of

Ciudadela in Menorca. *Photo* Anne Hammick

beginners cannot get together with more experienced crews and arrange a cruise in company.

Harbours and anchorages

Around the islands there are now numerous marinas, as well as fishing harbours and *calas* (rocky inlets). Mallorca is the most developed of the three major islands with numerous marinas all the way around the coast. Palma is one of the hubs of yachting in the western Mediterranean and is a cosmopolitan place. Out of Palma you will be surprised at some of the wonderfully isolated and beautiful places to be found, something belied by the huge numbers of tourists which

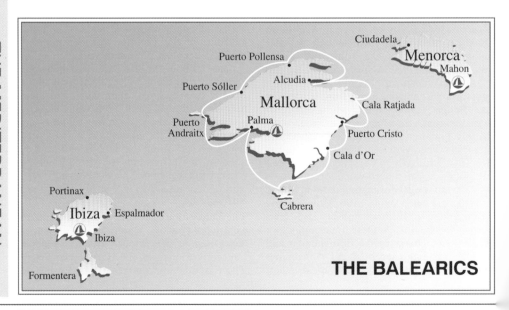

arrive here in the summer. In some of the anchorages you will be anchoring with a long line ashore as there is no room to swing. Berthing in the harbours is stern- or bow-to using laid moorings in the marinas and your own anchor in a few other harbours.

Main charter bases

Mallorca/Palma The main charter base for most companies. Scheduled, charter and internal flights. Transfer time is around 30 minutes.
Menorca/Mahón Small charter base. Transfer time around 20 minutes.
Ibiza/Ibiza Small charter base.

Sailing area

Most yachts will content themselves with sailing around Mallorca. Some will venture across to Ibiza or Menorca before returning to Mallorca unless on a one-way charter.

A typical two-week intermediate itinerary is as follows:

Palma – circumnavigation of Mallorca – Palma (total 180 miles)
Starts at Palma
- *Puerto Andraitx* Large steep-sided bay with a yacht harbour at the NE end. Restaurants.
- *Puerto Sóller* Enclosed bay with a fishing harbour tucked into the NE corner. Restaurants.
- *Puerto de Pollensa* Yacht harbour in the NW corner of the magnificent Bay of Pollensa. Restaurants.
- *Puerto de Alcudia* Marina in the NW corner of the magnificent Bay of Alcudia. Restaurants.
- *Lay day* – sail around the bay or just relax ashore.
- *Cala Ratjada* Short hop around the eastern corner of Mallorca. Restaurants.
- *Puerto Cristo* A dogleg *cala* where the marina is hidden from view until you are right up to the entrance. Restaurants.
- *Lay day* – visit the Caves of Drach.
- *Cala d'Or* Another dogleg *cala* with a marina tucked into the west creek. Restaurants.
- *Cabrera Island* You will need a permit to visit here. Moorings. A maritime reserve. Alternatively, go to Puerto de la Rápita.
- *Two lay days* – there are several bays and harbours around the south coast.
- *Palma*

The itinerary can be significantly extended by including Ibiza. It is around 65 miles from Palma to Puerto Ibiza. Remember to allow for getting back in the event of unsettled weather.

Land excursions

Palma This large city offers much to do and see, including the huge cathedral, various churches, good markets, shopping galore, Bellver Castle and an outdoor reconstructed Spanish village/museum.
Cuevas del Drach A labyrinth of caves explored by boat. Near Puerto Cristo.
La Cartuja Chopin lovers will want to visit this monastery in the highlands where Chopin and his lover George Sands spent the winter of 1838, described in Sands' *A Winter in Majorca*.

Onward routes

Some charter companies arrange one-way routes between the Balearics and Barcelona, but you will need to have experience of night sailing to do the overnight trip. It is around 125 miles from Barcelona to Palma. One-way trips can sometimes be arranged between Palma and Ibiza and Palma and Menorca.

Other charter bases

There are small charter bases at Barcelona and Valencia. Cruising here is usually along the coast and back again to the charter base. There are numerous marinas all along the coast and some fishing harbours and a few anchorages. The Costa Brava around Barcelona is an attractive cruising area with some spectacular scenery.

France

South of France

FOR
- Sympathetic marinas and harbours in chic resorts
- Cuisine ashore that is superb, often superlative, and excellent value for money
- Good wines at good prices
- Easy sailing along a coast dotted with marinas
- Festivals and exhibitions
- Settled summer weather patterns

Villefranche on the French Riviera.
Photo Rod Heikell

AGAINST
- Marinas and harbours often crowded in the summer
- Few anchorages which will all be hideously crowded in the summer
- The Golfe du Lion area can be windy in the summer and very windy in spring and autumn

Corsica
FOR
- Settled summer weather patterns and consistent winds
- Lots of wonderful anchorages and clear turquoise water
- Breathtaking mountain backdrop
- A cruise can easily encompass Corsica and Sardinia from one of the more southerly charter bases
- A good mix of marinas and harbours in between anchorages
- Good food and convivial bars ashore

AGAINST
- Chance of strong winds and heavy seas in spring and autumn
- Some navigation is tricky in the rock-strewn Strait of Bonifacio

Types of charter
- Flotilla
- Bareboat
- Skippered
- Luxury

Along the Mediterranean coast of France there are probably more marinas per mile than anywhere else in the Mediterranean (or the world for that matter). However, the large offshore island of Corsica with a good mix of harbours and anchorages extends the cruising area with almost as much coastline again and significantly adds to the attractions of cruising in Mediterranean France. Charter mostly tends to be concentrated around a number of marinas along the Côte d'Azur and Riviera and the southern half of Corsica although there are small operations all along the mainland coast as well.

When to go
The season in France runs from around mid-May to mid-September although really settled weather can only be expected from June to early September.

Early season Mid-May to mid-June. Day temperatures are warm, around 22–29°C in the day, but drop at night. Sea temperatures have not yet warmed up at around 13–17°C. Wind patterns are irregular and there is the likelihood of gale-force winds from the north (the *mistral*) or south. There are, on average, 4–8 days of rain per month.

High season June to mid-September. Day temperatures are hot, often around 26–30°C, and the evenings are balmy. On windless days it can feel very hot. Sea temperatures are around 21–23°C. Wind patterns have settled down and there is usually an onshore sea breeze. Along the Golfe du Lion and around Marseille the *tramontane* or *mistral* may blow, occasionally up to Force 6–7 (22–33 knots), making it feel a lot cooler.

Late season To the end of September. Air temperatures are around 25–28°C and sea temperatures remain as for the high season. The *mistral* and *tramontane* is more likely to blow and a depression may pass through, bringing strong southerlies.

At Marseille

	Av max °C	Av min °C	Highest recorded	Relative humidity	Days 0·1mm rain	Sea temp °C
Apr	18	8	29	54%	7	12
May	22	11	31	54%	8	13
Jun	26	15	37	50%	4	17
Jul	29	17	39	45%	2	20
Aug	28	17	37	49%	5	22
Sep	25	15	34	54%	6	22
Oct	20	10	29	61%	8	20
Nov	15	6	23	66%	9	17

At Ajaccio (Corsica)

	Av max °C	Av min °C	Highest recorded	Relative humidity	Days 0.1mm rain	Sea temp °C
Apr	18	7	29	66%	9	13
May	21	10	33	69%	8	13
Jun	25	14	37	65%	4	17
Jul	27	16	37	65%	1	21
Aug	28	16	39	64%	2	22
Sep	26	15	36	64%	6	23
Oct	22	11	31	63%	10	22
Nov	18	7	26	66%	11	18

Getting there

There are daily scheduled flights and charter flights to Marignane (Marseille) and Nice from many European airports. There are internal flights to Perpignan, Montpellier, Marignane, Hyères and Nice. For nearby European countries it is an easy enough drive to the south of France or there are good rail connections.

Some European flights and charter flights in the season to Ajaccio, Bastia and Figari in Corsica and internal flights from France to Calvi, Ajaccio, Figari and Bastia. It is also possible to get a ferry to Calvi, Ajaccio or Bastia from the south of France or Italy.

Getting to the charter base will usually involve a train, bus or taxi trip. If the charter company offers a transfer service this should be taken as it is much the easiest way of getting from the airport to the charter base, especially on Corsica.

Eating and drinking

I hardly need to recommend French cuisine although I believe its reputation outshines the reality in many restaurants. That said, most French food is of superior quality and exceptional value. Even Corsican food, which once had a bad reputation, has improved significantly. The French are serious about food, sometimes to the point of pomposity, and you should indulge yourself and immerse your palate in the national hobby of eating good food and drinking good wine. This is a country for gourmets and gourmands alike.

A French meal usually has an *hors d'ouevre* which can range from a salad to finely prepared seafood or pates, the main course which is nearly always meat or fish accompanied by a garnish or vegetables, and a dessert. As you go up the scale of restaurant more dishes can be jammed between these. Many restaurants offer a tourist menu, usually with a choice of dishes for each course, and these can be exceptional value.

Seafood should be sampled somewhere along the way and preferably several times over. The French know about seafood and, if nothing else, you should try a few oysters, a *moules marinière*, fish soup or *bouillabaise*, and a freshly caught fish or crustacean of some description.

French wine is a bargain although restaurants add a substantial percentage on top of the base price. Local wine by the carafe is usually good value, after which you can start by price, region, variety or just at random to begin sampling the massive choice available. Most of it is good, all of it is relatively cheap for the quality, and some of it is just exquisite. French beer is of the lager type, light and fizzy, and eminently palatable. Spirits are relatively cheap. The coffee is good and an institution.

Provisioning

All provisions are easily found in the larger towns and resorts and most supermarkets will have recognisable brands, all clearly priced. Unfortunately the large supermarkets are often in out-of-town sites and can be difficult to get to from a harbour without a car. At a number of harbours there are supermarkets which will supply yachts and deliver goods to you on the boat. In somewhere like Antibes you can order everything from groceries to handmade chocolates to be delivered to the boat. If possible go to the local *Les Halles* for fresh fruit and vegetables, cheeses (of which there are many regional varieties) and good fresh fish and shellfish. And, of course , there are all the local *boulangeries, patisseries, charcuteries* and *poisonneries*.

Costs

The overall cost of living is medium on EU averages and, for food, is particularly good value. Typical costs for eating out range from £8 a head and upwards for a half-reasonable *Menu Turistique*. For £15-20 a head you can find exceptional value for money. Local wine is around £3·50–£4 a bottle and beer is around £1 a *demi* in a bar. Provisioning is on a par with other EU countries except for wine and beer which is cheap in supermarkets. Cured meats and cheeses are excellent and good value, and seafood is reasonably priced and invariably fresh.

Public transport is reasonably priced, comfortable and efficient – this is after all the land of the TGV *(Train a Grande Velocitie)*. Taxis are expensive as are hire cars at around £25 a day. Mountain bikes can be rented in a few places.

Crime and personal safety

Muggings and petty theft exist in France (foreign cars seem to be a speciality for break-ins) but, on the whole, the charterer afloat is unlikely to encounter much in the way of local crime. Care should be taken to lock the boat and remove all expensive items from the deck or, alternatively, lock items like outboard motors and dinghies to the boat as any loss will probably come off your safety deposit. When wandering around larger cities like Marseille and Cannes care should be taken not to ostentatiously display valuables such as cameras, camcorders and expensive watches and jewellery.

Sailing guides and charts

There are numerous guides to Mediterranean France. Obtaining English guides in France can be difficult except in places like Antibes and Beaulieu, so they are best purchased before going on charter. The following may be useful.
Mediterranean France & Corsica Pilot Rod Heikell. Imray. Covers Mediterranean France and Corsica in detail
South France Pilot (three volumes) Robin Brandon. Imray. Covers the south of France and Corsica in detail
Livre du Bord French Almanac (annual) with detailed coverage of Mediterranean France and Corsica. In French with some English
Admiralty charts cover all areas only just adequately. French hydrographic (SHOM) charts give more detailed coverage. *Navicarte* yachtsmen's charts are available in many areas.

Essential information

Time zone UT +1 DST Apr–Sep
Language French. Italian and English spoken in some areas
Telecommunications Automatic dialling. Code 33. Good public phone service (phone cards) and fax *(tele-repondeur)* service widely available. Mobile phones with a GSM card work all along the mainland coast and for most of Corsica.
Health Medical services are excellent. Reciprocal medical care for EU nationals with *Form E111*. You are advised to take out private medical insurance for the trip as medical costs are high. Most charter operators will be able to organise something and flotilla operators and some bareboat operators make travel insurance mandatory.
Money The unit of currency is the French franc and rates have been reasonably stable over the last five years. You can obtain francs before you go, but there is little advantage over obtaining them in France.

Banks are open 0830–1200 and 1400–1700 Mon–Fri although hours may vary in the summer. Exchange offices and travel offices operate outside these hours. Post offices will exchange traveller's cheques, Eurocheques, Postcheques, and cash. All major credit and charge cards are commonly accepted. ATM machines are common and work with most major credit cards (try *Credit Lyonnais* and *Credit Agricole* machines).
Documentation Members of the EU must carry their passport or identity card although there are no real controls on internal EU borders. Most non-EU countries do not require visas.

In some cases proof of competence to handle a yacht will be asked for although this is rare. All other boat documentation will be provided by the company although it will rarely be asked for. Occasionally, customs *(Douane)* will make spot checks on boats and, in this case, all documents should be presented.

Charter areas

There are no obvious clusters of charter boats with bases being distributed all along the coast.

Wind and sea

Along the Côte d'Azur and Riviera from Toulon to the Italian border, the prevailing wind is a sea breeze, the *vent du midi*, blowing on to the land from the S–SE–E. From Toulon to the Spanish border the prevailing wind is from the N–NW although a SE sea breeze blows when the NW wind is not blowing. The sea breeze typically gets up around midday, blows at Force 3–5 (7–21 knots) and dies at night. The NW wind blows

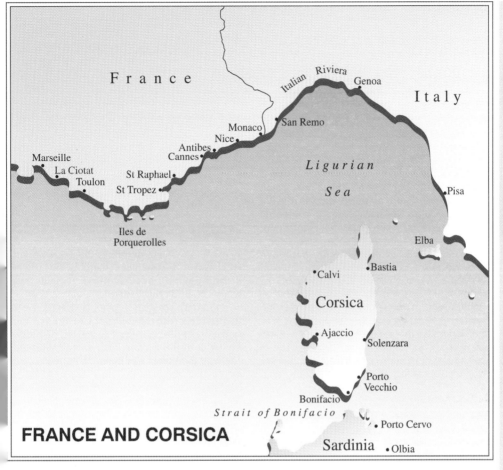

FRANCE AND CORSICA

at Force 4–6 (11–27 knots) although at times when the *tramontane* and *mistral* blow (from the N–NW) the wind often gets up to Force 6–8 (22–40 knots). The latter are more frequent in spring and autumn and blow infrequently in the summer.

Seas are moderate with the sea breeze although some of the harbours with entrances in comparatively shallow water in the Gulf of Lions will have a confused swell at the entrance. With a strong *tramontane* and *mistral* there are heavy confused seas along the coast.

Suitable for...

The area east of Toulon is suitable for intermediate and experienced sailors. The Golfe du Lion is really only for experienced sailors because the weather can change so quickly and the wind can get up very quickly to strong to gale-force winds and heavy seas.

Harbours and anchorages

There are few anchorages around the coast (except for the *calanques* east of Marseille and a few other anchorages such as around Iles des Lerins) and you will invariably be in a marina for the night. Marinas are reasonably priced and provide all facilities. Berthing is stern- or bow-to using laid moorings tailed to the quay or a buoy and, in some cases, posts.

Main charter bases

A large number of harbours have small bareboat fleets. Some of the more important charter bases are at Argeles, Marseille, Bandol, Le Lavandou, Hyères, Toulon, Saint Mandrier, Cogolin, Cannes, Antibes, and Nice. This list is not exhaustive and new bases come and go every year. There are major airports handling European flights at Marignane (Marseille) and Nice and smaller airports at Perpignan and Hyères. There are good road and rail connections all along the south of France.

Sailing areas

Effectively you will be sailing either east or west along the coast and then back again (unless you are doing a one-way charter). The south of France is typically thought of as being all Nice and Cannes and St-Tropez, elegant old resorts with elegant people and lifestyles to match. In fact, the coast varies considerably depending on where you are. Around the low sandy shores of the Golfe du Lion are the new resorts built in the 1960s and 70s to bring employment to the area. They are not elegant but do provide a useful string of harbours around the coast. From Marseille to Toulon there are a mix of marinas, old resorts and commercial harbours. The area has a number of spectacular anchorages in the *calanques* east of Marseille and some gems of harbours. Both the Golfe du Lion and the area around Marseille are subject to the *tramontane* or *mistral* and it can get very windy at times.

The area from Toulon to the Italian border, encompassing the Côte d'Azur and the Riviera, is the most popular area with all the well-known names. It can get crowded in the summer but there is much to do and see ashore and it is this area I would recommend.

Land excursions

For the most part, visitors will just want to wander around the old resorts, sit in a café to watch the sun go down, and enjoy a slow evening meal with a good bottle of wine while people-spotting. This is the best part. Apart from that, think about the following.

Aigues-Morte 13th-century walled town built for Louis IX as a base from which to set off during the crusades. Preserved more or less intact although now prettied-up for the tourists. Taxi from La Grande Motte or Port Camargue. Recommended.

Sainte-Maries de la Mer Site of gypsy church and annual gypsy festival deep in the Camargue. From Port Gardian.

Grasse Centre of the perfume industry in the hills behind Cannes. Tours of the perfume houses can be arranged. By bus or taxi from Cannes or nearby ports.

Fort Royal and Monastery of St Honorat/Iles de Lerins Anchor off Iles de Lerins or take a boat from Cannes. Fort Royal was where the 'Man in the Iron Mask' was imprisoned and the monastery was founded in the 4th century by St Honorat. Recommended.

Chapel of St Peter Decorated by Jean Cocteau. Near Villefranche.

Villa Kerylos Facsimile of an ancient Greek villa, built by the eccentric Theodore Reinach. Furnished as per ancient times. Near Beaulieu.

Monaco The old town, casino, palace and oceanographic museum are all worth a visit. Recommended.

Onward routes

One-way routes can usually be organised along the south of France so you do not have to retrace your steps. A charge may be made for the service.

Corsica

Corsica has been described as a mountain surrounded by sea and there is no better description. It is everywhere rugged and steep-to and few islands rival it for a spectacular coastline. Yachts based here frequently cruise the south of Corsica and the northern end of Sardinia so I have included the latter in this section. The area around the Strait of Bonifacio has been described as the best cruising area in the western Mediterranean and it is difficult to disagree with this. There are numerous bareboat companies and some sailing in company in the area. The climate is generally warmer than the south of France and temperatures frequently reach 30–32°C in the summer.

Wind and sea

The prevailing summer wind is a sea breeze blowing from the W onto the west coast, although it is channelled to the SW in the north and the NW in the south of the island. It is generally from the west through the Straits of Bonifacio. It usually gets up at midday and blows anything from Force 3–6 (7–27 knots) before dying at night. On the east coast there is generally a light SE sea breeze unless the stronger breezes on the west coast climb over the mountains and fall down onto the east coast. The sea breeze is often augmented in the summer by the *libeccio*, a strong W–SW wind which can blow up to Force 7–8 (28–40 knots) and usually blows for several days. Occasionally, a strong *mistral* may reach Corsica although it has usually lost a good deal of its strength by this time.

Seas can be substantial along the west coast when westerlies have been blowing for some time and there is frequently a large

Lavezzi in the Strait of Bonifacio between Corsica and Sardinia. *Photo* Rod Heikell

swell running. Around Cap Corse, care is needed of large and confused seas in strong winds.

Suitable for...

Corsica is for intermediate to experienced sailors who will usually find enough wind to satisfy them and some interesting navigation in the rock-strewn Strait of Bonifacio.

Harbours and anchorages

Corsica and Sardinia have a good mix of marinas, harbours and anchorages around the coast and it is not too difficult to arrange an interesting itinerary. Many of the anchorages are fringed by above- and below-water rocks requiring care with navigation and some expertise in rock-hopping. In some of the anchorages you will be taking a long line ashore as there is no room to swing. Berthing in the harbours is stern- or bow-to using laid moorings which are usually tailed to the quay or a small buoy. In a few harbours you will have to use your own anchor.

Main charter bases

There are numerous charter bases around the island.
Calvi Internal flights to Calvi from France. Transfer time around 20 minutes.
Ajaccio Some European and internal flights from France. Transfer time around 20 minutes.
Macinaggio Internal flights to Bastia. Transfer time around 1 hour.
Bastia European and internal flights including flights from Paris. Transfer time around 20 minutes.
Solenzara Some European and internal flights to Bastia or Figari. Transfer time around 2 hours from either.
Porto Vecchio Some European and internal flights to Figari. Transfer time around 1 hour.
Bonifacio Some European and internal flights to Figari. Transfer time around 20 minutes.

Sardinia

Cannigione Bareboat base. Some European and internal flights to Olbia. Transfer time around 30 minutes.

Porto Rotondo Bareboat base. Some European and internal flights to Olbia. Transfer time around 15 minutes.

Sailing area

Most yachts based near the south end of Corsica (on either the west or east coast) will cruise south to the Strait of Bonifacio and will usually cross to the northern coast of Sardinia as well. This way you get a bit of Corsica (nominally French) and a bit of Sardinia (nominally Italian) in the one cruise. Despite their proximity, both islands are a totally different mix of culture and cuisine. There are sufficient harbours and anchorages along the way so that you hardly ever have to revisit a place on the return leg.

A typical two-week intermediate itinerary is as follows:

Solenzara – Sardinia – Solenzara
(total 130 miles)

Starts at Solenzara

- *Golfe de San Ciprianu* Large bay with a sheltered anchorage in the north or south. Clear turquoise water. Restaurant. You may have to go around into Baie de Stagnolo in the Gulf of Porto Vecchio if there are strong easterlies.
- *Port de Rondinara* Well-sheltered bay. Care needed of rock in the middle. Restaurant.
- *Bonifacio* Difficult to see the entrance. Magnificent fjord-like bay and harbour. Restaurants.
- *Two lay days* – explore anchorages along the coast. Climb up to the old town above the harbour.
- *Lavezzi* Leave early to find a place in one of the anchorages. Care needed of above- and below-water rocks everywhere.
- *Saint Teresa Gallura* Long inlet with a harbour at the end. Restaurants.
- *Porto Pollo* Anchorage behind an islet. Bad holding.
- *Cannigione* Lively village at the bottom of Golfo di Arzachena. Other anchorages nearby. Restaurants.
- *Porto Cervo* Playground of the very rich. Anchor off on the north side inside the buoys or go into the marina if you are feeling excessively wealthy. Restaurants.
- *La Maddalena* Main town of the Maddalena archipelago. Anchorages all around the nearby islands with clear water and good walks ashore. Restaurants.
- *Porto Vecchio* Difficult approach. Marina at the head of the bay. Also good shelter in Baia di Stagnolo. Restaurants.

- *Solenzara*

The itinerary can be easily shortened by cutting out some of the places on Sardinia.

Land excursions

Calvi A wander up to the citadel, now a base for the Foreign Legion, is undemanding and interesting.

Bonifacio A wander around the citadel and old town above the harbour is fascinating with wonderful views from the cliff-top (not for sufferers of vertigo).

Porto Cervo The jewel of the Costa Smeralda, gives a fascinating glimpse at the habitat of the rich. You can anchor free of charge on the north side of the bay.

Onward routes

Some companies arrange one-way routes between bases on Corsica. Occasionally yachts can do one-way routes from Corsica to the Tuscan islands or adjacent coast of Italy.

Italy

FOR
- Fine old resorts and enchanting villages and towns around the coast and islands
- Wonderful cuisine, every bit as good as France
- Good restaurants and bars with the best coffee in the world
- Settled weather patterns in the summer

AGAINST
- Inconsistent winds except around Sardinia
- Costs for eating out and in marinas and harbours is expensive
- Marinas and harbours can be very crowded in the summer

Types of charter
- Bareboat
- Skippered
- Luxury

For the length of coastline Italy has few established charter areas. Skippered yachts will often visit areas like the Italian Riviera or the Bay of Naples, but not in numbers. The only really well-established charter area for bareboat charter is around the north of Sardinia in the Strait of Bonifacio including Corsica. There is also skippered and bareboat charter out of Genoa and nearby marinas on the Italian Riviera, at Portoferraio

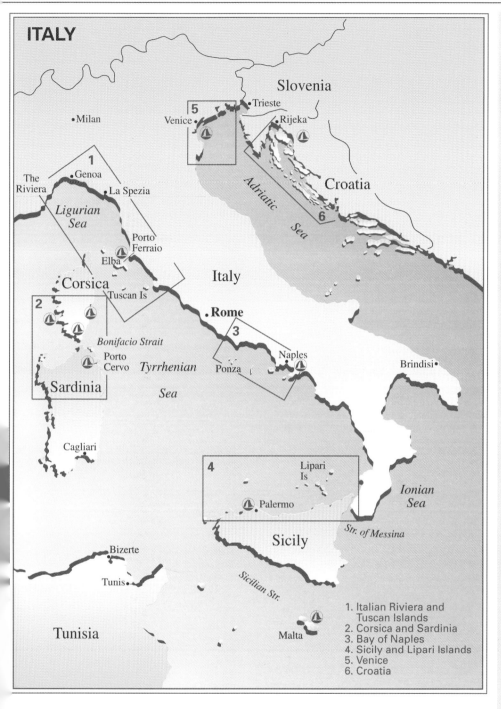

ITALY

Milan

The Riviera

Genoa

La Spezia

Ligurian Sea

Porto Ferraio

Elba

Corsica

Tuscan Is

1

2

Bonifacio Strait

Porto Cervo

Sardinia

Tyrrhenian Sea

Cagliari

Italy

. **Rome**

3

Ponza

Naples

Slovenia

Trieste

Venice

5

Rijeka

Adriatic Sea

Croatia

6

Brindisi.

Bizerte

Tunis.

Tunisia

4

Palermo

Lipari Is

Ionian Sea

Str. of Messina

Sicily

Sicilian Str.

Malta

1. Italian Riviera and
   Tuscan Islands
2. Corsica and Sardinia
3. Bay of Naples
4. Sicily and Lipari Islands
5. Venice
6. Croatia

on Elba and nearby mainland marinas, in the Bay of Naples and on Sicily, and from marinas around Venice. Many of these operations are small scale and really aimed at the home market so it can be difficult to track them down.

When to go

The season in Italy runs from around mid-May to the middle of September. At the beginning and end of the season the weather can be unsettled when a depression passes close by and you can expect periods of stronger winds and rain.

Early season Mid-May to mid-June. Day temperatures are warm, around 18–24°C in the day, but drop at night. Sea temperatures have not yet warmed up and are around 16–18°C. Wind patterns are irregular although westerlies predominate. There is a good possibility of a depression passing nearby and bringing gale-force winds. There are, on average, 4–6 days of rain per month.

High season June to mid-September. Day temperatures are hot, often around 25–32°C, and evenings are balmy. It can feel very hot on windless days. Sea temperatures have warmed up to around 23–25°C. Wind patterns have settled down with a prevalence of westerlies. The sea breeze is common along much of the coast although the local topography can significantly alter the direction of the wind.

Late season To the end of September. Usually much as for the high season with slightly lower air temperatures but similar sea temperatures.

At Naples

	Av max [C	Av min [C	Highest recorded	Relative humidity	Days 1mm rain	Sea temp [C
Apr	18	9	27	61%	8	13
May	22	12	32	63%	7	15
Jun	26	16	35	58%	4	17
Jul	29	18	36	53%	2	22
Aug	29	18	37	53%	3	24
Sep	26	16	34	59%	5	23
Oct	22	12	29	63%	9	22
Nov	17	9	26	68%	11	19

Getting there

There are daily scheduled flights to Rome and Genoa from most European airports and from most major overseas airports. There are less frequent scheduled flights and some charter flights to Rome, Olbia on Sardinia, and to Naples.

It is also possible to fly to Ajaccio on Corsica and travel from there to Sardinia although it is a bit tortuous.

Getting to the charter base will usually be by bus or taxi. If a charter company offers a transfer service this is well worth taking as buses are irregular in places such as Sardinia and taxis are not cheap.

Cape Palinuro on the Italian coast between the Bay of Naples and Sicily. *Photo* Rod Heikell

THE MEDITERRANEAN

It is, of course, possible to drive from neighbouring European countries and this is not unduly arduous if you have the time and inclination.

Eating and drinking

Italy offers the gastronome a cuisine on a par with and, according to some, superior to, French cuisine. Italian food is certainly an experience not to be missed with many regional variations. Part of the art of Italian cuisine lies in blending what often appear to be diverse ingredients – pasta and seafood for example – to produce wonderfully subtle dishes.

An Italian meal usually starts with an *antipasto* or pasta dish, then the main dish of meat or fish, followed by dessert. The prices shown on a menu do not include the *coperto* (cover charge) or service charge, both of which will be added at the end of the bill. Many restaurants offer a *menu turistico* – usually three courses from a limited choice at a fixed price. These are good value and, often, you will be offered a limited choice of the *à la carte* menu for less than the total it would otherwise cost. In any restaurant enquire if there is a pasta freshly made in the restaurant as some of these are simply mouthwatering.

Categories of restaurant vary and the old titles do not carry the indication of quality or price that they used to. *Pizzerias* are still around the bottom rung and usually have a selection of other dishes apart from pizzas and pasta. Traditionally a *trattoria* meant a middle-priced place that featured home cooking without pretension, but many restaurants now call themselves *trattorias* to impart a homely atmosphere.

Italian wine is always drinkable and often excellent. Many restaurants will have a local wine by the carafe and this is usually good. Otherwise equip yourself with a guide to the wines of Italy and pick your way through the wine list. Italian beer is of the light lager type, usually *Peroni* or *Nastro Azzurro*, and eminently drinkable. Spirits are relatively cheap and measures are generous. The coffee is the best in the world.

Provisioning

All provisions are easily found in the larger towns and villages and most supermarkets will have recognisable brand names as well as all those wonderful Italian cured hams, salamis and cheeses. Prices will all be clearly marked and, in general, shopping is as much a delight as a chore.

Costs

The overall cost of living is at the top end of EU averages although costs have remained static in recent years and so, in real terms, have come down somewhat. Typical costs for eating out are £8–£15 a head at the lower end, local wine is around £2·50–£5 a bottle, and beer is around 80 pence to £1·20 for the local brew. Provisioning is about on a par with, or slightly higher than, other EU countries, but the quality of many goods – such as cured hams and cheeses – is high.

Transport varies with taxi fares being on the high side. Car hire is expensive at around £25–30 per day. Hire motorbikes and bicycles are not common.

Crime and personal safety

Italy has a crime problem in the shape of muggings and petty theft, but these do not usually affect the visitor afloat. You might get the impression – with the recent Mafia trials and thieves on scooters in Naples who snatch jewellery and valuables from people – that you must constantly be vigilant, but the Mafia are not concerned with tourists and in only a few places, notably Genoa, Rome and Naples, do you need to be on your guard against purse-snatchers and pickpockets. If you take normal precautions and do not wear jewellery ostentatiously, keep a firm hold on your camera and camcorder, and put your wallet and credit cards in an inside pocket, you are unlikely to be troubled.

Sailing guides and charts

There are several sailing guides to Italy although most are in Italian. Obtaining these guides in Italy can be difficult outside of large yachting centres, so it is best to obtain them before you go on a charter. The following may be useful:

Italian Waters Pilot Rod Heikell. Imray. Covers all Italian waters, including Sardinia and Sicily, but not the eastern Adriatic coast

Imray Mediterranean Almanac ed. Rod Heikell. Imray. Covers most Italian marinas including those on the east coast.

Pagine Azzure An annual almanac with harbour plans. In Italian only

Vade-Mecum for Nautical Tourism in Italy Ministry of Tourism. A free guide from the Italian Tourist Office

Admiralty charts cover all areas and are available from Admiralty agents.

Italian charts, which are beautifully produced but expensive (around £15 each), are available in the larger yachting centres.

Essential information

Time zone UT +1 DST Apr–Sep

Language Italian. French, German and English spoken in some areas

Telecommunications Automatic dialling. Code 39. Generally good service. Public telephones with phonecards. Fax services possible from marinas and travel agents. Mobile phones with a GSM card supported.

Health Medical services are generally good. Reciprocal medical care is available for EU nationals with *Form E111*. You are advised to take out private medical insurance for the trip as medical costs are high. Travel insurance (including medical cover) is mandatory with many bareboat companies.

Money The unit of currency is the *lira* and rates have been reasonably stable over the last five years. You can obtain *lira* before you go to Italy, but there is not a lot to choose between getting it beforehand or changing money once there.

Banks are open 0830–1330 Mon–Fri. Exchange offices operate outside these hours. Post offices will exchange Eurocheques, postcheques, traveller's cheques and cash. Major credit and charge cards can be used in some places, but are not as widely accepted as in most other European countries. Most ATM machines will not work with foreign credit cards although some do.

Documentation Members of the EU must carry their passport or identity card although there are usually no real controls on internal EU borders. Most non-EU countries do not require visas.

In some cases, proof of competence to handle a yacht will be asked for, although this is rare. The yacht charter company can usually provide something suitable once it is convinced of your ability to handle a yacht. All other boat documentation will be provided by the company. Charter documentation and clearance does not usually take very long and, once cleared, you are unlikely to be checked for paperwork in subsequent harbours.

Charter areas

Sardinia

This area is covered under Corsica in the section on France. Many of the charter yachts based in Corsica normally cruise between the bottom end of Corsica and the top end of Sardinia.

Italian Riviera and Tuscan islands

Situated between the border with France and down around the coast to the island of Elba. Charter here is bareboat or skippered. The season gets going fairly late and finishes early. The climate is significantly cooler than further south and not as settled as that south of Rome.

Wind and sea

The prevailing wind in the summer is a sea breeze blowing on to the coast from the SW–SE. It is not consistent or developed at all times although, in July and August, it will usually blow at Force 4–5 (11–21 knots) in the afternoon. There are often days of calm. In the early and late season no one direction prevails although a *libeccio* can frequently blow strongly from the SW.

Seas are often confused when the wind blows and, even with calms, there can be some ground swell. Strong southerlies heap up dangerous seas along the coast and can make entry to some harbours difficult.

Suitable for...

The area is suitable for intermediate and experienced sailors.

Harbours and anchorages

There are only a few anchorages around the coast and islands and, for the most part, you will spend the night in a marina or yacht harbour. Berthing is stern- or bow-to, normally with a mooring tailed to the quay or a buoy except in a few places where you will use your own anchor.

Main charter bases

Bareboat charter is based around Genoa, Viareggio, Elba and Cala Galera. There are no real clusters of charter boats and all bases are fairly small-scale affairs. There are major airports handling European flights at Genoa, Firenze, Elba and Rome. International flights go to Genoa and Rome.

Sailing area

The area cruised depends, to an extent, on where the base is situated. Genoa-based yachts go either west along the Italian Riviera or south to Portofino and La Spezia. Viareggio-based yachts generally go south to the Tuscan Islands and Elba-based boats likewise cruise the islands and adjacent mainland coast. Cala Galera-based yachts also usually head north for the Tuscan Islands and adjacent coast.

If you had to pick an area, the Tuscan islands and adjacent coast is the best cruising area with numerous attractive harbours and some anchorages within easy sailing distance. For the more ambitious the east coast of Corsica is not that far away.

Land excursions

Around the coast and islands the old Ligurian villages and towns are wonders in themselves, all pastel-washed buildings and brightly tiled entrances. Most have attractive waterfronts with lots going on where you can sit and watch the locals going about their daily business. Outside the villages and towns there are a few well-known sites to look at.
Loano/Caves of Toirano Labyrinth of caves with traces of Neanderthal occupation. Close inland from Loano.
Pisa Leaning Tower of Pisa and associated buildings. Easily visited from Viareggio.
Portoferraio/Villa dei Mulini Napoleon's House when he was exiled on Elba.

Onward routes

One-way routes are sometimes arranged between bases in the Tuscan islands and Naples depending on the charter company. They are generally less common than elsewhere.

Bay of Naples

The Bay of Naples and offshore islands of Capri and Ischia are well known and all sorts of images and historical footnotes come to mind immediately. The area in the Bay of Naples and the coast to the south makes up a useful cruising area and some one-way trips are organised to Sicily. The climate is warmer than further north and temperatures often reach 30–33°C in July and August. Out of the wind it feels very hot.

Wind and sea

The prevailing summer wind is, again, a sea breeze blowing from the SW–SE depending on the local topography. It generally gets up around midday and blows at Force 3–4 (7–16 knots). In the early and late season weather patterns are less settled and there may be stronger winds, particularly from the north, when a depression passes nearby. The *sirocco* also blows at times from the south and can blow up to Force 7 (33 knots) and set up a considerable sea.

Seas on the whole are small except when the *sirocco* blows as indicated.

Suitable for...

The area is suitable for intermediate to experienced sailors although some frustration may be expressed by the more experienced over the calms encountered. Experienced sailors can also do one-way trips to Sicily where distances are greater and there is more wind.

Harbours and anchorages

The area has a mix of marinas and fishing or commercial harbours around the coast and islands. There are few well sheltered anchorages. Many of the fishing harbours and commercial harbours have a section of quay devoted to yachts and prices equivalent to marina prices will be charged here. Berthing is stern- or bow-to using laid moorings if provided or otherwise your own anchor.

Main charter bases

Procida A small bareboat charter base on the island of Procida. Charterers normally fly into Naples and transfer by ferry to the island. Transfer time around 1 hour.
Nettuno A marina south of Rome. Yachts usually cruise south through the Pontine islands to the Bay of Naples. Charterers fly into Rome. Transfer time 1½ hours.

Sailing area

From Nettuno, yachts normally head down south through the wonderful (and popular) islands of Ponza and Ventotene to the Bay of Naples. From Procida yachts will want to visit Ischia and Capri and can then head off north or south. South of the Bay of Naples there is a wonderful cruising area along the coast to Amalfi, Salerno, Agropoli, Acciaroli, Camerota, Scario and Sapri. Some yachts will want to head for the Lipari islands.

In the season harbours near major cities like Naples and Rome can get very busy, but south of Naples the concentration of yachts thins out dramatically.

Land excursions

There is really only one must-see in the area. *Pompeii/Herculaneum* Well worth the effort. The ancient city, preserved under lava and volcanic ash when nearby Vesuvius erupted in AD79, is fascinating to walk around, even for those who do not like old bits of Roman rock. It is probably easiest to reach from the charter base at Procida where you can safely leave your boat and get a ferry and train to the site. Alternatively leave your boat at Torre del Greco.
Ventotene The old harbour is the old Roman harbour excavated from the rock.
Paestum The ruins of ancient Greek Paestum are said to be the finest Greek architecture in Italy. Can be visited from Agropoli.

Onward routes

Nettuno One-way charters are sometimes arranged between Nettuno and the Bay of Naples or vice versa. Easily accomplished within two weeks with a total of around 150 miles.
Sicily One-way charters are sometimes arranged between the Bay of Naples and Sicily via the Lipari islands. Yachts normally go to Portorosa or Palermo. Total of around 240 miles with a long overnight passage to the Lipari islands and some other longish day passages.

Other charter areas

Sicily At Portorosa and Palermo there are small bareboat operations. The cruising area is usually along the northern coast of Sicily and around the Lipari islands. Charterers normally fly into Palermo. Transfer time to Palermo is around 30 minutes and to Portorosa around 3 hours.
Venice From the marinas around Venice a number of small charter companies operate. The cruising area can be along the coast as far as Slovenia and of course a foray into the channels around Venice itself. There are a number of marinas close to the centre of Venice.

Malta

FOR
- Interesting sights ashore
- Good-value food and drink
- Long summer season

AGAINST
- Restricted cruising area
- Seas can be uncomfortable and winds strong

Types of charter
- Bareboat
- Skippered

A small charter fleet is based in Msida Marina at Marsamxett. Yachts can cruise around Malta and Gozo though this is not a ready-made cruising area. Navigation can be difficult at times and winds are usually fresh.

When to go

The season runs from May to October.

At Valletta

	Av max °C	Av min °C	Highest recorded	Relative humidity	Days 1mm rain	Sea temp °C
May	22	16	34	63%	2	15
Jun	26	19	39	60%	0	17
Jul	29	22	39	60%	0	22
Aug	29	23	40	62%	1	25
Sep	27	22	37	64%	3	25
Oct	24	19	33	65%	6	22

Getting there

There are scheduled flights from Britain and Italy and charter flights in the summer. Ferries run from Siracusa and Reggio in Italy to Malta. Transfer time is around 30 minutes to Marsamxett.

Sailing guides and charts

Italian Waters Pilot Rod Heikell. Imray. Covers Malta in detail
Imray Mediterranean Almanac ed Rod Heikell. Imray. Covers Malta
Admiralty charts cover Malta well.

Essential information

Time zone UT +1 DST Apr–Sep
Language Maltese. English spoken by nearly everyone
Telecommunications Automatic dialling. Code 356.
Documentation Members of the EU must carry their passport or identity card. Malta is not an EU member but EU nationals and most non-EU nationals do not require a visa.

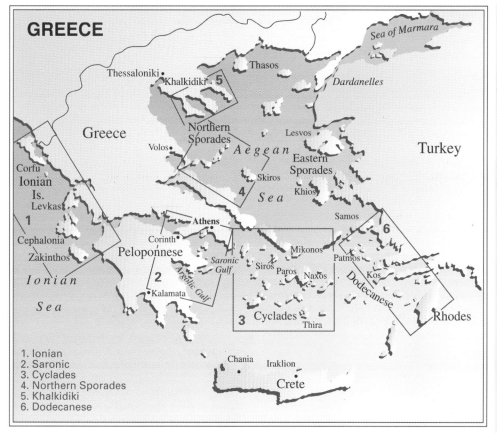

GREECE

Thessaloniki
Khalkidiki **5**
Thasos
Dardanelles
Sea of Marmara

Greece

Northern
Sporades
Volos

Lesvos

Aegean

Turkey

Corfu
Ionian
Is.
Levkas

1

Skiros

Eastern
Sporades

Khios

Sea

Samos

6

Cephalonia

Corinth
Athens

Zakinthos
Peloponnese
Argolic Gulf
2

Saronic
Gulf
Siros
Paros
Mikonos
Patmos

Naxos
Kos
Dodecanese

Ionian

Sea

Kalamata

3 Cyclades
Thira

Rhodes

Chania   Iraklion

Crete

1. Ionian
2. Saronic
3. Cyclades
4. Northern Sporades
5. Khalkidiki
6. Dodecanese

Sailing area

Charter yachts based in Malta will usually circumnavigate the islands of Malta and Gozo. It may be possible to organise a cruise along the southern or eastern sides of Sicily by prior arrangement. There are few useful anchorages around the Maltese islands and there is nearly always a swell running, making it a lumpy place to sail around. Experienced sailors will enjoy the challenge, especially some of the intricate navigation needed. Beginners and intermediate sailors should take on a skipper.

Greece

FOR

- Settled summer weather patterns and a long season
- Range of winds across the different areas, suitable for beginners to experienced sailors
- Longest coastline in the Mediterranean with harbours and anchorages everywhere
- Magnificent scenery and lots of anchorages with clear blue water and the possibility of getting away from the crowds
- Informal and enjoyable life ashore
- Numerous packages available with all types of charter catered for, from flotilla to skippered luxury yachts

AGAINST

- Some areas crowded in the summer
- Cyclades and Dodecanese can be very windy in July and August
- Cuisine ashore often of poor quality and overpriced

Types of charter

- Flotilla
- Bareboat
- Skippered
- Luxury

A long-established charter area with all types of charter and numerous different bases amongst the islands and on the mainland. Large skippered yachts have toured Greece since the 19th century. In the 1960s, small skippered yachts appeared and, in the late 1970s, bareboats and flotillas started to operate here. Greece has more coastline than any other Mediterranean country – nearly 7,400 miles if you unravel the coastline of all those islands – and, importantly, a much-indented coastline providing an abundance of natural harbours and anchorages around the mainland coast and islands. Add to this a settled summer climate and constant prevailing winds and you wind up with a wonderful sailing area. There are few people who do not return to Greece having once chartered there.

When to go

The season in Greece normally starts around mid-April and runs through to the middle of October. In general it is more settled and warmer in the Dodecanese in the east than in the Ionian in the west and Northern Sporades.

Early season April to May. Day temperatures are warm, around 19–24°C, but drop at night when a sweater will be needed. Sea temperatures have not yet warmed up and are generally around 18–19°C. Wind patterns have not settled down and there is the possibility of a depression coming through, bringing strong winds and rain.

High season June to September. Day temperatures are hot, around 26–32°C, and evenings are warm. Some nights will be hot and it takes a while to get used to sleeping in these temperatures. Sea temperatures have warmed up to around 21–26°C. Wind patterns are dependable and the prevailing winds constant in direction and strength. There are few days of rain.

Late season October. Day temperatures are still hot, around 21°C in the west and 23–24°C in the east. Sea temperatures remain warm around 22–24°C. Wind patterns are relatively settled although there is the possibility of a depression passing through bringing strong winds and rain.

At Athens

	Av max °C	Av min °C	Highest recorded	Relative humidity	Days 0·1mm rain	Sea temp °C
Apr	20	11	32	48%	9	14
May	25	16	36	47%	8	15
Jun	30	20	42	39%	4	18
Jul	33	23	42	34%	2	22
Aug	33	23	43	34%	3	24-25
Sep	29	19	38	42%	4	24
Oct	24	15	37	52%	8	23
Nov	19	12	28	56%	12	20

Getting there

There are daily scheduled flights to Athens international airport from most major European airports and less frequent scheduled flights from major overseas airports. In the summer there are frequent charter flights from many European airports and these are substantially cheaper than scheduled flights. Charter flights connect not only with Athens, but with many smaller airports including Corfu, Preveza, Kalamata, Thessaloniki, several of the Cyclades islands, Crete, Kos and Rhodes.

Greek civil aviation law requires that users of charter flights spend their holiday in Greece and do not travel outside the country if they want to use the return portion of their flight. Consequently it is not possible to get a flight to Kos, for example, and then travel to Turkey.

The journey to the charter base will usually be by bus, taxi, ferry, or a combination of these. If a charter company offers a transfer service this is well worth using to take the hassle out of arranging your own transport to and from the airport and will usually cost around the same as or less than arranging your own transfers.

Eating and drinking

Greece is not a gourmet destination, but eating out is an essential part of the Greek experience and tavernas are often sited in the most wonderful places. You will frequently be able to eat out close to the harbour or trek a bit further and find shaded courtyards or wonderful views. Greek food majors on charcoal-grilled meat and fish, pre-cooked dishes such as *moussaka*, *pastitsio*, lamb and beef stews, and stuffed peppers, all of which will be served with the ubiquitous chips and Greek salad. Food presentation is not high on the list of *taverna* protocol, but Greek food should be considered part of the overall experience of sitting in a wonderful location on balmy nights and gently mellowing amidst

The man who cooks your fish dinner.
Photo Rod Heikell

the chaos of waiters rushing hither and thither.

Most Greek wine is acceptable. It is rarely fine or consistent and, while you may find one bottle quite quaffable, the next may be nearly undrinkable. Greek beer is of the lager type, often with a recognisable German or Scandinavian name but usually brewed in Greece, and eminently thirst quenching when cold. *Ouzo*, the aniseed-flavoured aperitif common throughout the Mediterranean, is the national drink and is usually mixed with a little water. If you can find an old-fashioned *ouzerie* that serves little *mezes* with the *ouzo* then so much the better. Greek brandy, generically referred to as *Metaxa* (the most common brand) is an acquired taste, being somewhat sweeter and less tangy than brandy proper.

Provisioning

Most provisions are easily found in the larger towns and resorts in Greece and gone are the days when you needed to arrive stocked up with coffee and tea and your favourite brand of baked beans. There is not the choice of items you might find in your local supermarket, but most major brands of goods are commonly found and probably a few interesting substitute brands as well.

Stocking up the boat can usually be accomplished in just one nearby supermarket and, close to the major yacht charter bases, you will generally find one or two supermarkets which will deliver once you have made your purchases. Some of the yacht charter companies will provide an order list which you tick in the appropriate places and the goods are bought and delivered to the boat before you arrive.

Costs

The overall cost of living is somewhat below the EU average although not as low as it used to be. Typical costs for eating out are £6–£10 a head, local wine is around £3–£5 a bottle, and beer is around 60–90 pence for the local brew.

Provisioning is about on a par with other EU countries and many imported items are now available for little more than you would expect to pay at home. Some locally produced items – yoghurt, dried fruits and nuts, and spirits like *ouzo* – are good value.

Transport varies with taxi fares being somewhat below other EU countries, but car hire being relatively more expensive at around £25–£30 per day. Hire motorbikes are fairly cheap, around £6–£10 per day, but the price usually reflects the poor condition of the steed in question. Hire bicycles, including mountain bikes, can be hired in many places at around £3–£5 per day.

Crime and personal safety

Greece is a safe and relatively crime-free country to visit. There are few instances of mugging, rape, and petty theft and those that do occur are unlikely to touch the visitor afloat. In the cities and larger tourist resorts – Athens, Thessaloniki, Corfu and Mikonos, some north-coast resorts on Crete, and Rhodes – take normal precautions and do not ostentatiously carry valuables with you. Thefts from boats are few and far between and it is extremely unlikely that you will have anything stolen from your boat.

Sailing guides and charts

There are several sailing guides to Greece and charts cover all areas. Obtaining these guides and charts in Greece can be difficult except in Athens and a few other places such as Corfu, Levkas and Rhodes, so it is best to obtain them before you leave. The following may be useful:
Greek Waters Pilot Rod Heikell. Imray.
    Covers all Greek waters in detail
Ionian Rod Heikell. Imray. Covers the
    Ionian from Corfu to Zakinthos in detail
Saronic Rod Heikell. Imray. Covers the
    Saronic Gulf (around Athens) and eastern
    Peloponnese in detail
Admiralty charts cover all areas and are available from Admiralty agents.
Imray-Tetra charts cover all the charter areas on a scale suitable for yachtsmen and are available from Imray or chandlers.

Essential information

Time zone UT +2 DST Apr–Sep
Language Demotic Greek. English and German also spoken
Telecommunications Automatic dialling. Code 30. Adequate public telephone service with phonecards. Telephone and fax services from travel agents or other private agencies. Mobile phones with a GSM card supported.
Health Medical services range from good in the cities to poor in the smaller towns. Reciprocal medical care is available for EU nationals with *Form E111*. You are advised to take out private medical insurance for the trip and most charter operators can arrange this.

Travel insurance (including medical cover) is mandatory with all flotilla operators and many bareboat companies.
Money The unit of currency is the *drachma* and rates have been reasonably stable over the last five years. You can obtain *drachma* before you go to Greece, but there is not much to choose between getting it beforehand or changing money at a bank in Greece. Changing money at information or travel agents will not give you such a good rate of exchange.

Banks are open 0800–1300 Monday to Friday. Exchange offices and travel agents operate outside these hours. Post offices will change Eurocheques, postcheques, traveller's cheques and cash. All major credit and charge cards, Eurocheques and traveller's cheques are accepted. ATM machines can be found in the larger towns and work with most credit cards.
Documentation Members of the EU must carry their passport or identity card. Non-EU nationals must have a valid passport. Most non-EU countries – including America, Canada, Australia, New Zealand, Norway, Austria and Switzerland – do not require visas.

In some cases proof of competence to handle a yacht will be required although this is rare. The yacht charter company can usually provide something suitable once it is convinced of your ability to handle a yacht. All other boat documentation will be provided by the company. It can take several hours for clearance of the charter documentation before you leave. It is normal for the representative of the charter company to arrange this and to advise on procedures at subsequent harbours.

Charter areas

Ionian

Situated on the west of Greece, the Ionian has long been a popular charter area for flotilla, villa flotilla, and bareboat charter. The climate is cooler than the areas to the east although temperatures are still high in July and August with averages of around 30–31°C. The area does not correspond to stereotyped images of Greece with a significantly greener aspect to it and an Italianate feel to the older buildings. Newer buildings are of the pour-and-fill variety

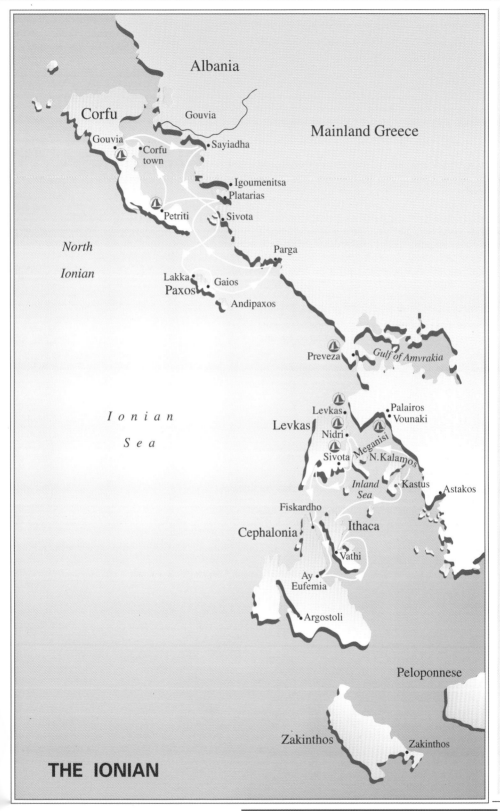

Albania

Corfu

Gouvia

Gouvia

Corfu
town

Sayiadha

Mainland Greece

Igoumenitsa
Platarias

Petriti

Sivota

North

Ionian

Parga

Lakka
Paxos

Gaios

Andipaxos

Ionian

Sea

Preveza

Gulf of Amvrakia

Levkas

Levkas

Palairos
Vounaki

Nidri

Sivota

Meganisi

N.Kalamos

Inland
Sea

Kastus

Astakos

Fiskardho

Cephalonia

Ithaca

Vathi

Ay
Eufemia

Argostoli

Peloponnese

Zakinthos

Zakinthos

THE IONIAN

common throughout Greece although most must have a red tile roof – eventually.

Wind and sea

The prevailing wind in this area, the *maistro*, is less boisterous than the prevailing *meltemi* in the Aegean. Between June and September the wind blows from the NW–W down throughout the whole area. It usually gets up about midday and blows hardest at around Force 4–6 (11–27 knots) in the afternoon. It dies down around sunset. In the morning there is invariably a calm that is useful if you have to motor north. In early and late season the *maistro* is less-developed and some days barely blows at all. At this time a depression may pass over the area and will often bring strong to gale force southerlies which can abruptly swing around to strong northerlies. There may also be thunderstorms with gale-force squalls although they rarely last longer than a couple of hours.

Seas in the area are the typical short Mediterranean chop with longer and higher waves in the sea areas not protected by the outer islands.

Suitable for...

The combination of predictable winds providing a good sailing breeze, a calm at night and in the morning, and a cruising ground protected from large seas by the string of islands running down the coast, makes this an ideal flotilla area for beginners and families and for flotilla or bareboat charterers who like to enjoy a good sail with a calm anchorage at night. This is proper gentleman's sailing with the calm in the mornings making it easy to motor back to the north if you don't want to bash to windward. Don't get the impression it is a nursery area for would-be sailors though, as the sailing can be exhilarating under the lee of the islands when the afternoon breeze is fully developed.

Harbours and anchorages

There is an abundance of fishing harbours and well-protected anchorages on both the islands and the adjacent mainland coast. The whole area is literally peppered with bays and coves and, despite the numbers of yachts operating in the area, it is still possible to get away and find less crowded spots. Berthing in the harbours is everywhere stern- or bow-to using your own anchor.

View from a Taverna. Koroni on the Peloponnese.
Photo Rod Heikell

Sailing Holidays Ltd
the flotilla specialists

Meandering around the Greek Ionian Islands

Informal flotillas, independent sailing or a combination of the two!

A relaxed introduction to sailing in the safest of environments.

We offer super deals for couples on our 27ft Jaguars - having a yacht to yourselves (without having to win the Lottery to do it!).

Singles, couples and groups will also be able to have the time of their lives on our 29, 32 or 36ft Beneteau fleets.

Wander from island to island, village to village, taverna to taverna at your leisure.

Fabulous sailing in this most beautiful of areas

Phone for a chat or drop us a line for our brochure

☎ **0181 459 8787**

Write to 105 Mount Pleasant Road, London NW10 3EH or Fax: 0181 459 8798

ATOL 2580 1038
FULLY BONDED

Main charter bases

There are two major charter bases and several other smaller bases.

Corfu The principal charter base on Corfu is Gouvia Marina close to Corfu town. It is a short distance from Corfu airport with around a 15-minute transfer time. On the east coast, Petriti is also used by a flotilla company with around an hour transfer.

Preveza A small charter base close to Aktion Airport. Around 15 minutes' transfer time.

Levkas The other main charter base in the Ionian. There are charter fleets based at Levkas town, Nidri and Sivota. From Aktion Airport it is around 30 minutes to Levkas town, 45 minutes to Nidri and 1 hour to Sivota.

Palairos (Zaverda) A charter base on the mainland opposite Levkas. It is around 1 hour transfer from Aktion Airport.

Vounaki Flotilla and bareboat base close south of Palairos.

Zakinthos A small charter base at Zakinthos town. It is around 45 minutes' transfer time from Zakinthos Airport.

Sailing area

The area is fairly neatly divided up into the north and south. Yachts based in Corfu do a northern itinerary around Corfu, Paxos and the adjacent coast. Yachts based in Levkas and nearby do a southern itinerary around the inland sea bordered by Levkas and Zakinthos. Inevitably there is some crossover with yachts cruising part of the northern and southern areas.

Typical two-week itineraries are as follows.

Corfu – Corfu (total 100 miles)
A cruise in the sea area between Corfu and Paxos and the adjacent mainland coast
- *Starts at Gouvia marina*
- *Ay Stefanos* A small wooded bay on the NE end of Corfu. Anchor off. Tavernas ashore.
- *Lay day* – anchor off in one of the bays south of Ay Stefanos for lunch or overnight.
- *Sayiadha* Small fishing port on the mainland known for its seafood. Several tavernas.
- *Mourtos/Sivota* Anchorage inside the Sivota islands or on the quay at Mourtos village.
- *Lakka* Large bay on the N of Paxos island. Clear turquoise water. Tavernas ashore.

- Gaios Small capital of the island. Busy in the season so get here early.
- Two lay days – sail around Paxos to look at the caves on the west side of the island or across to unspoiled Andipaxos for lunch and a swim. Return to Gaios or Mongonisi for the night.
- Parga On the mainland opposite Paxos. Small harbour in the west bay or anchor off. Bustling watersports centre. Several tavernas nearby or walk into the village for supper.
- Platarias Small harbour on the mainland coast opposite Corfu. Tavernas ashore.
- Petriti On Corfu opposite Platarias. Anchor off in the attractive bay or there may be room in the harbour. Tavernas ashore.
- Corfu town Smelly harbour but near to the facilities and shopping in Corfu town. Tavernas and nightlife.
- Gouvia marina

Inland Sea (total 120 miles)
A cruise in the area called the Inland Sea, bounded by Levkas, Cephalonia, Zakinthos and the adjacent mainland coast.
- *Starts at Nidri on Levkas.*
- *Sivota* A dogleg bay hidden from seawards on the SE of Levkas. Go on the quay or anchor off. Tavernas ashore.
- *Vassiliki* Small fishing harbour on the SW of Levkas. A green well-watered spot. Tavernas ashore. World-ranked sailboard centre.
- *Fiskardho* Sheltered bay and harbour on the north end of Cephalonia. The only place to escape the devastating 1953 earthquake on Cephalonia and thus retain the Italianate-style buildings of the island. Tavernas.
- *Lay day* – walk around to good swimming bays or sail around to Assos.
- *Ay Eufemia* Ferry and fishing harbour on the east side of Cephalonia. Tavernas.
- *Vathi* Main harbour on the E side of Ithaca inside a massive land-locked bay. Lunch stop at Parapigadi. Boisterous sail later into Vathi. Tavernas.
- *Kioni* Small fishing harbour surrounded by steep slopes on the north end of Ithaca. Tavernas.
- *Kastus* A small island with a small harbour and bay on the SE side. Tavernas.
- *Two lay days* – cruise around Kastus and nearby Kalamos and return for the night to Kastus, Kalamos, or Port Leone.

- *Atheni* A large bay on the NE tip of Meganisi. Anchor off with a long line ashore. Taverna about 30 minutes' walk away.
- *Sivota*
- *Nidri*

Land excursions

There are comparatively few land excursions in the area.

Corfu Parts of the old town deserve a wander around and tours can be arranged to the over-the-top kitsch casino.

Preveza/Nikopolis Visit the ruins of Nikopolis, the huge city built by Augustus Caesar after his victory over Antony and Cleopatra in the sea area off Aktion. Most people are a little disappointed by the scattered remains of the city.

Katakolon/Olympus The port on the NW side of the Peloponnese opposite the bottom of Zakinthos. From here it is possible to arrange a tour of this ancient city remembered in our modern-day Olympics. Recommended if you do not mind a lot of sailing getting down to Katakolon and back to the charter base.

Onward routes

One-way routes are often arranged between Levkas or Zakinthos to Athens. Yachts will either go through the Gulf of Patras, Gulf of Corinth and the Corinth Canal into the Aegean or sail around the Peloponnese and up the eastern side of the Peloponnese to Athens. On either route there is a lot of sailing involved for a two-week trip with a total of around 180 miles through the Corinth Canal and around 270 miles around the Peloponnese.

Saronic

The gulf south of Athens and generally extended as an area down the east coast of the Peloponnese. Its proximity to Athens and Athens Airport has meant it has always been a popular area. Despite being close to Athens the area has many small and relatively untouched harbours and anchorages as well as the more sophisticated resorts. The geography of the area is rugged and rocky with the mountains of the eastern Peloponnese rising abruptly from the sea and providing a magnificent backdrop. The climate is hotter than the Ionian and, in July

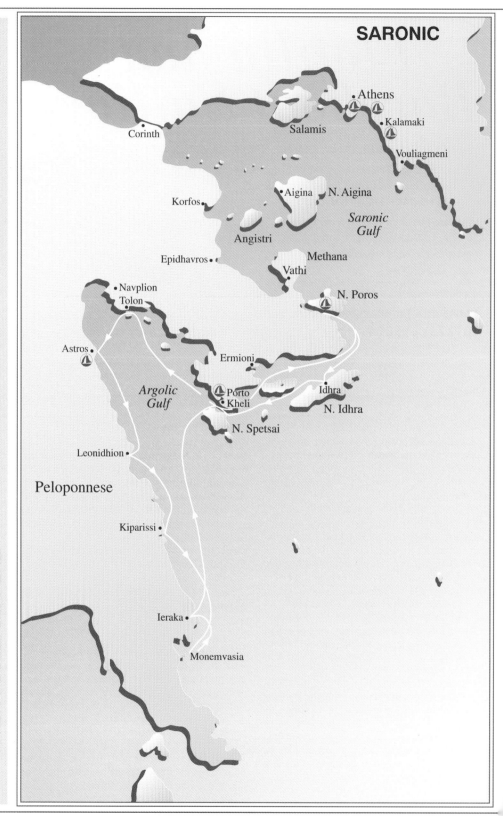

SARONIC

Corinth

Athens

Kalamaki

Salamis

Vouliagmeni

Korfos

Aigina

N. Aigina

*Saronic
Gulf*

Angistri

Epidhavros

Methana

Vathi

N. Poros

Navplion

Tolon

Astros

Ermioni

Idhra

*Argolic
Gulf*

Porto
Kheli

N. Idhra

N. Spetsai

Leonidhion

Peloponnese

Kiparissi

Ieraka

Monemvasia

and August, temperatures can reach a sizzling 33–35°C.

Wind and sea

There is a mix of prevailing winds over the area. In the Saronic Gulf down to Poros the *meltemi* will often blow, although this is the limit of the area the wind blows over. The *meltemi* blows from the NE at around Force 4–6 (11–27 knots). It will frequently blow day and night although it generally dies off at night towards Methana and Poros. If the *meltemi* does not blow there will often be a S–SE sea breeze. In the area between Poros, Hydra and the Argolic Gulf the prevailing wind is a sea breeze blowing from the SE. It usually gets up about midday, blows at Force 3–5 (7–21 knots) and dies down at sunset. Down the eastern Peloponnese from Kiparissia to Monemvasia the prevailing wind is a NE morning breeze around Force 4 (11–16 knots) turning around to a SE sea breeze, around Force 4, in the afternoon. In July and August the *meltemi* will sometimes blow on to this coast at anything up to Force 6–7 (22–33 knots).

Seas here vary according to the area. Behind the islands and in the Argolic Gulf the seas are typically short and sharp but of no great height. Seas in the Saronic Gulf are a little fiercer when the *meltemi* is blowing. Along the eastern Peloponnese the seas are higher and can become confused when the *meltemi* blows onto the coast.

Suitable for...

This area, with a mix of winds and numerous well-sheltered harbours and anchorages, is suitable for beginners and families as well as intermediate and experienced sailors. In the area encompassed by Poros, Hydra, Spetsai and the Argolic Gulf, the predictable afternoon breeze and morning calm makes it an ideal flotilla area with longer excursions down the Peloponnese or up to Aegina for the more adventurous. Like the Ionian there is plenty of exhilarating sailing to be had in the area with the morning calm providing the opportunity to motor to windward if desired.

Harbours and anchorages

The area has a mix of yacht harbours, fishing harbours and anchorages amongst the islands and the adjacent coast. Around the coast near Athens are numerous marinas, although most charterers will only use these as a base from which to leave and return. Some of the harbours close to Athens, notably Aegina,

Poros, Hydra and Spetsai, are overcrowded in the summer and especially at weekends when Athens-based boats pour out of the capital for the unpolluted air of the islands. Berthing in the harbours is everywhere stern- or bow-to using your own anchor, except for the marinas where laid moorings are installed.

Main charter bases

The main bareboat and skippered charter bases are in the marinas near Athens. There are a few other flotilla and bareboat bases amongst the islands and on the Peloponnese.
Athens In the marinas around Athens there are numerous bareboat and skippered charter companies based at Zea Marina, Flisvos (Faliron), Alimos (Kalamaki) Marina, and Glifadha 4. The attraction of these charter bases is not the surroundings – which are noisy, dirty and subject to noise pollution from the planes taking off and landing at Athens Airport – but the convenience of stepping off the plane and on to your yacht. Transfer times are from 10 minutes for Glifadha 4, 15 minutes for Alimos and 20 minutes for Flisvos, to 30 minutes for Zea.
Poros A flotilla and bareboat base in the harbour sandwiched between Poros Island and the Peloponnese. Around 2–2½ hours' transfer time on the hydrofoil or fast ferry from Piraeus.
Porto Kheli A flotilla base in the natural harbour opposite the island of Spetsai. Around 4 hours' transfer time.
Astros Flotilla and bareboat charter base in the NW corner of the Argolic Gulf. Around 3 hours' transfer time.

Sailing area

The area has a fairly standard run from Athens following the coast of the eastern Peloponnese and off-lying islands until turning around and heading back. There are sufficient harbours and anchorages along the way so that you do not have to revisit places on the return leg of the route. Depending on how much sailing is desired, a yacht can cruise up into the Argolic Gulf and/or south down to Monemvasia.

A typical two-week intermediate itinerary is as follows.
Poros – Monemvasia – Poros
(total 125 miles)
- *Starts at Poros*
- *Idhra* An exquisite gem preserved much as it was in the 19th century and where no cars are allowed on the island. A popular

destination and you need to get here before 1500 to get a berth although, after that, boats stack up from the quay out, up to three deep. Tavernas.

- *Spetsai* Anchor in Baltiza Creek as the inner harbour is usually crowded. Attractive 19th-century merchants' houses. Tavernas and nightlife.
- *Tolon* Stop for lunch at one of the bays in the gulf until the afternoon breeze fills in. Tolon harbour is usually full so anchor off the beach. Tavernas and nightlife ashore.
- *Astros* A short sail across the gulf. Attractive harbour with good swimming beach nearby. Tavernas.
- *Lay day.*
- *Leonidhion* A small fishing harbour. A bit uncomfortable but delightful. Tavernas.
- *Kiparissi* A huge bay with a pier. Anchor according to the wind and sea. Tavernas.
- *Monemvasia* A Gibraltar-like headland jutting out from the coast. A small marina on the south side or anchor off. Visit the old town on the peninsula for an evening meal.
- *Lay day* – explore the old fort and old town on the peninsula or anchorages in the bays to the north.

- *Ieraka* Fjord-like inlet between Monemvasia and Kiparissi. Tavernas.
- *Porto Kheli* An enclosed bay opposite Spetsai. Watersports centre. Tavernas.
- *Poros*

Land excursions

Athens The ancient capital of Greece and the birthplace of democracy, although it is difficult to discern the ancient bits amongst the high-rise buildings. Yet a visit to the Parthenon and surrounding buildings is a must.

Epidavros A taxi can be arranged from the harbour of Palaia Epidavros to visit the theatre, an acoustically perfect piece of ancient engineering. Also worth a look are the buildings of the Askeplion and the little museum. Recommended.

Mycenae An excursion can be arranged from Navplion. An impressive and important site, the centre of the Mycenean civilisation. Navplion itself is a smelly harbour, but the old town and the impressive Venetian citadel of Palmidhi above it merit a visit. Recommended.

Ieraka on the eastern Peloponnese.
Photo Rod Heikell

Leonidhion From here you can arrange a taxi to visit the Monastery of Elona tucked into the cliffs in the mountains behind the port.

Monemvasia The old town on the headland, now a protected site, and the citadel on the summit are a marvellously preserved piece of Byzantine architecture with later Turkish and Venetian additions. Recommended.

Onward routes

Athens is the centre of yachting in Greece and one-way trips are common to several other areas.

Ionian One-way routes are often arranged between Athens to Levkas or Zakinthos. Yachts will either go through the Corinth Canal to the Gulf of Corinth, Gulf of Patras and into the Ionian or sail around and up the western side of the Peloponnese. On either route there is a lot of sailing involved for a two-week trip with a total of around 180 miles through the Corinth Canal and around 270 miles around the Peloponnese.

Dodecanese One-way routes are common through the Cyclades to either Kos or Rhodes. This route is fairly windy although heading SE to the Dodecanese the wind is mostly aft of the beam when the *meltemi* is blowing. Around 250 miles.

Northern Sporades Not a common route. It involves a lot of uphill work against the *meltemi* in summer. Yachts usually take the inshore route inside Evia where there are more harbours and anchorages to visit. Around 170 miles on a straight run which you will emphatically not to do in the summer against the *meltemi*.

Cyclades

The scattered archipelago of islands in the central Aegean. These are the islands that correspond most to our picture of Greece, with white-cube houses sprouting from a rocky landscape and lapped by the blue Mediterranean. Everyone has probably heard of Mikonos and possibly of Thira (Santorini), Paros, Naxos and Milos. But there are many many more islands in this group that are just as wonderful as these and which are less popular (for which read less crowded) and more suited to exploration by yacht. The two names that roll off everyone's tongue, Mikonos and Thira, are paradoxically least suited for a visit by yacht. Mikonos harbour is overcrowded, exposed to

the full force of the *meltemi*, and has a lot of wash from the constant coming and going of large ferries. Thira has no good comfortable anchorage and is best visited briefly before going to spend the night in a safe harbour nearby.

The area is hot in the summer with temperatures averaging 33–36°C in July and August although the cooling *meltemi* blowing over the islands makes it appear less.

Wind and sea

Between mid-June and the end of September the Aegean is subject to the full force of the *meltemi*. This a constant wind formed by the pressure difference between the Azores high and the low of Pakistan when the SW monsoon is established and not a typical thermal sea breeze. It regularly blows at Force 6–7 (22–33 knots) and gusts off the lee side of high islands can be considerably more. It is not to be underestimated. It blows in an arc through the Cyclades, from the NE in the north, turning to N and then NW in the S and W. It does have some thermal component and may die off to Force 4–5 (11–21 knots) at night although you cannot count on it. The *meltemi* is less well developed at the beginning and end of the season and, for this reason, this is the best time to visit the Cyclades.

The *meltemi* causes a steep breaking sea that can be difficult to beat against to windward. Around headlands and through channels there can be exceptionally confused seas where the direction of a local wave train is different to the main swell further out.

Suitable for . . .

In the summer the Cyclades should be attempted by experienced sailors only. I used to make a living bringing bareboats back from the islands where desperate charterers had abandoned their yachts and, with them, their deposits. If you set out for the Cyclades and decide it is just too uncomfortable to continue and enjoy it, then remember you can head west to the Saronic and eastern Peloponnese where winds are lighter and it is generally calm at night.

Harbours and anchorages

Nearly all of the islands have at least one main harbour and many have numerous harbours and/or protected anchorages. Communication by boat was once the only means of communication for these islands and the harbour was the lifeline to the outer world. Berthing in the harbours is everywhere stern- or bow-to using your own anchor.

Main charter bases

Athens Athens is the main charter base although yachts can do one way trips to or from Rhodes or Kos and Athens. There are also small bareboat bases on Siros and Paros. Getting back from the Dodecanese against the *meltemi* is a long hard bash to windward and for experienced and hardy sailors only.

Sailing area

There are no obvious routes through the Cyclades for a two-week cruise and charterers can pick-and-mix according to preference. What is important is to leave enough lay days and a suitable period of time to get back against the *meltemi* to the charter base, usually Athens. There is nothing more calculated to ruin a relaxed holiday than several days of beating to windward against a Force 7 and, early on, the skipper should take stock of how his crew or guests are reacting to the wind and sea. If there are muttered threats about mutiny and catching the ferry back, then it is always possible to shorten the trip and do shorter legs back against the wind to Athens.

Northern Sporades

A string of islands in the NW Aegean off the top of Evia. This group is a popular charter area because the *meltemi* blows with less force here and there are numerous harbours and anchorages along the lee side of the chain of islands. The islands are also greener than the parched rock of the Cyclades with pine covering large areas and a number of fine sandy beaches. The architecture, typically red-tiled houses with pitched roofs, instead of the square cubes of the Cyclades, lends an individual character to the area. Temperatures in the summer are moderate although they reach 32°C in July and August. In the spring and autumn, temperatures are considerably cooler than further south and you will need a pullover in the evenings.

Wind and sea

The prevailing wind in the summer is the *meltemi* blowing from the N–NE over the islands. It blows more fitfully here, usually Force 4–5 (11–21 knots), with numerous days of calm or light southerly breezes. At the beginning and end of the season there may be unsettled weather and strong northerly or southerly winds when a depression passes over.

The seas here are typically a low short chop in the lee of the islands with no great force or height to them. In the passages between the islands or out of their lee the seas can be higher, but usually of no consequence in the summer.

Suitable for . . .

The settled wind patterns and moderate winds mean that this is a popular area for flotilla and bareboat charter for beginners and intermediate sailors. If venturing out of the area – say down to Skiros and the east coast of Evia where the *meltemi* is considerably stronger and the seas proportionately higher, more sailing experience is necessary.

Harbours and anchorages

There are numerous well-protected harbours and anchorages along the chain of islands and in and around the northern Evia channel on the mainland opposite. The harbours and anchorages on the main islands of Skiathos, Skopelos and Alonnisos can get crowded in the summer while the harbours on the mainland and Evia are never crowded. Berthing in the harbours is nearly everywhere stern- or bow-to using your own anchor.

Main charter bases

Skiathos The main charter base is Skiathos where there is an airport with direct European flights. Transfer time is around 15 minutes.
Volos There is also a flotilla and bareboat base at Milina in the Gulf of Volos and bareboats at Volos.

Sailing area

The sailing area is under the lee of the chain of islands with a trip south to Skiros for the more experienced or west into the northern Evia channel and Gulf of Volos for those who want to venture further. From Skiathos, most yachts head for Glossa or one of the anchorages on the SW side of Skopelos, around to Skopelos depending on the strength of the *meltemi*, to Patitiri on Alonnisos, and then to Pelagos. After that it is a matter of deciding whether you will stay under the lee of the islands and potter, or head off west to the northern Evia channel and Gulf of Volos, or south to windy Skiros and the east side of Evia.

Onward routes

Not common. It is possible to do a one-way route to Athens, usually down the inside of Evia.

Dodecanese

The string of islands lying down the eastern side of the Aegean close to the Turkish coast. The islands have had a chequered history and were occupied by the Italians up until the Second World War when they reverted to Greece. In recent years the area has become increasingly popular for yacht charter and, because mild weather can be expected later in the season, it can be as busy here in late September as it is in August in other areas. The climate here can be very hot in summer and is still warm in late September and October. Temperatures in July and August typically reach 34–36°C although, like the Cyclades, it feels less because of the cooling *meltemi* blowing over the islands.

Wind and sea

The prevailing wind in the summer is our old friend the *meltemi*. In the SE corner of the Aegean it has curved around to blow from the NW–W. It usually blows at Force 5–7 (17–33 knots) in the summer with stronger gusts off the lee side of the high islands. As in the Cyclades, it blows with less force and frequency at the beginning and end of the season.

Seas around the Dodecanese are short and sharp, similar to those in the Cyclades and difficult to beat against to windward. In the summer a fairly constant current flows northwards up the Turkish coast and the prevailing winds blowing against this current can create confused seas, especially around headlands and capes.

Suitable for . . .

Like the Cyclades the Dodecanese are for experienced sailors. The strong summer winds and short seas create conditions that can make it difficult to go north. Most yacht charter here is bareboat or skippered charter although there is a flotilla running out of Kos.

Harbours and anchorages

As in the Cyclades, communication by sea was essential in the past, and all the islands have at least one harbour and frequently more. There are also numerous well-sheltered anchorages and the charterer will have no problem arranging an itinerary around the islands. Berthing in all harbours is stern- or bow-to using your own anchor.

Main charter bases

Rhodes The main charter base is at Rhodes in cluttered and crowded Mandraki. There are frequent European flights to Rhodes airport with a transfer time of around 45 minutes to Rhodes harbour.
Kos Charter yachts are also based at Kos where there is around a 25-minute transfer from Kos airport to Kos harbour.
Samos Bareboat base at Pithagorion.

Sailing area

The sailing area extends north from Rhodes to Samos for hardy sailors who want to keep on beating to windward to get this far. There is a wide choice of harbours and anchorages all along the chain of islands and starting at Rhodes has the advantage that you get the windward leg of the cruise out of the way first and can then coast back south to Rhodes with the wind aft of the beam. From Kos you can go either north or south depending on your inclination and how far you want to sail. A typical two-week itinerary is as follows.

Rhodes – Kalimnos – Rhodes
(total 180 miles)
- *Starts at Rhodes*
- *Simi* Until you get up to the entrance you will not see the building-block town around the sides of the steep-to inlet that forms the natural harbour. Tavernas.
- *Lay day* – potter around to any of the bays on the east or south of the island or just relax at Simi town.
- *Nisiros/Palon* A small fishing harbour on the north side of Nisiros. Several tavernas.
- *Lay day* – visit the crater at the summit of the island.
- *Kos* The main harbour of the island. Crowded and chaotic. Tavernas and nightlife.
- *Kalimnos/Vathi* A fjord-like inlet on the SE corner of the island. If there is no room on the small quayed area anchor fore and aft further into the inlet. Several tavernas.
- *Kalimnos* Main harbour of the island. Tavernas and nightlife.
- *Two lay days* – potter around the island or go further north to Leros.
- *Kos/Kamares* Small harbour and bay tucked under the SW corner of Kos. Berth in the harbour or anchor in the bay. Several tavernas.

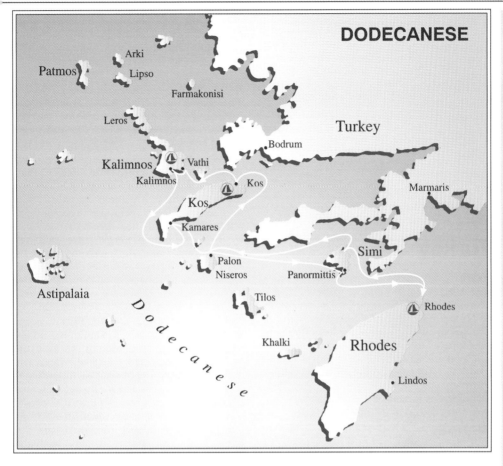

- *Palon on Nisiros or Tilos* Tilos is not a good harbour with a strong meltemi so make your choice depending on the wind.
- *Simi/Panormittis* An enclosed anchorage on the SW corner of Simi. Monastery ashore. Taverna.
- *Rhodes*

Land excursions

Rhodes The old walled town and castle of the Knights of St John is one of the finest surviving pieces of medieval military architecture. Just wander around and try to avoid the touts.

Nisiros A visit to the crater is well worth the effort and you get magnificent views over the sea and islands as well. There is an occasional bus from Mandraki or a taxi from Palon can be arranged. Do not leave your yacht unattended in Mandraki harbour which is exposed to the *meltemi*. Recommended.

Kos Around Kos town are bits and pieces of the ancient city and the castle built by the

Knights of St John. A visit to the famous Ascelepion, made famous by Hippocrates, is easiest by taxi.

Patmos The fortified monastery of St John is easily reached by bus or taxi from Skala, the main port on the east side of the island. Recommended.

Onward routes

It is possible to charter a yacht in Rhodes and sail up through the Cyclades to Athens. In the summer, when the *meltemi* is blowing, this is a long hard slog against the prevailing wind and can only be recommended for experienced sailors. Those less experienced can contemplate it in early or late season. Around 250 miles.

Other charter areas

Peloponnese Small flotilla and bareboat fleets operate out of Githion. These may not always operate for the whole season depending on weather conditions. Kalamata Airport is nearby with about a 1-hour transfer time.

Khalkidikhi A small charter fleet operates out of Porto Koufo and another out of Porto Carras. Thessaloniki Airport is nearby with about a 2-hour transfer time. Mostly bareboat.

Lesvos Small bareboat base.

Crete Small bareboat base.

Turkey

FOR

- Settled summer weather patterns and a long season
- Numerous packages available with all types of charter catered for from flotilla to skippered luxury yachts
- Good and interesting food with a flavour of the east and exceptionally good value
- Magnificent mountainous scenery with numerous attractive anchorages
- Lots of things to do and see ashore

AGAINST

- Some areas crowded in the summer
- Long transfers to some charter bases

Types of charter

- Flotilla
- Bareboat
- Skippered
- Luxury

A more recent charter area, now a well-established charter destination in the Mediterranean. It supports all types of charter from flotilla, through bareboat to skippered charter with a number of charter bases around the coast. Although Turkey has few islands it does have a much-indented coastline with deep gulfs making up for the lack of islands. A few skippered yachts cruised Turkey in the 1960s and 70s but it was not until the 1980s that yacht charter expanded in Turkey and flotilla and bareboat fleets were introduced. The area is well suited to yacht charter with a settled summer climate and a magnificent mountainous coastline, covered in pine in many places. For most people it is a gentle introduction to Asia Minor and most people come away surprised at the subtle blend of east and west. In recent years a number of marinas have been built and these rank with any in the Mediterranean for services and facilities.

When to go

The season in Turkey starts around mid-April and runs through until the end of October. The weather is warmer and more settled here later in the season than it is in the western Mediterranean.

Early season April to May. Day temperatures are warm, around 22–27°C in the day, but drop at night and a sweater will be needed. Sea temperatures have not yet warmed up and are generally around 19–20°C. Wind patterns have not yet become fully established although there is still a preponderance of northerlies. There is a possibility of a depression passing nearby and bringing gale-force winds, often southerlies, for a few days accompanied by rain and, frequently, thunderstorms.

High season June to September. Day temperatures are hot, around 33–36°C in July and August, and evenings are warm. On days when there is no wind or in harbours which shut out the wind it can feel very hot. Along the eastern Turkish coast, temperatures are higher, often 35–36°C in the day, and a higher humidity saps the energy and can make sleeping at night difficult until you get used to it. Sea temperatures have warmed up to around 22–25°C and shallow water that gets the sun all day is positively tepid. Wind patterns are dependable and the prevailing winds are constant in direction and strength. There are few days of rain.

Late season October. Day temperatures are still hot, around 25–27°C, although the evenings are cooler. Sea temperatures remain warm around 24°C. Wind patterns are still constant although there is the possibility of a depression passing through bringing gale-force winds, rain and frequent thunderstorms.

At Izmir

	Av max °C	Av min °C	Highest recorded	Relative humidity	Days 1mm rain	Sea temp °C
Apr	21	9	33	48%	5	14
May	26	13	41	45%	4	15
Jun	31	17	41	40%	2	18
Jul	33	21	42	31%	0	22
Aug	33	21	42	37%	1	24-25
Sep	29	17	39	42%	1	24
Oct	24	13	37	49%	4	23
Nov	19	9	32	58%	6	20

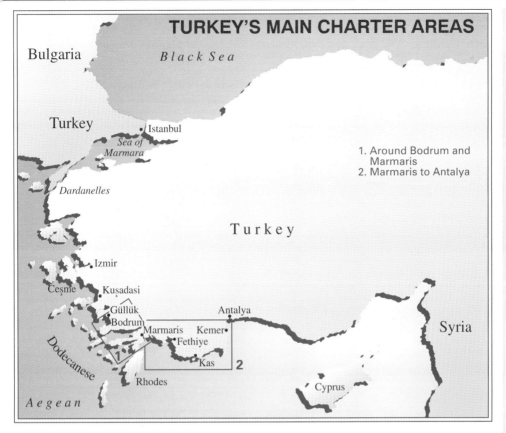

TURKEY'S MAIN CHARTER AREAS

1. Around Bodrum and Marmaris
2. Marmaris to Antalya

Getting there

Although Istanbul is the main international airport for Turkey, it is too far from the popular charter areas to be useful for most people on a two-week holiday. Most charterers arrive through one of the smaller airports that have European flights, principally Izmir, Dalaman or Antalya. Bodrum Airport is now open although there are few international charter flights at the time of writing. It is likely there will be charter flights in 1998. Internal flights from Istanbul connect with these airports on a regular basis.

The journey to the charter base will usually be by bus, minibus or taxi. If a charter company offers a transfer service this should be taken as it removes the hassles of arranging your transport to and from the airport and will usually cost around the same or less than arranging your own transfers.

Eating and drinking

Eating in Turkey is a delight. The cuisine is as celebrated in the east as French cuisine is in the west. The food is varied and inexpensive and the service invariably good. Turks are natural entrepreneurs and, if half a dozen yachts visit an anchorage, a makeshift restaurant will spring up there in no time. In the villages and towns there is usually a good choice of restaurants of all types. *Lokantas* are the traditional eating place, usually serving an interesting variety of pre-cooked soups, stews, and oven dishes as well as grilled dishes. Restaurants are more upmarket and usually have fewer pre-cooked and more grilled dishes. Pizza places may serve the traditional Turkish *pide* and/or adaptations of the Italian pizza. Between these are many shades of grey.

Starters in Turkey are many and varied. There will often be different vegetables in a vinaigrette, salads of all descriptions, including seafood and chicken salads, small hot dishes like *borek* (cheese wrapped in *filo* pastry and deep fried), cooked vegetables like aubergines which are chopped and combined into dips . . . the list is long and satisfying.

Cooked dishes often revolve around stewed dishes or *pilaf* combinations. Lamb, beef and chicken are used, but not pork as this is, at least nominally, a Moslem country. Grilled meat can be beef, spicy meatballs, kebabs, lamb, chicken or liver. Fish is invariably grilled. Many restaurants will have their own speciality dishes and these can be very good. Most people are impressed by the variety and finesse of Turkish cuisine and a cruise along the Turkish coast can become as much a gastronomic tour as a sailing holiday.

Turkish wine is just acceptable. It is neither fine nor consistent and you will often find that one bottle is different to another – sometimes dramatically so. Turkish beer, mostly *Efes* or *Tuborg*, is of the lager type and eminently thirst quenching. *Raki*, the aniseed-flavoured aperitif similar to *ouzo*, is potent and drunk in surprisingly large quantities by Turkish males. Turkish gin and vodka is adequate, but Turkish brandy is only really palatable if you like something that tastes like cough mixture.

Provisioning

Most provisions can be found except in some out-of-the-way places. Local produce, especially fruit and vegetables, is excellent.

Imported goods can be found in the larger towns and resorts, but naturally prices are substantially higher than you might pay in Europe. In the towns there is a market day once a week (usually Friday) where local produce – fruit and vegetables, dried fruit and nuts, local cheeses, herbs and spices, and local handicrafts, as well as the ubiquitous range of plastic goods and knick-knacks found all over the world – is on sale. It is worth a visit just for the colour and interesting stalls even if you don't intend to buy anything.

Stocking up the boat can usually be accomplished at a few nearby shops and many will deliver. Some of the charter companies will provide an order list so that the boat is already provisioned when you arrive.

Costs

The overall cost of living is below EU averages although prices have been rising, particularly in some of the restaurants in the larger resorts or where there is a captive market. With a little time you can inspect a number of restaurants and make your choice

you can get just about anywhere by bus or *dolmuş*. Hire cars are relatively expensive at £20–30 per day. Hire motorbikes and bicycles are rare.

Crime and personal safety

Turkey is a safe country to visit with few instances of mugging, rape and petty theft. In recent years there has been a rise in the incidence of sexual assaults on lone women in the larger resorts and normal precautions should be taken – do not stay alone in out-of-the-way nightclubs and bars until the wee hours and do not walk home unaccompanied late at night. Taxis run all through the night in most resorts and are cheap. Theft from boats is rare and you are unlikely to have anything stolen from your boat.

Sailing guides and charts

There are several guides to Turkey and charts cover all areas. Obtaining these guides and charts in Turkey can be all but impossible and, if you do find them, they will cost you a good deal more than in your own country. The following may be useful:

Turkish Waters & Cyprus Pilot Rod Heikell.
     Imray. Covers all Turkish waters in detail
The Turquoise Coast of Turkey Rod Heikell.
     NET. A guide to what to see along the
     coast from Bodrum to Kekova
Admiralty charts cover all areas and are available from Admiralty agents.
Imray-Tetra charts cover all the charter areas on a scale suitable for yachtsmen and are available from Imray or chandlers.

Essential information

Time zone UT +3 DST Apr–Sep
Language Turkish (using the Roman alphabet since 1928). Kurdish and Arabic. English, German and some French in tourist resorts
Telecommunications Automatic dialling to most areas. Code 90. Public telephone system with phonecards. Telephone and fax service from marinas and travel agents. Mobile phones with a GSM card work in most populated areas.
Health Medical services in the cities and tourist resorts range from average to poor depending on which doctor you see. Try to get a recommendation before seeing a doctor or dentist as there are some good ones around with well-equipped surgeries. You are advised to take out private medical insurance for the trip and most charter operators or travel agents can arrange this.

Serçe Limani on the coast down from Marmaris.
Photo Rod Heikell

at leisure. Typical costs for eating out range from around £3 a head in a small *lokanta* or restaurant to £10 a head in a restaurant. Wine can easily push up the cost as it is frequently £4–£6 for a pretty ordinary bottle. Beer is 50–90 pence for a large glass. Spirits are cheap although you may find the label on the bottle does not reflect what is in it.

Provisioning is cheap if you stick to local produce and locally produced staples, but any imported items are expensive. Few spend a lot of time on board cooking because the food ashore is relatively cheap and good, so most provisioning only needs to be for breakfast and lunch.

Transport in Turkey is cheap. Taxi fares are low now that most taxis have meters. Buses run to many destinations and *dolmuş* (shared minibuses running on a more or less fixed route – *dolmuş* literally means 'stuffed') run the locals and tourists alike everywhere else. The low level of car ownership means

Travel insurance (including medical cover) is mandatory with all flotilla operators and many bareboat companies.

Money The unit of currency is the *lira*. Turkey has had a problem with raging inflation for the last ten years and, on average, there is some 40–70 per cent inflation per annum. For this reason it is hardly worth obtaining Turkish *lira* before you leave and, in any case, many banks do not hold it because it devalues so quickly.

Banks are open 0830–1200 and 1330–1700 Mon–Fri. Exchange offices, marina offices, and travel agents operate outside these hours. All major credit cards, charge cards, Eurocheques and traveller's cheques are accepted. ATM machines can be found in the larger towns and tourist resorts and work with most major credit cards.

Documentation All visitors to Turkey must have a valid passport. EU members may carry an identity card. Most visitors do not need a visa except for UK nationals. This visa can be obtained when you go through immigration and, at the time of writing, cost £10·00 sterling.

In some cases proof of competence to handle a yacht will be asked for although this is rare. Ask your yacht charter company for advice and, if it believes documentation is necessary, it will usually be able to provide something suitable. All other boat documentation will be provided by the company. It can take several hours for clearance of the charter documentation before you leave and, as your passports will be required, this cannot be done beforehand. At subsequent harbours you will be responsible for clearing in and out as required if not on flotilla. It is not unusual for the coastguard, the *Sahil Guvenlik*, to check your papers in anchorages.

Charter gulet in Değirmen Bükü in the Gulf of Gökkova. *Photo* Rod Heikell

Charter areas

Bodrum

Bodrum sits at the entrance to the Gulf of Gökkova opposite the Greek island of Kos. A number of charter fleets are based at and around Bodrum from where they can explore the Gulf of Güllük to the north, the Gulf of Gökkova or, further south, the Gulf of Hisaronu. The climate can be very hot in the summer and the season lasts well into September and October. Temperatures in July often reach 34–36°C and, out of any cooling breeze, it does feel hot. Bodrum sits protected by a semi-circle of high land and is a dusty breathless place in July and August.

Wind and sea

The prevailing wind in the summer is the *meltemi*. It blows down the coast from NW to W, tending to curve and blow down into the gulfs. It usually blows at Force 5–7 (17–33 knots) in the summer with stronger gusts off the high land on the north side of the gulfs.

At the head of the gulfs it tends to run out of steam. At the beginning and end of the season, when the *meltemi* does not blow, winds still tend to be northerly although there may also be a S–SW sea breeze. Also at the beginning and end of the season a depression may pass through bringing gale-force winds, frequently from the south.

Seas around the coast are the typical short chop of the Mediterranean which can be difficult to beat against to windward. In the summer a fairly constant current flows northwards up the Turkish coast so that around headlands and capes and in narrow channels, the prevailing wind blowing against the current can kick up a confused sea.

Suitable for

The area is suitable for beginners, intermediate and experienced sailors. On a skippered *gulet* charter complete novices can go along. In the *meltemi* season the wind can at times be strong and, off the capes, considerable confused seas can be raised. Yacht charter here is a mix of flotilla,

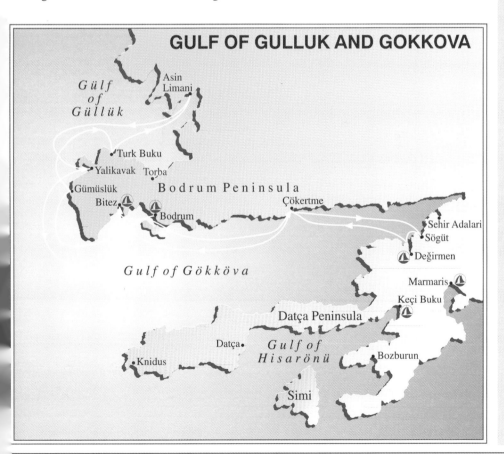

GULF OF GULLUK AND GOKKOVA

Gülf of Güllük — Asin Limani — Turk Buku — Yalikavak — Torba — Gümüslük — Bitez — Bodrum — **Bodrum Peninsula** — Çökertme — Sehir Adalari — Sögüt — Değirmen — Marmaris — Keçi Buku — *Gulf of Gökköva* — Datça Peninsula — Datça — *Gulf of Hisarönü* — Knidus — Bozburun — Simi

bareboat and skippered with the local boats – the *gulets* – running what amounts to a mixture of yacht charter and mini-cruises.

Harbours and anchorages

There are a number of harbours around the gulfs and a large number of sheltered anchorages. In most of the anchorages, yachts anchor and take a long line ashore. Berthing in harbours is stern- or bow-to using your own anchor, except where laid moorings have been installed.

Main charter bases

Bodrum Bareboat and skippered charter out of Bodrum marina. There are also numerous *gulet* charters out of here. Close to Bodrum in Bitez there are flotilla and bareboat charter bases. If flying into Bodrum Airport transfer time is around 40 minutes. Alternatively there are flights to Izmir and Dalaman with a transfer time of around 3½-4 hours depending on traffic.

English Harbour (Değirmen Bükü) Flotilla and bareboat base. Transfer time of around 3 hours from Dalaman Airport.
Güllük Small bareboat base.

Sailing area

The sailing area tends to revolve around the two gulfs of Güllük and Gökkova. The gulfs are deep, (the Gulf of Gökkova is over 40 miles long and mostly over 10 miles wide), and much indented, providing numerous sheltered anchorages. The coast is mostly mountainous and much of it is extensively wooded in pine. Although there are relatively few harbours, there are numerous restaurants dotted around the various bays. Provisions are more hard to come by, except in the few settlements.

A typical two-week itinerary is as follows.

Bodrum – Bodrum (a cruise in the Gulf of Güllük and Gulf of Gökkova)
(total 170 miles)
- *Starts at Bodrum*

Kale Koy in Kekova in the SE of Turkey.
Photo Rod Heikell

- *Bitez* A bay just a few miles along the coast from Bodrum. Gives you a chance to get used to the yacht. Watersports centre. Restaurants.
- *Gümüşlük* An enclosed bay on the western end of Bodrum peninsula. Care needed of the submerged breakwater in the entrance. Anchor with a long line ashore or, in calm weather, go bow-to the wooden jetty. Restaurants.
- *Turk Bükü* Large bay on the south side of the Gulf of Güllük. Restaurants and bars.
- *Asin* Narrow inlet in the SE of Gulf of Güllük. Ruins of Iassus. Restaurants.
- *Lay day* – visit the ruins of ancient Iassus above the harbour or sail to nearby bays.
- *Yalikavak* Squeeze into the small harbour or anchor in the bay to the north. Restaurants in the village.
- *Bitez/Gümbet/Bodrum* Stock up on provisions.
- *Cökertme* Large bay on the north side of the Gulf of Gökkova. Restaurants. Carpets made ashore.
- *Söğüt* Pine-clad bay. Restaurants.
- *Lay day* – visit Snake and Castle Islands. Return to Söğüt for the night.
- *Değirmen Bükü* Anchor in one of the bays. Restaurant in the east bay.
- *Cökertme*
- *Bodrum*

Land excursions

Bodrum Visit St Peters Castle by the harbour. Excellent museum of underwater archaeology within. Recommended.

Ephesus Excursions can be arranged from Bodrum. It is a full-day excursion usually visiting other sites such as the Church of the Virgin Mary. Ephesus is crowded, but recommended.

Iassus Can be visited from Asin harbour. The setting is exquisite.

Didyma Can be visited by taxi from Altinkum on the northern side of the Gulf of Güllük. Largest Ionic temple.

Snake and Castle Islands (Sehir Adalari) Ruins of ancient city and necropolis in an idyllic site. Cleopatra's beach. Recommended.

Knidos Site of the ancient city is immediately above the ancient harbour on the end of the Datça peninsula. Recommended.

Onward routes

One-way routes are often arranged between Bodrum and Marmaris. This is easily within the compass of a two-week cruise and is not a taxing trip. From Bodrum you have the wind aft of the beam for most of the trip. Around a 110-mile trip without excursions into the gulfs. The total mileage is easily extended by sailing into the gulfs.

Marmaris

Marmaris sits tucked up in a large bay opposite the island of Rhodes. A number of charter fleets are based at the marina or around the large bay. From here, yachts can explore either west towards the Gulf of Hisarönü or SE towards the Gulf of Fethiye. The climate here is very hot in the summer and is still warm in September and October. Temperatures can reach 34–36°C and it feels hot and sticky out of any breeze.

Wind and sea

The prevailing wind in the summer is the *meltemi* although here it often has a distinct diurnal component and dies off to some extent at night and in the early morning. Often the wind will not penetrate all the way to Ekinçik until the afternoon. On the more exposed coast, especially along the coast running down to Bozburun, the *meltemi* will blow from the NW–W at around Force 4–6 (11–27 knots) in July to September. When the *meltemi* does not blow there will often be a sea breeze from the S–SE. In early and late season a depression may pass through, bringing gale-force winds, frequently from S.

Seas in the area are short and sharp and can become confused around capes and through narrow channels where the prevailing wind blows against the north-going current. Where there is no wind around the coast between Marmaris and south of Ekinçik there will often be a confused sea, the result of wind further out to sea.

Suitable for . . .

The area is suitable for all from novice to intermediate to experienced sailors. Yacht charter here is a mixture of flotilla, bareboat and skippered charter as well as *gulet* mini-cruises.

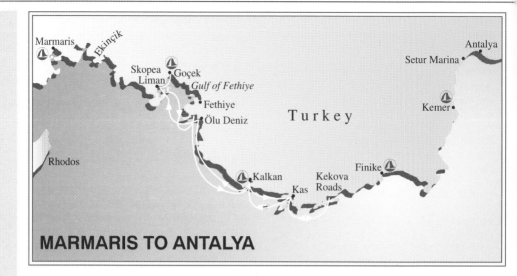

MARMARIS TO ANTALYA

Harbours and anchorages

There are few harbours around the area and, for the most part, you will be visiting anchorages. As around Bodrum you will frequently have to anchor with a long line ashore. Berthing in the harbours is stern- or bow-to using your own anchor except where laid moorings are supplied, as at Marmaris Marina.

Main charter bases

The main charter base is Marmaris Marina with a few other bases scattered around the large bay. Flights are normally to Dalaman Airport with around a 3-hour transfer from the airport to Marmaris.

Sailing area

Yachts tend to head for either the Gulf of Hisarönü to the west or go SE down to the Gulf of Fethiye. The adventurous in search of sea miles can combine the two. In common with the Bodrum area the deep and much-indented coast provides a large cruising area despite the lack of islands to cruise around. Most of the coast is steep-to and wooded in pine. Although there are few harbours, there are typically numerous restaurants in the bays.

Land excursions

Caunos From Ekinçik, local boats take you up a reed-lined river to the ancient site of Caunos. En route you will see Lycian rock tombs in the cliffs above the river. Recommended.

Onward routes

Bodrum One-way routes to Bodrum. The one-way trip to Bodrum is against the prevailing wind but is not overly arduous at around 110 miles without detours into the gulfs.

Fethiye/Göçek The one-way trip to Fethiye or Göçek is around 70–80 miles which can easily be extended.

Fethiye/Göçek

The Gulf of Fethiye is tucked into the coast approximately 40 miles east of Rhodes. A number of charter fleets are based here with access to the cruising area to the NW and SE and, importantly, close to Dalaman Airport. The climate here is very hot in the summer with temperatures often reaching 34–38°C. Further south and east, the season extends well into October.

Wind and sea

The prevailing wind here is the *meltemi* blowing from the W–SW. It has a distinct diurnal component in many parts of the area and often will not reach some areas at all. The *meltemi* blows strongest through August and September at around Force 4–6 (11–27 knots) although there will be days when it is lighter or does not blow at all. Effectively you are on the limit of the *meltemi* area here. In early and late season, winds are commonly from the north or south with a light sea breeze from a southerly direction often blowing. In early and late season a depression may pass through, often bringing gale-force winds, frequently from the south.

Seas along the coast are short and sharp, but moderate with one exception. When the *meltemi* is blowing strongly there can be heavy seas running along the coast between the Gulf of Fethiye and Kekova, especially off Yedi Burunlar, the Seven Capes.

Suitable for . . .

The area is suitable for beginners and experienced sailors. Beginners in the area should stay clear of the Seven Capes and destinations SE of the Gulf of Fethiye in the *meltemi* season. Yacht charter here is a mixture of flotilla, bareboat and skippered charter as well as *gulet* mini-cruises.

Harbours and anchorages

There are a few harbours along the coast but, for the most part, you will be visiting anchorages. As is the case further north, anchoring with a long line ashore is the norm in many places. Berthing in the harbours is stern- or bow-to using your own anchor except where laid moorings are supplied.

Main charter bases

Göçek A small village in the north corner of the Gulf of Fethiye that has developed into an important charter base. Transfer time is around 30 minutes from Dalaman Airport, the short transfer time making it a popular place for charter fleets.

Fethiye The large town in the east corner of the gulf. There are charter fleets at Fethiye Marina or in nearby locations around Fethiye Bay. Transfer time from Dalaman Airport is around 45 minutes.

Kalkan A small charter fleet further down the coast. Transfer time from Dalaman Airport is around 1½ hours and from Antalya Airport around 2 hours.

Sailing area

Yachts tend to potter around the NW side of the Gulf of Fethiye amongst the islands and bays and then head either NW towards Marmaris or SE towards Kekova. The coast is, as elsewhere, mountainous and largely wooded in pine.

A typical two-week itinerary is as follows.

Göçek – Kekova – Göçek

(total 160 miles)

- *Starts at Göçek*
- *Skopea Limani/Deep Bay* Short leg to attractive bay. Good swimming. Restaurant.
- *Skopea Limani/Kapi Creek* Sail to Wall Bay for lunch. End up in Kapi Creek. Restaurant.
- *Gemiler Adasi* Anchor in Karacaoren Bükü for the night. Restaurant.
- *Kalkan* Small resort and harbour. Provisions. Chic restaurants.
- *Lay day* – arrange a trip to Patara and/or Xanthos.
- *Kaş* Small resort under steep-to mountains. Provisions and restaurants.
- *Kekova Roads* Anchor for the night in Uçağiz. Restaurants.
- *Lay day* – potter around and return to Uçağiz or Gökkaya.
- *Kaş*
- *Kalkan*
- *Olü Deniz* Yachts often leave very early in the morning to get up this difficult stretch of coast. Anchor with a long line ashore outside the entrance.
- *Skopea Limani/Tomb Bay* Spectacular bay with rock tombs on the slopes. Good swimming. Restaurant. Short distance back to Göçek.
- *Göçek*

Land excursions

Fethiye Home to a few sarcophagi and a large rock tomb behind. The market in the town is colourful.

Patara A huge city, now mostly covered in sand. You pass by it on the way down the coast. Taxi from Kalkan.

Xanthos The ancient capital of Lycia in a wooded valley. Surrounded by numerous sarcophagi. Taxi from Kalkan. Recommended.

Kale Köy A small castle and miniature theatre amid a vast necropolis. Yachts anchor off in the bay below. Recommended.

Onward routes

Marmaris A popular one-way route for many charterers. Around 70–80 miles.

Kemer or Setur Antalya Marina A one-way route that, although not common, poses no problems. Around 140–150 miles.

Other charter areas

Kuşadasi A small charter fleet operates out of Kuşadasi. Izmir Airport is nearby with about a 1-hour transfer. Most charters are skippered although bareboats are available. Yachts either head north towards Ceşme or south to Bodrum.

Finike Small bareboat base.

Kemer/Setur Antalya Small numbers of charter yachts operate out of these two marinas. Antalya Airport is nearby with about a 30-minute transfer time. Most charter is skippered although bareboats are available.

Istanbul Bareboat and skippered charter.

Ceşme peninsula Bareboat and skippered charter.

Other Mediterranean charter areas

Croatia

Before the break-up of the old Yugoslavia and the bloody civil war which announced the formation of Serbia, Slovenia and Croatia, this coast was a popular charter destination. Since the fragile peace treaty in Bosnia Herzegovina and between Croatia and Serbia, yachts have returned to the area and there is some limited yacht charter with a number of major charter companies looking at the area for the future. Croatia has the lion's share of the coast and it is likely that, in the future, if the peace holds, it will once again become a popular charter area.

The Croatian coast is much indented with hundreds of offshore islands. Some of these are quite large and support sizeable towns and villages. There are a good number of marinas, other harbours which a yacht can use and numerous anchorages. The summer season is settled with consistent winds, mostly from the north. It is a cruising area as good as anywhere in the Mediterranean.

At present there is only limited bareboat and skippered charter out of the more northern marinas of Cres, Opatija, Split and Pula. In the future it is likely that flotilla and bareboat charter will reappear. For further information try the sailing magazines or a charter agent.

References

Adriatic Pilot T & D Thompson. Imray
Imray Mediterranean Almanac ed. Rod Heikell. Imray

Cyprus

There is limited bareboat and skippered charter out of Larnaca and Limassol Marina in the southern (Greek) half of Cyprus. One of the problems with this area is that there are very few places to visit along the coast. For what really amounts to day-sailing or a bit of coastal cruising the area has a long, settled summer season.

For further information try the sailing magazines or a charter agent.

References

Turkish Waters & Cyprus Pilot Rod Heikell. Imray

Tunisia

There is some limited skippered charter out of El Kantaoui and Monastir. Charter has never really taken off in Tunisia for no good reason. The country is relatively stable, there are wonderful cruising areas and interesting things to do and see ashore.

For further information try the sailing magazines or a charter agent.

References

North Africa Pilot RCC Pilotage Foundation/Hans van Rijn. Imray
Imray Mediterranean Almanac ed. Rod Heikell. Imray

Morocco

There is limited skippered charter out of the new marina at Marinasmir. There are few places to go along the Moroccan coast so a one week charter is about all you need except if you go across to Spain. Flights to Tangier.

References

North Africa Pilot RCC Pilotage Foundation/Hans van Rijn. Imray.
Imray Mediterranean Almanac ed. Rod Heikell. Imray.

Portugal

Not quite the Mediterranean but with a similar summer climate. There is some skippered and bareboat charter out of Vilamoura Marina.

References

Atlantic Spain and Portugal Oz Robinson Revised by Anne Hammick/RCC Pilotage Foundation. Imray.

Contributed by Chris Doyle and Nancy Scott

US and British Virgin Islands

FOR
- Consistent trade-wind sailing
- Numerous well-protected anchorages a short distance apart
- Good restaurants and bars ashore
- Clear tropical waters and good diving

AGAINST
- Crowded in the season
- Unsettled weather in the hurricane season

Types of charter
- Bareboat
- Skippered
- Luxury

The island group of the Virgin Islands is comprised of two separate island territories, the United States Virgin Islands and British Virgin Islands. The islands sparkle with beautiful beaches and have some of the best anchorages and protected sailing in the Caribbean.

Bareboat chartering has become very popular in these islands due to the protection of the Sir Francis Drake Channel from ocean swells. Many first-time charterers get their feet wet here because of the relatively benign sea conditions, the consistency of the trade winds and sunny weather.

The island recognises the importance of the boating industry to the local economy and, therefore, many businesses cater to yachts, enabling one to provision with ease, arrange dive and snorkelling trips, have meals and drinks at the many island anchorages and, of course, repairs and parts for yachts are readily available.

When to go

The change in season is subtle. Typically the months from July through October and even into November tend to be wetter and less consistently sunny. December through February can bring what is referred to as 'Christmas winds' where the trade winds can get a bit stronger than the rest of the year, ranging from 15 to 25 knots.

April, May and June are usually sunny, gentle with consistent trade winds blowing 12 to 15 knots. The hurricane season begins on 1 June and lasts until November. Most hurricanes brew during the months of August, September and October and necessitate vigilance for the skipper. Warnings are made well in advance and the prudent skipper has plenty of time to prepare for the chance of a hurricane.

Getting there

Air services from Europe and the US are generally through another island. The major airlines fly into Puerto Rico, St Thomas and St Croix several times a day from the United States and a commuter airline services the British Virgin Islands and most of the other Caribbean Islands from San Juan.

Visitors arriving from the United Kingdom generally fly to Antigua and then hop on to a commuter flight to either the US or British Virgin Islands, French visitors fly through Martinique or Guadeloupe before hopping over to the Virgins.

Eating and drinking

A vast array of restaurants and dining experiences await the visitor. From fast-food chains in the US Virgins to sophisticated dining, even on somewhat remote islands. Dining is varied and generally good. Local fish, lobster and conch are served as well as typical European meals. The local cooking is a wonderful mixture of Spanish influence from Puerto Rico, Indian dishes from the many East Indian people living in the Caribbean and, combined with the local fruits and vegetables, makes for a delightful, flavourful style of Caribbean cuisine.

Although wine can be somewhat more expensive than you may be accustomed to, spirits – rum, gin, scotch, vodka and so on – are comparatively inexpensive. Meals out, however, can make up the difference. Because many of the ingredients are shipped from Europe and the US, the end price tends to be high.

Provisioning

Large supermarkets are available in St Thomas and St Croix. The British Virgin Islands also have a few large markets which supply the island with virtually everything one may require and more. Because of the charter trade in the Virgins, speciality provisioning stores concentrate on the yachting and charter markets. They have extensive lists of food items and can assist in choices and quantities and they will deliver provisioning by car to your yacht.

Costs

As most items must be shipped to the islands from elsewhere and are subject to customs duties, prices are generally more expensive than in Europe and the US. An increase of anywhere from 20 to 50 per cent higher with the exception of liquor and local fruits and vegetables can be expected.

Eating out typically costs £10 per person or more at most tourist restaurants, however, one can pay less at a local restaurant that caters to local clientele. Drinks can vary from being quite expensive in the more elite hotels to quite reasonable at local pubs and bars.

Taxis tend to be quite expensive, and have no meters. It is advisable to check with the driver ahead of time to be sure you are in agreement on the fare. The taxi associations do have published fares and you may ask to see them before accepting a taxi. There are local buses which are quite reasonably priced by contrast.

Crime and personal safety

Violent crime is somewhat rare in the islands, but, as in many places, theft is all too common. It is advisable not to bring expensive jewellery or cash with you. Thieves are mainly looking for these commodities. The tourist who has just had a few too many Pina Coladas and is immersed in the tropical moonlight is fair game for muggers. Be as attentive as if you were in any typical town in the US and you shouldn't run into problems. Using credit cards and traveller's cheques will be a safer way to pay for things in the islands. Check with your charter company or hotel regarding safety in a particular area of the islands.

Essential information

Health There is a hospital in St Thomas, US Virgin Islands and also a hospital in Road Town, Tortola, BVI. Several well-trained doctors reside in these islands should you have a problem. Emergencies are either handled locally, although sometimes it is necessary to fly a patient to San Juan, Puerto Rico for specific problems.

Money The US dollar is used in both the US and British Virgin Islands. Traveller's cheques and credit cards are widely accepted at almost all establishments in the islands. The British Virgins are a centre for offshore banking and derive much of the islands' income from that business.

Banks are plentiful in both the US and British Virgin Islands and are accustomed to working with tourists.

Documentation A passport is usually sufficient for most EC countries, the US and Canada. All others should check to ensure a visa is not required before embarking on their trips.

The passport as well as ship's papers are required when travelling between the United States and the British Virgin Islands. Customs and immigration clearance between these two island countries is a firm requirement, but the process has been streamlined and is not too time consuming.

Suitable for

For bareboat chartering the skipper will need a working knowledge of basic navigation. The islands are all within sight of each other making the job fairly simple. However, it is necessary to be able to read a chart, plot your position and take compass bearings. The only passage that takes you out of sight of land briefly is from Virgin Gorda to Anegada. This passage requires more attention owing to the proximity of Horseshoe Reef which has claimed more than its fair share of boats.

A one-week charter will give you a delicious taste of the Virgin Islands, but to really experience the many anchorages, beaches and cays one should spend a minimum of two weeks. For charters starting in Tortola, British Virgin Islands, most skippers head for North Sound, Virgin Gorda, visiting the outlying islands of Jost Van Dyke, Marina Cay, Norman, Peter and Cooper Islands on the way out and on the

At anchor in the British Virgin Islands.
Photo Pat Collinge

way back. The anchorages are all within a couple of hours of each other making the trips short, leaving plenty of time for snorkelling, diving and exploring. Many of the anchorages either have restaurants catering for the yachting crowd or aren't far from a restaurant or bar.

Charters starting in St Thomas, USVI will probably work their way to St John in the US Virgin Islands. Three-quarters of the island is National Park and boasts some of the most beautiful beaches in the Caribbean. The town of Cruz Bay is full of quaint shops and restaurants. Cruz Bay is a good place to clear customs in and out of the British and US Virgin Islands. The British Virgins are a stone's throw across the Sir Francis Drake Channel and customs clearance into the country can easily be accomplished at Sopers Hole, West End.

Land excursions

St Johns – The National Park Service sponsors many hikes throughout the park, visiting the remains of plantations and sugar mills. Contact the National Park Office for a schedule.

Tortola – The National Parks Trust provides trails with breathtaking views from Sage Mountain, a rainforest at the highest point in Tortola. Another interesting visit is Callwood's Rum Distillery in Cane Garden Bay where rum is made using the cane from the surrounding hills. The O'Neal Botanical Gardens across from the police station are lovely and peaceful, featuring exotic plants and flowers of the Caribbean.

Virgin Gorda – Coppermine Point is a short drive from the Virgin Gorda Yacht Harbour and has the remains of a 16th-century copper mine which mined ore until 1867.

Sailing guides and charts

Cruising Guide to the Virgin Islands Simon and Nancy Scott. Cruising Guide Publications. Colour aerial photos and pilotage information. Available locally.

Virgin Anchorages Aerial photos of 41 anchorages. Cruising Guide Publications.

Puerto Rico, Passage and Virgin Islands D M Street Jnr

Imray-Iolaire and American charts are available locally.

Windwards

FOR
- Consistent winds, warm temperatures and abundant sunshine all year round
- Numerous anchorages
- A wide range of restaurants, from elegant gourmet to cheerful waterfront bars
- Varied topography, with steep mountain

rainforests, rich agricultural land and sunny sand cays
- Mixture of French, Caribbean and English cultures
- Wonderful diving, snorkelling and swimming all year round

AGAINST
- Weather needs watching carefully during the hurricane season (June–November)
- The consistent trade winds of up to 20 knots can be heavy for beginners
- Time spent clearing customs on some routes

Types of charter
- Bareboat
- Skippered
- Luxury
- Head-boat
- Occasional flotillas

The Windward Islands include four separate countries. Martinique, at the north end of the island chain, is a department of France. St Lucia, St Vincent (together with the Grenadines) and Grenada are all independent countries. The main islands are mountainous and verdant with lush rainforest at the middle elevations. The swimming, diving and snorkelling are excellent year round.

The Grenadines lie between St Vincent and Grenada and consist of many smaller islands with flawless beaches. In this group are the Tobago Cays, four small islands in a large area of water protected by a vast horseshoe reef. This anchorage typifies for many the ideal Caribbean cruising destination.

The weather is generally very pleasant with steady winds. This, combined with a variety of anchorages, makes for perfect cruising.

Diving and snorkelling are excellent all year round and there are many friendly and fully accredited dive shops to choose from.

When to go
There are two seasons – the dry (February to mid-June) and the wet (mid-June to December). These are not clearly differentiated, but you do get significantly more rain in the wet season. There is also a 'high-price' season (December to April) and a 'low-price' season (May to November), linked to demand. Temperatures year round are 25–30°C and sea temperatures 25–29°C. Humidity is high, but never oppressive because there is a constant breeze.

December to March These are the most popular times owing to the demand for a winter break. December is still in the rainy season and there is a chance of some rainy weather. Winds during this period tend to be at their strongest, especially in December and January. Occasional northerly swells during December and January make a few anchorages uncomfortable.

March to early June This is usually when Caribbean sailing is at its best. The winds are quite consistent and not as strong, and the weather is dry and sunny.

July to November While there can be excellent sailing during this time, it is the hurricane season and close attention to the weather forecasts is essential. Hurricanes pass through the northern Windwards once every six years on average and the southern Windwards about once every 50 years. However, there are many more warnings that must be heeded, even though they may turn out to be false alarms. August to November is the rainiest time of the year and people coming for just one week take a chance on the weather. Over longer periods rain is always mixed with bright sunshine.

Windward Islands
At Soufrière (St Lucia)

	Av max °C	Av min °C	Highest recorded	Relative humidity	Days 1mm rain
Jan	28	21	31	70%	18
Feb	28	21	32	68%	13
Mar	29	21	32	65%	13
Apr	31	22	35	64%	10
May	31	23	36	65%	16
Jun	31	23	36	69%	21
Jul	31	23	35	71%	23
Aug	31	23	34	69%	22
Sep	31	23	34	70%	21
Oct	31	22	33	69%	19
Nov	29	22	32	75%	20
Dec	28	21	32	71%	19

Getting there
Martinique is well served by daily flights from Europe and the US. St Lucia and Grenada have several flights a week from Europe and daily flights to the US. St Vincent cannot take the larger planes, so it is necessary to change planes on one of the other islands or fly via Barbados, which also serves as a hub for Grenada and St Lucia when there are no direct flights. It should be noted that St Lucia has two airports: Hewanorra, the big international airport in the south, and Vigie, a smaller airport in the north. Vigie is much closer to the charter companies than

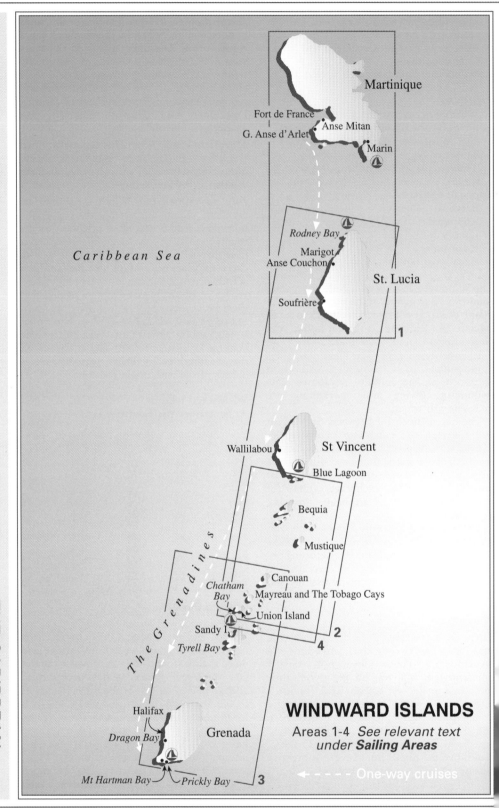

Martinique

Fort de France
Anse Mitan
G. Anse d'Arlet
Marin

Caribbean Sea

Rodney Bay
Marigot
Anse Couchon
St. Lucia
Soufrière

1

Wallilabou
St Vincent
Blue Lagoon

Bequia

Mustique

Canouan
Chatham Bay
Mayreau and The Tobago Cays
Union Island
Sandy I.

2

Tyrell Bay

4

The Grenadines

Halifax

Dragon Bay
Grenada

WINDWARD ISLANDS

Areas 1-4 *See relevant text under* **Sailing Areas**

Mt Hartman Bay
Prickly Bay

3

← – – – – One-way cruises

Hewanorra, so flying here when possible saves an hour-long taxi ride.

Eating and drinking

The people in the Windwards have come from Europe, Africa, East India and China. The local Creole cooking reflects these origins and is generally spicy. Curries are available in most places and a Caribbean speciality is the *roti* – curried chicken, beef or lamb (*conch*) wrapped in a wheatflour tortilla-like shell. Chicken, seafood and lobster in season, together with local vegetables are the basic ingredients of most Creole cooking. In Martinique there is also traditional French cuisine and this has spread to the more sophisticated restaurants in other islands. Add to this more recent arrivals of pizza, *Kentucky Fried Chicken* and, in Martinique, *McDonald's*, and there is something for everyone.

Provisioning

Martinique has vast modern supermarkets and Grenada has some smaller, excellent ones. There is perfectly adequate provisioning in St Lucia, St Vincent and even Bequia but, for fancy delicatessen items, you may have to visit a speciality shop as well as a supermarket. Local fruits and vegetables are best bought in the local open-air produce markets which are lively and colourful. Even in the smaller islands you will not starve, though your choice of food will be more limited.

Costs

Many items on supermarket shelves will cost between 20 and 50 per cent more than in Europe, but there are exceptions. Local fruits, vegetables, frozen chicken and fresh fish are all relatively inexpensive as are rum and other liquors which cost £2·50–£5 per bottle.

Eating out typically costs £10 per person or more, though you can get a filling *roti* in a local bar for as little as £1·50. Beer is around 70 pence in a local bar and 50 pence in the supermarket. Wine costs £4 per bottle or more, except in Martinique where it is about 20 per cent more than French prices. Drinking in bars varies enormously with the surroundings and is about four or five times as expensive in a swish tourist hotel – where you can pay up to £3 for one drink – than it is in a local bar. Transport is inexpensive by local bus (less than £1 for a long ride). Local car hire costs about £27 per day on average.

Marigot Bay on St Lucia. *Photo* Yachting World

Taxi tours are available everywhere and, for four people, will cost about £25 per person for a full day.

Crime and personal safety

Theft is fairly common in the islands, the most frequent target being an unlocked dinghy or outboard. Boats do occasionally get robbed when people are ashore. The thieves are mainly looking for cameras or cash. You probably won't be affected but, to be on the safe side, do not bring large quantities of cash. Use credit cards and traveller's cheques instead. Insure cameras and binoculars for your holiday.

Violent theft is rare, but there are one or two areas where it is not safe to walk at night except in large groups. Ask your charter company for details before you set off.

Sailing guides and charts

Sailors Guide to the Windward Islands Chris Doyle. Cruising Guide Publications. Covers the Windwards in detail

Street's Martinique to Trinidad D M Street Jr. Charts for the area are good and easily available. Imray-Iolaire charts for the Caribbean Sea are widely available. British Admiralty and US DMA charts also cover the area .

Essential information

Time zone UT -4

Language In Martinique French is spoken; English in the other islands. St Lucians speak Patois in addition to English.

Telecommunications Card phones are available throughout the islands. Many charter yachts are also equipped with cellular phones.

Health There are adequate medical services for most common health problems in all the major islands. However, for serious and critical ailments it is necessary to get to Martinique or Barbados as fast as possible as they are the only islands with sophisticated facilities. Charter planes and air-ambulance services are available. Martinique, being part of France, has reciprocal medical benefits for some European nationals.

Money The currency in Martinique is the French franc. In all other islands it is the Eastern Caribbean (EC) dollar which is set at a fixed rate to the US dollar of EC2·65 to US$1. Nearly everyone accepts US traveller's cheques and US dollars and the larger hotels and restaurants will also take Pounds sterling. Credit cards are widely accepted, especially the Visa group (Visa, MasterCard, Carte Bleu and so on).

There are banks on any island with a population of a few thousand or more. They are open on weekdays, usually only from 0800–1300, but have extra hours on Fridays from 1500–1700.

Documentation For most people, a passport is sufficient to visit all the countries in the group. However, some nationals, including many from the Middle East, Russia and ex-Soviet Bloc countries will also need a visa. These are generally issued through British embassies.

When going from one country to another, customs formalities have to be dealt with. These are usually simple, but you have to fill out forms in every office you visit. You will need your passport, ship's papers and clearance from the last port.

Charter areas

The whole area is good for chartering, but the amount you see will depend on how long you have and the experience of the crew.

Harbours and anchorages

The harbours and anchorages lie on the western or southern side of the islands where they are protected from the regular trade winds and seas. They range from busy sociable marinas to deserted sand cays.

Wind and sea

The trade winds blow almost constantly from the easterly quadrant – a little more often north of east in the winter, and south of east in the summer. The trade winds are at their strongest during the winter months, particularly in December and January when they can sometimes blow for days on end at 20 knots. These winds intensify somewhat around the ends of islands, a phenomenon especially evident at the north end of St Vincent. While sailing in the lee of the larger islands may be gusty, the seas are smooth, making it both easy and exhilarating.

Suitable for . . .

For bareboating, basic navigational skills are necessary. You must be able to plot your position, take compass bearings and identify the islands and anchorages.

The passage between Martinique and St Lucia is about six hours with four hours in open water which is occasionally rough. This makes a charter from Martinique to St Lucia and back (or vice versa) suitable for just about everyone.

The passage between St Lucia and St Vincent is about five hours in open water. The north end of St Vincent can be very rough, especially in December and January. This passage is easy in the southerly direction when the wind is generally aft, but can be frightening for the inexperienced sailing north in rough conditions. Because of this, a trip from Martinique or St Lucia to St Vincent and the Grenadines and back should only be undertaken by those used to open-sea conditions.

However, one-way trips are also available, starting in Martinique or St Lucia and finishing in Union Island or Grenada, and these would be suitable for most.

Charters starting and finishing in St Vincent, which includes those visiting the Grenadines, have only short open-sea passages and are suitable for anyone who has reasonably good navigational skills. These islands have the added bonus of all being in one country so there are no customs to deal with.

Charters out of Grenada to see the Grenadines involve a slightly longer first-day passage to Carriacou, but they are also suitable for almost everyone.

Main charter bases

Martinique Anse Mitan and Marin
St Lucia Rodney Bay and Marigot Bay
St Vincent Blue Lagoon
Union Island Clifton
Grenada Prickly Bay and Mt Hartman Bay

Sailing areas

Many of the suggested itineraries overlap and in truth you can mix and match the following suggestions depending on time and inclination.

Grenada. *Photo* Yachting World

One week
Martinique and St Lucia starting in Marin

The same charter can be reworked to start in St Lucia
(About 120 miles)

- *Day 1 – Marin to Rodney Bay, St Lucia*
  Clear customs. Get a three-day permit which allows you to clear in and out at the same time. You will find a large marina with plenty of shoreside shops, bars and restaurants.
- *Day 2 – Rodney Bay to Soufrière*
  Tie up on one of the marine park moorings. Dive or snorkel, take a trip ashore, eat on board or ashore.
- *Day 3 – Soufrière to Anse Cochon*
  Lunch and snorkel in this deserted bay, then spend the night at Marigot where there are several bars and restaurants.
- *Day 4 – Marigot to Fort de France*
  Clear customs, go shopping and return to your boat in time to sail to Anse Mitan for the night. There are many restaurants serving French food.
- *Day 5 – Anse Mitan to St Pierre*
  This historic town was destroyed by a volcanic eruption in 1902. Visit the museum and enjoy town, the old ruins and the mountainous surroundings. Eat ashore or on board.
- *Day 6 – St Pierre to Grand Anse d'Arlet*
  Relax, swim, snorkel, eat ashore on or board.

- *Day 7 – Grand Anse d'Arlet to Marin*
  Enjoy a brisk beat to windward in fairly protected sea conditions.

Ten days
St Lucia to the Grenadines and back

For the experienced only
(About 200 miles)

- *Day 1 – Rodney Bay to Soufrière*
  Clear out at customs and sail to Soufriere. Dive, snorkel, eat out or on board. Charming town, mostly unaffected by tourists.
- *Day 2 – Soufrière to Bequia*
  Start early and sail to Bequia. Eat ashore or on board.
- *Day 3 – Stay in Bequia*
  Relax, stroll around town, go diving, snorkelling and/or hiking.
- *Day 4 – Bequia to Tobago Cays*
  Sail to the Tobago Cays. Eat on board – there are no restaurants. Snorkel, swim and enjoy the beaches.
- *Day 5 – Tobago Cays to Mayreau*
  Pleasant walks ashore and you can peruse the restaurants and decide whether to eat ashore or on board. More snorkelling, swimming or diving.
- *Day 6 – Mayreau to Palm and Union*
  Visit Palm Island where there are pleasant walks and a restaurant. Union Island has a small but busy town with several restaurants. Top up on provisions, fuel and water if needed.

- *Day 7 – Union to Canouan*
  Eat a pizza ashore in the Tamarind Beach Hotel, hike to the windward beaches.
- *Day 8 – Canouan to Wallilabou*
  Sail to Wallilabou in St Vincent and clear out at customs for St Lucia. Eat ashore or on board.
- *Day 9 – Wallilabou to Marigot*
  Set off early for your voyage to St Lucia. Reef well for the north end of St Vincent, especially if the winds have been strong. Spend the night in Marigot Bay. Clear in with customs.
- *Day 10 – Marigot to Rodney Bay*
  Visit Pigeon Island's old forts and museum on the way.

One week
St Vincent to the Grenadines and return
(About 80 miles)

- *Day 1 – Blue Lagoon to Bequia*
  Sail to Bequia, many shoreside attractions, excellent diving.
- *Day 2 – Bequia to Mustique*
  Enjoy hiking, snorkelling, diving and time on the beach.
- *Day 3 – Mustique to Tobago Cays*
  Sail to the Tobago Cays for excellent snorkelling and pretty beaches.
- *Day 4 – Tobago Cays to Petit St Vincent*
  Sail to Petit St Vincent. Make a side trip by dinghy to Petite Martinique. Dive or snorkel.
- *Day 5 – Petit St Vincent to Union Island*
  Stop at Palm Island for hiking and lunch and then sail to Union Island where Clifton, the main town, has restaurants, fuel, water and several small supermarkets. Or sail to Chatham Bay, a deserted anchorage with a pleasant beach and good snorkelling.

- *Day 6 – Union to Bequia*
  Sail to Canouan for an early lunch, then set off before 1300 for Bequia to make sure you arrive before nightfall.
- *Day 7 – Bequia to Blue Lagoon.*

Nine days
Grenada to the Grenadines and back
(About 100 miles)

- *Day 1 – half day*
  Start in Mt Hartman Bay. Clear customs outward bound. Overnight in Dragon Bay or Halifax Harbour on Grenada's west coast.
- *Day 2 – Grenada to Tyrell Bay, Carriacou*
  Many small bars and restaurants, friendly people, quiet streets for easy walking.
- *Day 3 – Carriacou to Union*
  Sail to Clifton, Union Island, clear customs. Good diving close by.
- *Day 4 – Union to the Tobago Cays*
  A short sail which will leave plenty of time for snorkelling and exploring the beaches. Eat on board.
- *Day 5 – Tobago Cays to Mayreau*
- *Day 6 – Mayreau to Petit St Vincent*
  Return to Clifton to clear customs, carry on to Petit St Vincent.
- *Day 7 – Petit St Vincent to Carriacou*
  Sail to Hillsborough to clear in, then on to Sandy Island for swimming, snorkelling or diving. Overnight in Tyrell Bay.
- *Day 8 – Carriacou to Grenada*
  Return to Grenada. Overnight in True Blue Bay and eat ashore.
- *Day 9 – Return to Mt Hartman Bay (half day)*

Onward routes

In addition to the above, one-way voyages, while a little more expensive for bareboaters, offer the best of all worlds, with easy reaching down the island chain. For a relaxed trip, two weeks are needed to enjoy the stretch from Martinique to Grenada. Ten days will do for Martinique to Union Island (116 miles) or St Lucia to Grenada (141 miles), and one week for St Lucia to Union Island (95 miles) or St Vincent to Grenada (81 miles). With luxury crewed charters you can usually pick up and drop off at your choice of ports at no extra cost.

Land excursions

There are several land excursions which will suit nature lovers and hikers.

Martinique A good road runs through a long section of rainforest, making it easy for those who prefer this form of sightseeing. Stop for a walk in the Jardin de Balata, beautifully designed and maintained gardens with a profusion of tropical plants.

St Lucia Hikes in the rainforest can be arranged through the Department of Forestry which will supply both a guide and transport for a fee ☎ 758 450 2231.

If in Soufrière, visit the Dasheen Restaurant and Bar at the Ladera Resort for a drink or meal. The view between the Pitons is almost straight down and is breathtaking.

St Vincent The hike to the top of the Soufriere volcano is spectacular. It is for the physically fit only and will take a whole day. Beginning in a banana plantation, the trail takes you through rainforest to the top of the 4000ft volcano, where only grasses and low plants survive the nearly constant cloud and high winds. Take a windbreak and lunch and spend as long a time at the summit as possible, waiting for a break in the clouds which will reveal spectacular views, both into the steaming crater and to the sea on both the east and west coasts.

Grenada Hikers will enjoy visiting one of Grenada's many rainforest waterfalls where you can take a bracing swim. This photogenic island is well worth a day's tour which will include views of St George's, the prettiest town in the region.

Other areas

Special group charters are arranged for Carnival in Trinidad (February) and for the Angostura-*Yachting World* Annual Race Week in Tobago (May). These offer an opportunity to see islands which are off the normal charter route.

Leewards

FOR
- Consistent winds, warm temperatures and abundant sunshine year round
- Numerous anchorages throughout
- A wide range of restaurants with cooking from all over the world
- A choice of areas offering different levels of difficulty and different kinds of scenery
- Several different cultures within a relatively small area
- Wonderful diving, snorkelling and swimming year round

AGAINST
- Weather needs watching very carefully during the hurricane season (June to November)
- Time spent clearing customs on some routes

Types of charter
- Bareboat
- Skippered
- Luxury
- Head-boat
- Occasional flotillas

The Leewards span an area of several hundred miles and include at least 14 sizeable islands. They are culturally and politically diverse with 11 different national governments. In the case of Sint Maarten/St Martin, one small island is divided in two: one part is partially independent under the Dutch and the other is French. The combined island is referred to as St Martin in this text.

Some parts of the Leewards are suitable for people without too much experience, while other areas are more difficult. It would take at least a month to visit all the islands and choices will have to be made.

Antigua, Barbuda, St Barts, St Martin and Anguilla are geologically more ancient islands. Worn down by time, they lack the lofty mountains needed to attract enough rain for rainforests. Instead, they generally have dry sunny weather and wonderful beaches.

Dominica, the western half of Guadeloupe, Montserrat, St Kitts and Nevis, St Eustatius (Statia) and Saba are younger islands with tall mountains, rainforests and dramatic topography. At the time of writing, volcanic rumblings have made Montserrat all but uninhabitable. Hiking is wonderful in these islands and the sightseeing interesting from either a foot trail or car window. Dominica and the Basse Terre part of Guadeloupe attract somewhat more rain than the other mountainous islands.

When to go

There are two seasons, the dry (February to mid-June) and the wet (mid-June to December). These are not clearly differentiated, but you do get significantly more rain in the wet season. There is also a 'high-price' season (December to April) and a 'low-price' season (May to November), linked to demand. Temperatures year round are 25–30°C, sea temperatures are 25–29°C. Humidity is high, but offset by the constant breeze.

December to March These are the most popular times owing to the demand for a winter break. December is still in the rainy season and there is a chance of some wet weather. Winds during this period tend to be at their strongest, especially in December and January. During this time the northwestern islands (Anguilla, St Martin and St Barts, Saba, Statia and St Kitts and Nevis) are affected by cold fronts moving southeast from the US. The weather before a cold front is generally wonderful: calm and sunny with light variable breezes. If the cold front makes it to the area – which happens about twice a year – the wind blows fairly hard from the northwest for some hours then goes to north and northeast, increasing in strength. This is accompanied by heavy showers and squalls. The weather has usually settled back down to normal within 24 hours. Even cold fronts that stall northwest of the area can produce ground swells that make some of the anchorages uncomfortable or even dangerous.

March to early June This is probably Caribbean sailing at its best. The winds are more consistent and not as strong, and the weather is largely dry and sunny.

August to November is the wettest time of year, though this is more noticeable in the larger islands of Guadeloupe and Dominica.

July to November While there can be excellent sailing during this time, it is the hurricane season and a close watch has to be kept on weather forecasts. Hurricanes go through this area about once every two to four years. They are much more likely in the months of August and September than at any other time. Forecasts usually give from one to three days' notice, giving adequate time to get to a hurricane anchorage. During the hurricane season, charterers should stay in touch with the charter base and follow their instructions should a hurricane approach. Riding out a hurricane can be a terrifying experience. Anyone who is unlucky enough to be in the path of a hurricane should leave the boat as instructed and find a safe place ashore. Air transport is often unavailable for several days after a hurricane.

Leeward Islands
At Plymouth (Montserrat)

	Av max °C	Av min °C	Highest recorded	Relative humidity	Days 1mm rain
Jan	28	21	32	65%	12
Feb	29	21	33	66%	9
Mar	29	21	34	59%	9
Apr	30	22	34	59%	8
May	31	23	36	60%	10
Jun	31	24	37	63%	13
Jul	31	24	37	64%	14
Aug	31	24	37	66%	16
Sep	32	23	36	66%	13
Oct	31	23	34	66%	14
Nov	29	23	37	68%	16
Dec	28	22	33	67%	13

Getting there

There are major airports in Guadeloupe, Antigua, St Kitts and St Martin. These are all well serviced with flights to the US as well as flights to and from Europe at least once a week. In the case of Guadeloupe there are daily flights to and from France. The small islands can be reached by smaller planes from these islands or via Puerto Rico which serves as a hub for the area.

Eating and drinking

Restaurants reflect spicy Creole traditions with Afro and East Indian roots, as well as traditional French cooking. Add to that the influences of the Dutch and of more recent arrivals who have set up establishments offering everything from New York steaks or Italian pasta to Brazilian specialities or

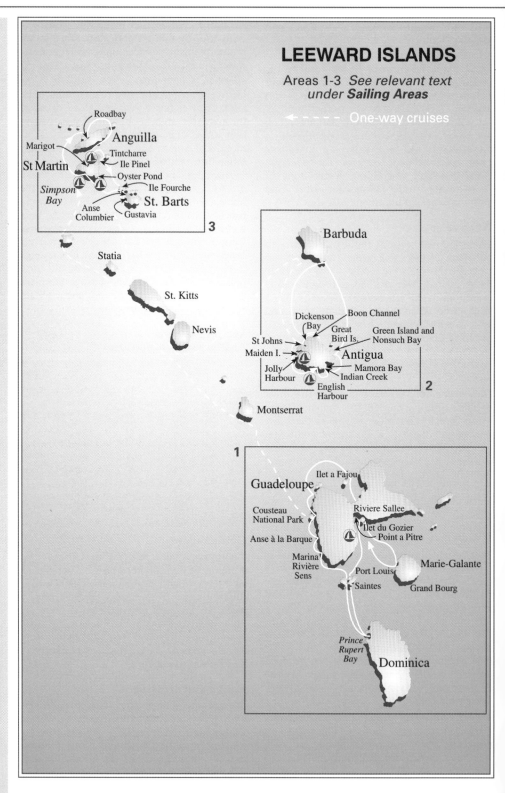

LEEWARD ISLANDS

Areas 1-3 *See relevant text*
under **Sailing Areas**

← - - - - One-way cruises

Roadbay

Anguilla

Marigot

Tintcharre

St Martin
Ile Pinel

Oyster Pond

Simpson Bay
Ile Fourche

Anse Columbier
St. Barts

Gustavia

3

Statia

St. Kitts

Nevis

Barbuda

Dickenson Bay
Boon Channel

Great Bird Is.
Green Island and Nonsuch Bay

St Johns

Maiden I.
Antigua

Jolly Harbour
Mamora Bay

Indian Creek

English Harbour

2

Montserrat

1

Ilet a Fajou

Guadeloupe

Riviere Sallee

Cousteau National Park

Ilet du Gozier

Anse à la Barque
Point a Pitre

Marina Rivière Sens

Marie-Galante

Port Louis

Saintes

Grand Bourg

Prince Rupert Bay

Dominica

English pub food and you have a wide enough choice to suit all tastes.

Provisioning

Excellent supermarkets can be found in all the larger islands and adequate ones in the smaller. Fresh fruits and vegetables are mostly imported and, therefore, somewhat expensive, with the notable exceptions of Dominica and Guadeloupe.

In St Martin, several of the large supermarkets will collect you from one of the marinas and drop you back with your shopping.

Costs

Many items on supermarket shelves will cost between 10 and 50 per cent more than in Europe, but there are exceptions. Liquor, for ewample, costs just £2·50–£5 per bottle.

Eating out typically costs £10 per head or more, though you can find less expensive local restaurants. Beer is around 70 pence in a local bar, 50 pence in the supermarket and less in St Martin. Wine is just a little over French prices in St Martin, St Barts and Guadeloupe but more expensive in the other islands, so it pays to stock up when in French territory.

Drinking in bars varies enormously depending on the kind of surroundings and is about four or five times as expensive in a swish tourist hotel as in a local beach-front bar. My record is £30 for two fruit punches and a beer in St Barts! Transport is very inexpensive by local bus. Local car hire averages about £27 per day. Taxi tours are available everywhere and for four people will cost about £25 per person for a full day.

Crime and personal safety

Theft is fairly common in the islands, the most frequent target being an unlocked dinghy or outboard. Boats do occasionally get robbed when people are ashore. The thieves are mainly looking for cameras or cash. To be on the safe side do not bring large quantities of cash. Use credit cards and traveller's cheques instead. Insure cameras and binoculars for your holiday. Violent theft is extremely rare.

Sailing guides and charts

Cruising Guide to the Leeward Islands Chris Doyle. Cruising Guide Publications, Covers this group in detail. Sketch charts of all the anchorages and many aerial colour photographs are provided. Shoreside information describes all the marinas and docks and most of the restaurants, bars and boutiques

Street's Martinique to Trinidad D M Street Jr. Charts for the area are good and easily available. There are the popular Imray Iolaire yachting charts as well as British Admiralty and US DMA charts for the area .

Essential information

Time zone UT -4 hours

Language In Martinique, St Martin and St Barts, French is spoken. English will be understood everywhere except Guadeloupe. English is the official language in all the other islands, though in Sint Maarten, Saba and Statia you'll also get along fine if you speak Dutch.

Telecommunications Card phones are available throughout the islands. Many charter yachts are equipped with cellular phones.

Documentation For most people, a passport is sufficient to visit all the countries in the group. However, some nationals, including many from the Middle East, Russia and ex-Soviet Bloc countries, will also need a visa for some islands.

When going from one country to another, customs formalities have to be dealt with. These are usually simple, but you have to fill out forms in every office you visit. You will need your passport, ship's papers and clearance from the last port.

Health There are adequate medical services on all the islands for most common health problems. Evacuation may be necessary for serious and critical ailments. Charter planes and air-ambulance services are available. Guadeloupe, being part of France, has reciprocal medical benefits for some European nationals.

Money There are three official currencies in this region: French francs, Dutch guilders, and Eastern Caribbean (EC) dollars. You will need French francs for Guadeloupe, and it is a good idea to have some EC dollars for Antigua and Montserrat. As for the rest of the islands, the US dollar is universally accepted and prices are often quoted in this currency. Nearly everyone takes US traveller's cheques and credit cards are widely accepted, (Visa, MasterCard, Carte Bleu and so on).

There are banks on any island with a population of a few thousand or more.

Local boats in Anguilla. *Photo* Pat Collinge

Opening hours vary from island to island but they nearly all open, in the mornings at least, on weekdays.

Charter areas

There are several clearly defined charter areas. Guadeloupe to Dominica is one, Antigua and Barbuda is another, and it is easy enough to do some sailing in each. St Martin, St Barts and Anguilla are another popular group, considerably further away. Those who like longer passages sometimes do one-way trips from Antigua or Guadeloupe to St Martin.

Wind and sea

Consistent trade winds make for delightful sailing. When the winds are at their strongest – during December and January – some of the open-sea passages can be a little rough, but it is easy to design a cruise where these passages take no more than two or three hours.

Suitable for . . .

Everyone can enjoy this area. Those who are a little nervous of the open sea can cruise the islands of St Martin, St Barts and Anguilla which are all close together. Otherwise they can sail round Guadeloupe. The more adventurous can cruise from Guadeloupe to Dominica and back, or do a one-way charter between these groups. Antigua and Barbuda, which is a gorgeous cruising area, does require considerable navigational skills, and the ability to eyeball through reef passages is essential.

Harbours and anchorages

Good anchorages abound in all the islands. Guadeloupe includes Marie Galante and The Saintes – smaller islands where cruising is delightful. Antigua not only has anchorages on the Leeward and southern shores, but also some delightful east- and north-coast bays protected by fringing reefs. It is one of the few areas in the Leewards where you can easily find a beautiful bay all to yourself. As a whole, the group offers a variety of anchorages, from deserted beaches and entertaining little villages with pleasant French restaurants to larger, more sophisticated towns. Those who like a lot of nightlife would do well to cruise around St Martin, which has many restaurants and casinos and a bustling social scene.

Main charter bases

Guadeloupe Pointe-à-Pitre (at the Port de Plaisance)
Antigua English Harbour and Falmouth on the south coast and Jolly Harbour on the west coast
St Martin Simpson Bay Lagoon, Port Lonvilliers, Oyster Pond

Suggested itineraries

Two weeks
Guadeloupe to Dominica and return
(About 200 miles)
● *Day 1 – Pointe-à-Pitre to Rivière Salée*
Shop, then set out in the afternoon and anchor close to the bridge at the beginning of the Riviere Salee.
● *Day 2 – Rivière Salée to Ilet à Fajou*
Wake up before light to get under the opening bridges. (They only open once a day, just before daybreak.) Motor through the Rivière Salée and through the channel which leads through Grand Cul de Sac Marin to the open sea. Anchor out of the channel close to Ilet à Fajou. Enjoy the peace and quiet, go snorkelling, eat dinner on board. (Those more interested in restaurants could choose to go on to Port Louis and anchor there.)
● *Day 3 – Ilet à Fajou to Deshaies*
Take an easy reach out to sea, gybe and sail to Deshaies. Walk to the river, eat in one of the small restaurants.
● *Day 4 – Deshaies to Cousteau National Marine Park*
Head south down the coast to the Cousteau National Marine Park. Spend the day snorkelling or diving. Eat on board or ashore.
● *Day 5 – Cousteau National Marine Park to Basse Terre*
Stop for lunch and a swim at Anse La Barque, continue to Basse Terre and spend the night in Marina Rivière Sens. Eat in one of the small restaurants ashore.
● *Day 6 – Basse Terre to The Saintes*
Sail to The Saintes. Anchor in the village or one of the quieter bays.
● *Day 7 – The Saintes to Prince Rupert Bay, Dominica*
Sail to Prince Rupert Bay.

● *Day 8 – Dominica*
Spend the day sightseeing ashore. Take a taxi tour round the island or arrange to go hiking.
● *Day 9 – Prince Rupert Bay to The Saintes*
Return to The Saintes, a charming group of islands, well worth a second stop.
● *Day 10 – The Saintes*
You will probably want to spend a whole extra day here.
● *Day 11 – The Saintes to Ilet du Gozier*
Sail to Ilet du Gozier, relax swim and snorkel.
● *Day 12 – Ilet du Gozier to Marie Galante*
Take the glorious reach out to Marie Galante, stopping in Anse Carnot for lunch, swells permitting. Anchor for the night in St Louis, or if that is uncomfortable behind the harbour wall in Grand Bourg. Eat ashore in one of the small bistros in either place.
● *Day 13 – Marie Galante*
Spend the day in Marie Galante, enjoying the gorgeous beaches, or rent a car or motor bike and explore the island.
● *Day 14 – Marie Galante to Pointe à Pitre*
A glorious sail back to base in Pointe-à-Pitre.

Ten days
Antigua and Barbuda
(About 100 miles)
● *Day 1 – English Harbour*
Stay in historic English Harbour, climb to Shirley Heights, enjoy the lively restaurant and social scene in the evening.
● *Day 2 – English Harbour to Indian Creek*
A short beat to windward to Indian Creek to get the crew in shape. Snorkelling, walking, peace and quiet. Those who prefer a more social scene can visit the large resort at Mamora Bay instead.
● *Day 3 – Indian Creek to Nonsuch Bay*
Another easy day. Sail up the east coast to Green Island and Nonsuch Bay. Find an anchorage all to yourself in the miles of protected water inside the offshore fringing reef.
● *Day 4 – Nonsuch Bay to Barbuda*
Get up early and head out to sea for Barbuda, arriving around midday. Enjoy the long white empty beaches, the snorkelling and the complete peace and quiet.
● *Day 5 – Barbuda*
Spend the day in Barbuda. Choose between seeing one of the other anchorages, going hiking, or arranging for a tour of the frigate bird colony and the island.
● *Day 6 – Barbuda to Dickenson Bay*
Sail to Dickenson Bay. Get back into the swing of civilisation by visiting the bars and eating ashore.

• *Day 7 – Dickenson Bay to Great Bird Island*
Sail through the Boon Channel to Crabbs, stock up on water and a few provisions if necessary, and carry on to Great Bird Island or back to the Maiden Island or Long Island anchorage.

• *Day 8 – Great Bird Island to Deep Bay*
Easy sail to St John's. Tie up at Redcliffe Cay. Pick out a restaurant for lunch while spending the morning in town, then sail to Deep Bay. Swim and snorkel on the wreck of the *Andes*.

• *Day 9 – Deep Bay to Jolly Harbour*
Stop for lunch at Maiden Island in Five Islands Harbour. Continue to Jolly Harbour for a sociable night in a marina. Eat ashore.

• *Day 10 – Jolly Harbour to English Harbour*
Sail back to English Harbour.

Seven days
St Martin, St Barts and Anguilla
(About 75 miles)

• *Day 1 – Simpson Bay to Road Bay, Anguilla*
Leave Simpson Bay and make the easy downwind sail to Road Bay in Anguilla. Clear in with customs.

• *Day 2 – Anguilla*
Spend the day in Anguilla and choose between day sailing to the offshore islands or taking a land tour. Eat ashore.

• *Day 3 – Anguilla to Marigot, St Martin*
Round the northern end of Anguilla and sail to Marigot on the French side of St Martin. Enjoy a good French meal ashore.

• *Day 4 – Marigot to Ile Pinel*
Sail to Tintamarre Island for lunch, spend the night in Ile Pinel, eat on board.

• *Day 5 – Ile Pinel to Ile Fourche*
Set sail for Ile Fourche near St Barts. Spend the day snorkelling or diving and enjoy a night in this remote island.

• *Day 6 – Ile Fourche to Anse Columbier*
Sail to Gustavia, for sightseeing and shopping, return in time sail to Anse Columbier.

• *Day 7 – Anse Columbier to Simpson Bay*

Land excursions

Dominica Dominica has the most dramatically beautiful topography in this group and there are wonderful trails in the rainforest. The really energetic will want to take the all day hike to the second-largest boiling lake in the world. The hikes to Trafalgar Falls or the Emerald Pool are easy, as is the trail that goes between the two large freshwater lakes. Dominica is home to the last of the Carib Indians and you can visit their reservation to buy handicrafts.

Guadeloupe Guadeloupe has beautiful rainforests and the hike to Chutes du Carbet is pleasant and easy.

Barbuda Barbuda has the largest nesting colony of frigate birds in the eastern Caribbean and anyone at all interested in these birds will want to schedule a tour to see them.

Onward routes

Several charter companies offer one-way trips from Guadeloupe to St Martin (about 180 miles) or from Antigua to St Martin (about 120 miles). These trips are for more adventurous sailors who want to put in several hours of sailing on most days. They also give you a chance to visit Montserrat, St Kitts and Nevis, and possibly even Saba and Statia.

USA

FOR

- Large choice of cruising areas from the Pacific Northwest to Chesapeake to San Diego and the Florida Keys
- Easy communications and excellent facilities in most places
- Friendly people and lots of interesting things to see ashore
- Good seafood
- Comparatively inexpensive once you are there

AGAINST

- Some areas crowded in the high season
- Some areas require experienced navigators
- Limited cruising area in a few places

Types of charter

- Flotilla/sailing in company
- Bareboat
- Skippered
- Luxury (in some areas)

The USA is, as everyone knows, a vast country with a long Atlantic and Pacific seaboard. Charter areas are scattered all along the eastern and western coasts as well as in the Great Lakes which straddle the US and Canada. The latter are really vast inland seas and it is something of a misnomer to call them lakes. Because of the size of the continent it is impossible to make generalisations about weather conditions and the sort of coast and harbours you will come across. For specific charter areas the relevant information will be included (although in abbreviated form) for some areas. Many Americans regard the Caribbean as their charter area of choice and most charter companies operating there are American.

When to go

This is covered under each charter area section.

Getting there

The USA has an extensive network of major international and smaller domestic airports with regular scheduled and charter flights operating everywhere. No country is better served by international and connecting flights. Information on relevant international and domestic airports is given under each charter area.

Eating and drinking

America is not often thought of as being a gourmet destination, but in my opinion – and that of others – it has very good food and, in many places, a wide range of ethnic restaurants serving wonderful inexpensive food. West-coast food is now a recognised style of cuisine and clam chowder and crab-cakes around the Pacific northwest and Chesapeake have long been famous. All along the coast seafood is excellent and generally fresh and cooked in interesting ways. From north to south and east to west the USA has a wide range of regional cooking and has adopted all the styles of its melting pot of immigrants over the years.

You can get affordable Japanese, Southeast Asian, Italian, Mexican, Creole, and good old American home cooking as well. Portions are always large as reflected in the girth of many of the inhabitants and institutions like the American breakfast are serious affairs. Then, of course, there are those American favourites like hamburgers and fried chicken although it pays to stay away from the brand names which now encircle the world and go to smaller establishments where this fare is infinitely better. Remember that a tip is expected in bars and restaurants (usually around 15 per cent of the bill). If you don't tip it is just plain embarrassing for all concerned, you will get dirty looks from staff and customers alike, and it means less in the pay packet for the waiter or waitress at the end of the week. When in Rome etc . . .

Californian wine is eminently quaffable and some of it very good although it is generally not cheap in restaurants. Avoid the brands commonly exported and go for smaller vintners. American beer is usually light lager and more of a refreshing cool drink than an alcoholic beverage. There are other stronger dark beers in some areas if you prefer a change to the ubiquitous *Budweiser*, *Miller* and *Schlitz*. Spirits are widely available and cocktails are popular in most places.

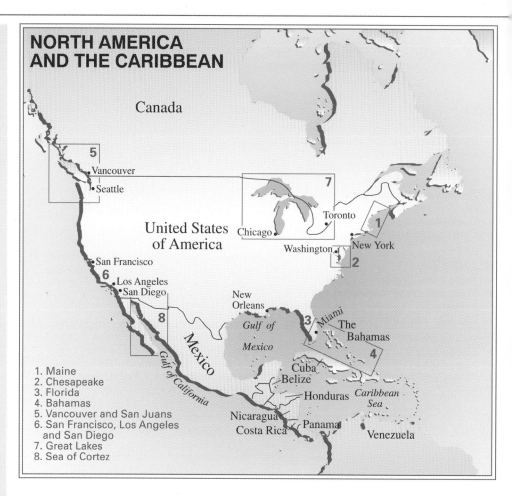

NORTH AMERICA AND THE CARIBBEAN

Canada

United States of America

5 Vancouver · Seattle

7 Toronto

Chicago ·

Washington New York 2

1

San Francisco

6 Los Angeles · San Diego

New Orleans

Gulf of Mexico

Miami

3 The Bahamas 4

8

Mexico

Gulf of California

Cuba
Belize
Honduras Caribbean Sea

1. Maine
2. Chesapeake
3. Florida
4. Bahamas
5. Vancouver and San Juans
6. San Francisco, Los Angeles and San Diego
7. Great Lakes
8. Sea of Cortez

Nicaragua
Costa Rica Panama
Venezuela

Provisioning

All provisions are easily found in larger towns and tourist spots although large supermarkets are usually out of town a bit. The smaller supermarkets will be able to supply nearly everything you want anyway. Delicatessens have a whole range of tempting treats in the way of cold meats, salamis and cheeses.

Many of the larger charter companies and some of the smaller ones can provision the boat for you on arrival. Normally you get either a list on which to tick off the items you want or a range of menus, from basic to luxury, with the items you get in each clearly stated. Getting the charter company to provision for you rarely costs too much more than doing it yourself and lets you get away from the charter base early. In any case there will be lots of opportunity in most places to restock the larder.

Costs

The overall cost of living is low to medium. Typical costs for eating out depend on the sort of place you go to, with small no-frills restaurants or cafes being good value and upmarket restaurants quite expensive. For breakfast go to a diner where a large serving will cost around $5–$10 (£3–£6.50). Lunch and snacks in a pizza place, Chinese or Southeast Asian restaurant with a set menu or salad bar will cost around $5–$15 (£3–£9·50) for a large portion. Evening meals in a restaurant can range from $10 (£6·50) for a cheap Japanese or Mexican meal with a beer to $50–$60 (£32–£38·50) for upmarket cuisine with wine. In between there are numerous variations but, on the whole, good quality food, including good seafood, is easily found at a price to suit your pocket.

Provisioning is relatively cheap for all items and meat and fresh fruit and vegetables are abundant and of good quality.

Transport is relatively cheap with air fares being the lowest in the world per air mile and rail and coach travel also good value. Car hire is the cheapest in the world with a compact normally costing around £10–£12 per day although, with deals arranged beforehand, car hire can be as low as £8·50 per day. Insurance must be added to these prices and varies from state to state. With petrol at just over $1 per gallon this is a very cheap and convenient way to get around. Hire bikes, including mountain bikes, are available in some places at a low cost.

Crime and personal safety

Although the US has a reputation for violent crime – and especially mugging – outside the major urban areas crime is not a big issue. In places like Washington, Los Angeles, New York, Miami and San Diego you need to be careful when out and about, especially at night. Don't flash money around, don't look as if you are lost, don't wear expensive jewellery and don't venture into any part of the city which is known to have a reputation for crime. If the worst happens and you are mugged do not get excited and make sudden movements – just hand over your money and valuables. The mugger will most likely be armed with a knife (guns are rare, despite the numbers in the USA) and probably just as scared as you – he only wants to get away with the dosh as quickly as possible.

When you leave the boat in harbour or at anchor to go ashore make sure it is securely locked and that any obvious temptations on deck have been stowed below. Leave the dinghy somewhere secure and chain it up if necessary. If you have an outboard on the dinghy ensure that it is padlocked on. Most marinas have security guards and it is unlikely you will have problems when berthed for the night.

Sailing guides and charts

Sailing guides are readily available in the US and can often be purchased from the charter company when you book your holiday. The relevant guides are mentioned for each area in that section.

Defence Mapping Agency (DMA) charts are widely available throughout the USA. There are many locally produced charts which have been cut down to A2 or A3 format and bound together to make useful chart-books for yachts. Many of these chart-books have harbour and anchorage plans, aerial photographs, notes on things to see

and do ashore, and even good restaurant recommendations. They can usually be found locally or ask the charter company you are booking with if this sort of publication is available.

Essential information

Time zone UT -5 to -8 depending on the state. Pacific standard time in California is -8 hours. Eastern standard time in New York is -5 hours. DST +1 in summer Apr–Oct

Language English. Spanish common in some areas

Telecommunications Automatic dialling. Country code 1. Public telephone service. Fax at bureaux and marina offices. Mobile phone system but the GSM system operates only in some places.

Health Good healthcare, although it is essential that you have health insurance as healthcare here is the most expensive in the world. Most insurance companies will add a premium to normal health insurance cover for the very high costs of care in the USA. You would be exceptionally foolish to travel in the USA without fully comprehensive health insurance and most charter companies will insist that you take out a full policy as part of their booking conditions.

Money The unit of currency is the universally recognised American dollar, the greenback, that can be used in almost any country in the world for goods and services. You can obtain dollars or dollar traveller's cheques before you go. All banks will change US dollar traveller's cheques, usually at face value. Traveller's cheques in other currencies and foreign cash will often be difficult to change or will involve a long and tedious process. Cash advances on major credit cards, Visa and MasterCard, and on charge cards like American Express and Diners Club, can be made. Most ATM machines accept Visa or MasterCard.

Banks are open 1000–1500 Mon–Fri although there may be variations in the summer between states. ATM machines are the best way of getting money in the USA with no hassles.

Documentation All non-American citizens must carry passports. Remember to take your passport (Americans included) if you are sailing across to the Bahamas from Florida, to Mexico from California, or to Canada from the Pacific Northwest. Most European passport holders, including UK citizens, do not require a full visitor's visa for a stay of 90 days or less. However nationals from

Australia, New Zealand, South Africa and even countries like Ireland, do require a full non-immigrant visitor's visa. Check with the US consulate if you are unsure.

Proof of competence to handle a yacht will not normally be required although you will have to satisfy the charter company you have sufficient experience to take out a bareboat. Some proof of competence may be required for longer passages, such as going across the Gulf Stream to the Bahamas or from California down to Mexico. It depends on the charter company and its assessment of your competence. All other boat documentation will be provided by the charter company. To go fishing, all states require you to have a fishing permit which can usually be obtained for a small fee locally for the length of your stay.

East Coast USA

Maine

The coast and islands in the state of Maine between Boston and Nova Scotia make up a spectacular cruising area although not one for the inexperienced. The area has its share of rocks and reefs, but the real problem is fog which can roll off the sea at any time. Neither is it spectacularly warm here, with July and August temperatures an average 24°–26°C in the day and 14°–16°C at night, although it can feel chillier than this.

The two main cruising areas are Penobscot Bay and Casco Bay further south. Both are dotted with islands. Many of these are uninhabited or have just an original house or two on them. Around the islands, navigation is fairly straightforward although there are shallow areas, rocky reefs and ridges, and the tides which can cause appreciable races between the islands. Fog is common through spring and summer when the prevailing southerlies bring moist warm air up over the cold Labrador current.

Facilities are limited except in the centres of population which are few and far between. There are international flights into Boston and feeder flights from New York.

New York/ Long Island

There are a number of yacht charter companies operating in this area for a mix of the Big Apple and cruising in Long Island Sound. The Sound has a mix of marinas, yards and some bays where you can anchor.

It is a busy area with not only local boats from the large surrounding population, but also commercial traffic headed for New York and onwards to the Hudson.

Sailing conditions are not the greatest here with a general lack of wind in high summer during July and August. The best sailing is reckoned to be during April-May and September-October when there are stronger winds. Winds are generally northerlies or southerlies in spring and autumn depending on the weather systems around. Winds in the summer are generally from the SW although there are many days of calm.

For more information look at American sailing magazines or talk to a charter broker.

Chesapeake Bay

At Washington

	Av max °C	Av min °C	Highest recorded	Relative humidity	Days 0·25mm rain
Apr	18	7	35	45%	11
May	24	12	36	48%	12
Jun	28	17	39	52%	11
Jul	31	20	41	53%	11
Aug	29	19	41	53%	11
Sep	26	15	40	53%	8
Oct	19	9	36	50%	9

Chesapeake Bay is an enclosed waterway extending over 200 miles from Norfolk in Virginia to past Baltimore in Maryland. It is much indented with a number of rivers and creeks running into it and it has a number of islands and islets. Much of it is very shallow and care is needed with your pilotage so you don't get stuck in the mud too often. The area is popular in the summer with lots of local boats around and there are numerous marinas and boat harbours to pull into for provisions and eating out. Eating out is part of the reason for being here with excellent crab, fish and shrimps, prepared in all sorts of tempting ways.

The season here lasts from April to October. May, June and September are reckoned the best months to sail here. Being inland it can get very hot in July and August and winds are the least reliable during high summer. For the most part, winds are from the south to southwest at 10–12 knots although there are numerous days of calm or very light winds. Thunderstorms are fairly frequent in the summer and may be accompanied by strong winds, often from west to northwest. There are tides in the area

Opposite Annapolis in the Chesapeake.
Photo Pat Collinge

with the strongest currents in the narrow channels at the southern end around Annapolis. Most navigation is straightforward with buoys, beacons or withies marking the channels. One thing to look out for is the large numbers of buoyed crab pots all around the area making it essential to keep an eye out most of the time. However the crab is so good ashore you won't begrudge the chore of zigzagging round the crab pots.

Chesapeake Bay has a wonderful mixture of cities and towns with all amenities, good maritime museums and excellent seafood restaurants. Marinas here offer just about every conceivable facility, including good showers and toilets, restaurants and bars, and most have swimming pools. There are smaller towns, some with small marinas or piers and lots of anchorages behind islands or up creeks. Many of the boats here have lifting keels or are shallow draught as getting stuck in the mud when exploring creeks and inlets is a common occurrence.

Around the remoter areas the vegetation is luxurious and the birdlife prolific – including egrets, herons and kingfishers. There are even supposed to be otters up some of the creeks. The heat and the thick vegetation does give rise to a few pests and 'noseeums' are a problem – pack a good insect repellent. Towards the end of the summer there can be lots of jellyfish around ruling out swimming and quite probably one of the reasons why a lot of marinas have pools.

There are a lot of places of note to visit around Chesapeake. From the south, Annapolis is considered by some Americans to be the boating capital of the USA, has a good maritime museum and is home to the American Naval Academy. The old historic centre of the city is well worth a visit and there are shops and boutiques aplenty. Around this area there are lots of examples of old maritime Chesapeake with many of the waterfront areas restored and in use for transient boaters exploring the area. Places like St Michaels and Oxford should not be missed. At the northern end of Chesapeake Bay it is possible to sail right up the Potomac to Washington DC although it is likely you will be more seduced by the charms of smaller places before the White House claims your attention. Baltimore, the capital of Maryland at the northern end of Chesapeake Bay, can also be visited by boat.

Most charter companies are clustered around Annapolis although there are companies operating out of the northern end of the Bay as well. There are international and feeder flights to Annapolis and internal communications by rail and coach are good. Alternatively, you can hire a car.

References

A Gunkholer's Guide. Cruising the Chesapeake Bill Shellenberger, Claiborne Young

Florida and the Bahamas

Florida and the Bahamas are lumped together here because charter boats from Florida often cross the Gulf Stream to cruise around the Bahamas. Crossing from Florida to the Bahamas is for experienced bareboat crews or skippered charter only and may be curtailed at times by the weather.

When to go

The season is year round although, in August to October at the height of the hurricane season, you may be held in check by the charter company and advised to cruise locally.

Low season May to mid-November. Paradoxically the summer months here are the low season as this is the wettest time of the year with slightly higher humidity. It is also the hurricane season which officially lasts from June to November. Hurricanes usually pass to the south of Florida and the Bahamas in June and July and the worst months are August to October. Winds are the easterly trades over the Bahamas and also over parts of the Florida coast. The trade winds tend to blow from east to southeast in the summer. Thunderstorms are common.

High season December to April. The mild winter temperatures make this a wonderful place to sail in the winter and water temperatures are still high. In fact the winter sea temperature is more refreshing than the high-summer sea temperatures which make it feel like you're swimming in warm soup. The easterly trades tend to be from the northeast at 10–20 knots. There can be winter gales influenced by depressions moving across the bulk of the USA to the north and these can bring strong southerly winds, commonly southeast, rain and cooler temperatures.

USA

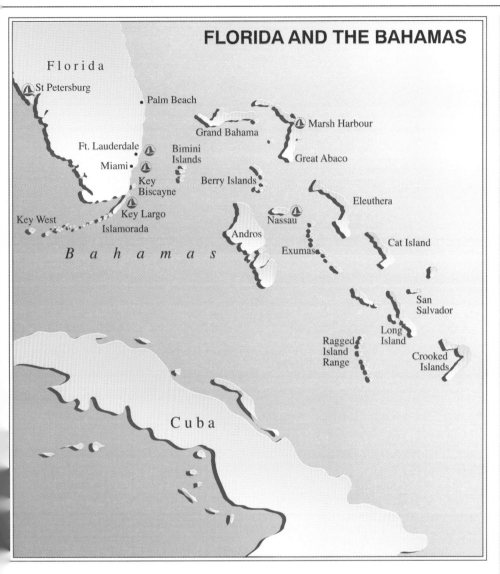

FLORIDA AND THE BAHAMAS

Florida

St Petersburg

Palm Beach

Grand Bahama

Marsh Harbour

Ft. Lauderdale

Bimini Islands

Miami

Great Abaco

Key Biscayne

Berry Islands

Eleuthera

Key West

Key Largo

Islamorada

Nassau

Andros

B a h a m a s

Exumas

Cat Island

San Salvador

Long Island

Ragged Island Range

Crooked Islands

Cuba

At Miami

	Av max °C	Av min °C	Highest recorded	Relative humidity	Days 0·25mm rain	Sea temp °C
Jan	23	16	29	66%	9	22
Feb	24	16	31	63%	6	23
Mar	26	18	33	62%	7	24
Apr	27	19	34	64%	7	25
May	29	22	34	67%	12	28
Jun	30	23	34	69%	13	30
Jul	31	24	36	68%	15	31
Aug	31	24	36	68%	15	32
Sep	31	24	35	70%	18	30
Oct	28	22	34	69%	16	28
Nov	26	19	31	64%	10	25
Dec	24	17	33	65%	7	23

Getting there

There are numerous daily scheduled and charter flights to Miami and Orlando from most important European and Pacific airports. There are some international flights to Tampa on the west coast. There are numerous domestic flights to Miami and Orlando on the east coast and to Tampa on the west. There are also some domestic flights to Key West and Marathon on the east coast and to Clearwater/St Petersburg on the west.

At anchor in the Bahamas. Yes the water really is that clear and in places that shallow.
Photo Yachting World

Charter areas

Charter yachts operate on both the east and west sides of Florida although most charter is concentrated around the east side and the Florida Keys. It is a popular charter area with excellent diving and fishing in the clear waters. It also offers a wide choice from the sheltered waters of the Intracoastal Waterway to offshore across the Gulf Stream, to the Bahamas. The Bahamas, just off the coast, are renowned for diving and fishing. Because much of the water around the Florida Keys and the Bahamas is shallow, many charter yachts have shoal-draught keels and catamarans are also popular for exploring the waters that deeper-draught craft have difficulty getting to.

Wind and sea

The prevailing winds in this area are the easterly trade winds. In the summer the winds blow from the east to southeast at around 10–15 knots, although the effects are lessened closer to the Florida coast where

there are often variable winds. Thunderstorms are common in the summer and can bring strong winds for a short period. Summer is the wet season and a fair amount of rain falls in the period from July to October. The hurricane season lasts from June to November, although August to October is the high-risk period for the Florida coast and the Bahamas. Hurricanes have hit this area and, in August to October, a close listening watch should be kept on the radio and on weather forecasts. (Weather forecasts are excellent for the area and you will be warned well in advance of any hurricane likely to hit Florida.) One thing you can be sure of is that you do not want to encounter the fury of a full-blown hurricane on a boat. The best policy in the event of a hurricane heading your way is to get the boat into a marina and head inland.

In the winter, the prevailing trades blow predominantly from the northeast at around 10–20 knots although, as above, the effect is lessened close off the coast of Florida. At times a cold 'norther' can blow down the coast from north to northwest and may at times reach gale force. Northers usually blow when the pressure starts to rise for the permanent winter anticyclone stationed over America. Strong southeast gales can also blow when depressions move out into the Atlantic from the American land mass.

Seas in this area range from nearly flat in the Intracoastal Waterway to quite rough when strong winds blow against the north-going Gulf Stream. In Hawk Channel, outside the Keys, seas are light to moderate. Over the Gulf Stream things can get very rough with a strong northerly and it is advisable to monitor weather forecasts carefully. Some charter companies will ban yachts going to the Bahamas if bad weather is forecast.

Suitable for . . .

The possibilities around the Florida Keys and the Bahamas offshore mean the area has something for everyone. Beginners can potter around the Intracoastal Waterway and out into Hawk Channel in settled conditions. Experienced sailors and crew can get some miles in crossing to the Bahamas and back again to Florida. There are a few semi-flotillas/sailing in company holidays although these are not like the organised flotillas of the Mediterranean. There are bareboats of all types and skippered charter from smaller yachts up to very large yachts. There are also instruction courses offered by some of the charter companies.

Harbours and anchorages

Harbours range from marinas with every facility laid on, to smaller yacht harbours and boat piers. Most marinas have all facilities including hot showers, restaurants and shops within the marina, as well as swimming pools. Even smaller, less flashy, harbours and piers will have some facilities and you will find the locals there go out of their way to help you. Anchorages vary from mud around the mangrove creeks to sand on the outer Keys and Bahamas. In the mangrove swamps there are lots of mosquitoes and 'noseeums' so take plenty of insect repellent. The locals reckon that the mosquitoes here arrive with napkins!

Main charter bases

The main charter bases on the east coast are in the marinas around Miami and Fort Lauderdale and along the main Keys at Key Largo, Islamorada and Key West. Many of the marinas are along the Intracoastal Waterway and there are charter bases at many of these. It is usually possible to arrange one-way charters between bases for an additional cost. On the west coast of Florida, most charter bases are near Tampa. There are domestic flights to Key West and Marathon on the east coast and to Tampa, Clearwater/St Petersburg Airport.

From Miami Airport there are airport shuttle services to downtown Miami and to most Key destinations. Normal coach services and airport limousine services (for which, read 'taxi') also operate along the coast. Probably the best way to do things is to have a hire car waiting at the airport and drive to your destination. It is sometimes possible to leave the car at the charter base after a few days and arrange to have another car waiting there on your return. From Miami it is around 1½ hours' drive to Key Largo and 3½ to Key West, depending on traffic.

Sailing area

On the eastern side there is a threefold choice of how you sail down the coast and Keys. The Intracoastal Waterway runs down between the Keys and the coast. Sheltered by the Keys it is comparatively flat water and there are numerous marinas and anchorages. This area is shallow in places and care is needed outside the channel. The channel itself is clearly marked with yellow triangles to starboard and yellow squares to port when heading south. The road bridges connecting the Keys open for boats so that you can get out into Hawk Channel. Between the Keys and the outer fringing reef is Hawk Channel which offers better sailing and deeper water. The outer fringing reef stops the worst of the swell but not the easterly trades. It is also possible to sail outside the fringing reef but there is little point to this.

Crossing to the Bahamas involves longer distances and some overnight sailing. It is around 50 miles to Bimini on the western side of the Bahamas where you can clear customs. From Bimini to somewhere like Great Stirrup Cay is 75 miles. After pottering around your chosen part of the Bahamas it is then necessary to get back to Bimini, clear out, and re-cross the Gulf Stream to the east coast. Really it is inadvisable to take less than two weeks over a Bahamas cruise because of the distances involved.

In the Bahamas there are several charter bases near island centres at Marsh Harbour on Great Abaco and Hopetown on Nassau. These bases are accessible by flights from Miami and get over the Gulf stream the easy way landing you right in the middle of the Bahamas and ready for a little cruising around the reefs and cays as soon as you get off the plane.

In the Bahamas you will find lots of local colour, but it is the local colour under the water which is the big attraction. Shallow waters allow snorkelling not far off the bottom and the clear waters and coral reefs are home to a wide variety of marine life. There are tropical fish everywhere.

The Bahamas have had a reputation as a drug-smuggling area that yachts should steer clear of. These days, the vigilant American coastguard has eliminated much of the drug-smuggling activity around here, but you will still need to be vigilant and it is best to stick to the more popular areas and, if possible, sail in company with another yacht.

On the west coast of Florida there are lots of small islands and mangrove creeks to explore. The area is less developed than the east coast and there are fewer tailor-made marinas and yacht facilities. The birdlife here is prolific with ibis, cormorants, pelicans, osprey and herons. This being Florida, there are also alligators.

A typical one-week itinerary from Miami to Key West is as follows.

Miami – Key West
(135 miles)
A cruise down the Florida Keys. Starts at Miami.
Elliot Key in Biscayne Bay
Anchor off the beach. Swim and explore the island.
Key Largo
Leave via Angelfish Creek to the Hawk Channel for a good sail south. Anchor behind Rodriguez Key or go into Marina del Mar for some nightlife.
Islamorada
Visit the Pennekamp Coral Reef State Park for snorkelling. Go to Holiday Isle Marina at Windley Key for the night. Restaurants.
Duck Key Sail to Hawks Cay Resort
Good beach and swimming.
Newfound Harbour
Anchor off Little Palm Island. Restaurant. Visit Big Pine Key to see the world's smallest deer.
Key West
Good snorkelling at Looe Key Marine Sanctuary. Go to Lands End Marina for the night. Restaurants and bars aplenty.

Key West
Explore the island and don't forget to visit Hemingway's house and the bar he frequented.

References
Cruising Guide to the Florida Keys Capt. Frank Papy
Waterway Guide: Lower Florida & The Keys Chartbook
Hidden Florida Keys and Everglades
Yachtsman's Guide to the Bahamas

West Coast
(For general information on the USA see USA East Coast section)

The west coast of America has a number of varied charter areas. Charter bases are in the San Juan Islands just under the Canadian border, San Francisco, Los Angeles and San Diego. The cruising conditions and climate vary considerably between the northern and southern areas with charter in the north confined to the summer and charter in the south extending over a longer period.

San Juan Islands and Seattle
At Seattle

	Av max °C	Av min °C	Highest recorded	Relative humidity	Days 1mm rain	Sea temp °C
May	18	8	33	56%	12	11
Jun	21	11	37	54%	9	13
Jul	22	12	38	51%	4	14
Aug	23	13	36	54%	5	14
Sep	19	11	33	61%	8	13
Oct	15	8	28	73%	13	12

Puget Sound, wrapping around the San Juan Islands just under the border with Canada, is a huge, much-indented cruising area. It is a popular area for yachting but it *is* possible to get away from it all. Effectively the area is increased by Vancouver and Vancouver Island just over the border and customs clearance between the USA and Canada is easy and quick. The islands are sheltered from the worst of the Pacific swell by Vancouver Island and Olympic Peninsula which enclose Puget Sound and extend down to Seattle. There are so many indentations around the coast and islands that it is always possible to find shelter.

The season runs from May to September although, in the spring and autumn, it can get chilly at times. It also rains a lot – a grey drizzle that doesn't show up in the statistics as much as it does when you are there. Day temperatures are pleasantly warm and at times it can get very hot, as a glance at the table above shows. The best time to visit is from June to September. Winds can be light and variable in July and August with more consistent winds in June and September. At times there will be a blow off the Pacific, more frequent in the spring and autumn than high summer.

Navigation amongst the islands is fairly straightforward except for strong tidal streams which can reach 4–5 knots in places such as the Spieden Channel. Tides are around 4·3m at springs. The area is well covered by yachtsman's guides and, if these are not on the charter yacht, then get hold of copies before you set off.

The islands are a wild area with lots of good walking and the opportunity to get away from it all. Dense forest covers much of the area and a number of the islands and much of the adjacent coast is national park . Large parts of the area were and some still are logging country and there are old logging towns scattered around the area. The region is actually semi-tropical rainforest, with a dense forest canopy under which lichens, mosses and ferns grow. There are lots of marked hiking paths and it is well worth allotting some time out from sailing for rambles ashore. The birdlife is prolific, including eagles and herons, and there are elk in places. The waters are home to all sorts of marine life including whales (orcas or killer whales frequent the area), dolphins and seals.

There are a number of yacht marinas, piers in places or laid moorings in the bays. Otherwise you are on your own and anchoring out. Facilities are limited away from the centres of population but there is usually somewhere you can get to for provisions and a bite ashore if you need it. All charter is bareboat or skippered and operates out of Seattle, Friday Harbour, Anacortes and a few other places. It is also possible to sail down from charter bases in Vancouver to the islands.

There are international and domestic flights into Seattle and Vancouver and some smaller connecting flights and seaplanes. Internal travel and communications are good whether by train, coach or car.

References
Evergreen Pacific San Juan Islands Cruising Atlas Charts and aerial photos. Available locally.
Emily's Guides to the San Juan Islands Set of three guides. Available locally.

San Francisco

The Bay is not the greatest place to sail out of because there are few places to sail to. It is a fair way to either the San Juans to the north or the harbours in the south. It is also prone to the notorious Bay Fog which rolls in off the sea on a good number of days in the summer, wafted in on the afternoon sea breeze. Those who sail around here love it, but you can't help thinking that they sail around here because they live here, not because it offers good sailing.

Los Angeles and San Diego
At San Diego

	Av max °C	Av min °C	Highest recorded	Relative humidity	Days 1mm rain	Sea temp °C
Mar	18	10	37	66%	7	15
Apr	19	12	36	68%	4	15
May	19	13	37	71%	3	16
Jun	21	15	36	72%	1	18
Jul	23	17	38	73%	1	19
Aug	23	18	34	73%	1	20
Sep	23	17	43	72%	1	19
Oct	22	14	36	71%	3	18
Nov	21	11	34	67%	4	17

The warm summers and temperate winters make this a more amenable charter area than the San Juans in the north but, while the climate is better, the cruising area is greatly restricted. You can basically go north or south along the coast. There are a few off-lying islands but no enclosed cruising area like Puget Sound or the area inside Vancouver Island. It is also hampered by the Pacific swell rolling in along the coast which provides good surfing conditions off the beaches but makes coastal passages in light winds uncomfortable and restricts the number of anchorages to those where an indentation provides shelter from the swell.

Winds in the summer are normally a sea breeze blowing onto the coast which rarely gets above 20 knots. Cruising from Los Angeles is usually south to San Diego taking in Catalina Island, Newport, Dana Point, Oceanside and Mission Bay along the way. Cruising from San Diego is either north to Los Angeles and Catalina Island or you can go south to Mexico and Ensenada and the Los Coronados Islands. It is worth taking a few days just to potter around San Diego Bay. There are numerous yacht marinas along the coast and mostly laid moorings in the few usable anchorages. The harbours and anchorages are popular in the summer and things can get very crowded. Marina del Rey in Los Angeles is the largest marina in the world.

It is possible to cruise in the winter but the Pacific swell rolling in tends to get bigger and there is always the possibility of the dreaded Santa Ana winds which blow over gale force and cause a large swell to beat on to the coast.

Communications are easy. Los Angeles Airport has international flights from all over the world. There are connecting flights to San Diego although it is a short trip by land. Trains and coaches serve the cities and towns although a hire car simplifies things greatly and hire cars in the USA are the cheapest in the world.

References

Charlie's US Pacific Coast Charlie's Charts. Distributed by Imray.

USA

Tahiti

(Society Islands)

FOR
- Exotic south seas scenery and ambience
- Good facilities and restaurants ashore
- Good sailing with consistent trade winds

AGAINST
- Some fairly long legs to get to destinations and some tricky reef entrances
- Can be expensive ashore in some places

Types of charter
- Bareboat
- Skippered
- Luxury

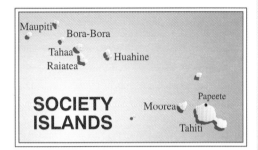

Properly these are the Society Islands of which Tahiti is just one island, but the name Tahiti has such connotations that it stands for the whole group. Tahiti has long been a magnet for northern Europeans of romantic persuasions and this includes many yachtsmen. Charter yachts have operated from Tahiti for some time although most of these have been skippered yachts. Bareboat and skippered yachts are now available to explore the islands and skippered yachts operate to the Marquesas as well.

The islands are of volcanic origin rising abruptly from the sea and are surrounded by fringing coral reefs. The scenery is spectacular and there is much to do and see ashore. The islands have been fairly well developed over the years for land-based tourism, so expect good facilities ashore and restaurants of a high standard and, likewise, high prices.

When to go

The season is year-round although many charter yachts do not run between August and October. The high season is generally considered to run from June to August and the mid-season from April to May. The prevailing trade winds blow across the islands from an easterly direction at around 15–20 knots in the wet season (May to August) and 10–15 knots in the dry season (September to April). It should be remembered that cyclones do sometimes hit the Society Islands during the months of December to March with January and February being the worst months. Temperatures are tropical with around 30°–32°C in January and December and 28°–30°C in June and July.

Tahiti: quintessential idea of the South Pacific.
Photo Yachting World

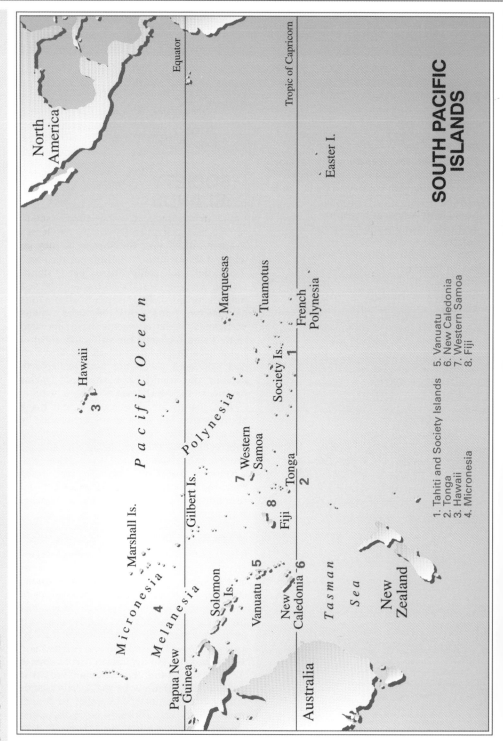

North
America

Equator

Tropic of Capricorn

Pacific Ocean

Hawaii
3

Marquesas

Tuamotus

Society Is.

French
Polynesia

Polynesia

Western
Samoa
7

Fiji
8

Tonga
2

Gilbert Is.

Marshall Is.

Micronesia
4

Melanesia

Solomon
Is.

Vanuatu
5

New
Caledonia
6

Papua New
Guinea

Tasman
Sea

Australia

New
Zealand

Easter I.

SOUTH PACIFIC
ISLANDS

1. Tahiti and Society Islands
2. Tonga
3. Hawaii
4. Micronesia

5. Vanuatu
6. New Caledonia
7. Western Samoa
8. Fiji

1

At Papeete

	Av max °C	Av min °C	Highest recorded	Relative humidity	Days 2·5mm rain	Sea temp °C
Nov	31	22	32	77%	13	27
Dec	31	22	33	78%	14	27
Jan	32	22	35	77%	16	27
Feb	32	22	33	77%	16	27
Mar	32	22	33	78%	17	27
Apr	32	22	33	78%	10	28
May	31	21	33	78%	10	28
Jun	30	21	32	79%	8	27
Jul	30	20	32	77%	5	26

Getting there

Tahiti is served by international flights from some European and American international airports and from Sydney and Auckland. Internal flights operate to some islands, including Raiatea.

Sailing guides and charts

Charlie's Charts: The Marquesas, Tuamotu, Pitcairn, Easter Is, Tahiti, Bora Bora and other Society Islands, the Australes, Cook Island. distrib. Imray
South Pacific Anchorages Warwick Clay. Imray. Harbours and anchorages south of the equator
Landfalls of Paradise. Earl Hinz
Admiralty and French charts cover the area well.

Essential information

Time zone UT -10
Language Tahitian and French
Telecommunications Direct dialling. Country code 689.
Electricity 110V 60Hz
Documentation Visas are not required from most countries – including EU countries, the USA and Australasia – if you are staying for less than 30 days. A valid passport is required for entry.

Sailing area

Charter yachts operate mostly from Raiatea and Papeete. Most of the sailing is between the islands – including Moorea, Huahine, Raiatea, Tahaa, Bora-Bora and Tahiti itself. The fringing coral reefs provide protection from the seas once you are inside them and there are numerous anchorages. Between the fringing reefs and the high jungle-clad volcanic islands the vistas are awe-inspiring and it won't take too long before old images of Gauguin, of Fletcher Christian and Bligh, of a dozen Hollywood movies set in the south Pacific, coming wriggling out of your subconscious. The islands are truly wonderful places and evocative of everything a south-sea paradise should be.

Because of the dangers of sailing amongst coral and the sometimes boisterous trade winds this area is suited to intermediate and experienced sailors for bareboats. There are often variable currents around the reefs – up to 3–4 knots in places – and this means that you must keep an eye on navigation. The channels through the reefs are well marked and buoyed, with red markers showing the outside of the reef and green markers the inside. Going through a reef entrance for the first time, with breakers and surf on either side of the pass, needs steady nerves and concentration. Less experienced sailors should take a skippered charter or at least a skipper for some of the time until they get used to the area.

For the most part you will be anchoring or picking up moorings. There is a marina on Raiatea at the Moorings base. There are a few jetties in places, usually off hotels or restaurants.

Ashore, costs are high and eating out in a restaurant can cost anything from £10 to £25 or £30 a head. With the French influence the food is, of course, very good in places. Provisioning is likewise not cheap.

Tonga

FOR
- Exotic south-sea islands
- Friendly locals ashore
- Tropical temperatures and waters

AGAINST
- Small sailing area

Types of charter
- Bareboat
- Skippered

Tonga is made up of three main islands between about 18° and 22°S. Charter boats operate from the Vava'u group in the north. It is a comparatively new charter area with just a small fleet of charter yachts operating. All sailing is either skippered or bareboat. Sailing in company with a lead boat to keep an eye on things can be arranged. The area is one of outstanding beauty with a multitude of wonderful anchorages amongst the islands and behind the reefs. It has become more popular in recent years so there are numbers of yachts around, but you can get away from the crowds with a bit of planning.

When to go

The season is year-round although it would pay to be careful during the typhoon months. It rains a good deal more frequently in the wet season in the Pacific islands than you might think. The prevailing southeast trade winds blow consistently across the islands between April and October at around 15–20 knots, and less predictably so from November to March. Typhoons occasionally pass through the islands with the worst months being those from January to March. Temperatures are tropical year round with 28°–30°C in December and January and 25°–26°C in June and July.

At Apia

	Av max °C	Av min °C	Highest recorded	Relative humidity	Days 1mm rain	Sea temp °C
Jan	30	24	33	79%	22	27
Feb	29	24	33	78%	19	27
Mar	30	23	33	78%	19	27
Apr	30	24	33	76%	14	28
May	29	23	32	76%	12	28
Jun	29	23	32	73%	7	27
Jul	29	23	33	75%	9	26
Aug	29	24	32	73%	9	26
Sep	29	23	32	75%	11	26
Oct	29	24	34	76%	14	26
Nov	30	23	33	75%	16	27
Dec	29	23	33	77%	19	27

Getting there

Tonga is served by international flights from Hawaii and New Zealand. Flights from Europe and the USA can connect through Hawaii.

Sailing guides and charts

Cruising Guide to the Vava'u Island Group in the Kingdom of Tonga The Moorings Distributed by Imrays
South Pacific Anchorages Warwick Clay. Imray. Harbours and anchorages in the Pacific south of the equator
Landfalls of Paradise. Earl Hinz
Admiralty and USA charts cover the area well.

Essential information

Time zone UT +13
Language Tongan and English
Telecommunications No direct dialling. Go through operator.

Opposite Tonga - one of the newer charter areas in the South Pacific that is proving popular.
Photo Yachting World

Documentation Visas are not required from most countries – including the EU, USA and Australasia – if you are staying for less than 30 days. A valid passport is required for entry.

Sailing area

Charter yachts operate around the northerly Vava'u group of islands where there are literally scores of wonderful anchorages. The actual sailing area is not huge and, because there are so many anchorages within a short distance, you can sail as much or as little as you like. Because of the danger of navigating amongst coral and the possibility of the southeast trade winds sometimes turning to the SW–W–NW, especially in the dry season and so making normally safe anchorages untenable, this area is not suited to inexperienced skippers for bareboats. Intermediate sailors worried about navigating in coral should take on a skipper, at least for part of the charter. The islands and anchorages themselves are a paradise and there is much to enjoy ashore. A traditional Tongan feast is usually part of the itinerary although it has become pretty much a set-piece for tourists in the main centres.

Other Pacific islands

Hawaii

In general, the Hawaiian Islands are not suited to yacht charter. The prevailing northeast trades blowing across the islands send in large rollers which, while welcomed by the surfing fraternity, make many of the anchorages at best uncomfortable and in some cases untenable. There is some skippered charter around the islands from a number of bases and this is the best way to enjoy Hawaii. There are international flights into Honolulu and numerous internal flights.

For more information, try American sailing magazines or a charter broker.

Further reading

Charlie's Charts Hawaii, Maui, Molokai and Lanai, Oahu and Kanai. distributed by Imray

Micronesia

Situated in the NW Pacific just above the equator, the island chain of Micronesia offers abundant sailing and diving opportunities. There are a number of small charter operations offering skippered charter and sail-dive charter. Most operations are out of Palau and, from here, there are so many possibilities that it is probably best to just sit back and allow the skipper to organise an itinerary. International flights into Palau.

For more information, try American and Southeast Asian boating magazines or a charter broker.

Vanuatu

The island chain of Vanuatu sits sandwiched between Australia and Fiji on the edge of the Coral Sea. There is some skippered charter out of Port Vila on Efate Island. The prevailing winds are the southeast trades and temperatures are much similar to Fiji (see climate chart). The best season is May to October and the islands are in the path of cyclones during the season from November to March. There are international flights into Port Vila,

For further information, see French and other sailing magazines or a charter broker.

Sailing Guides

South Pacific Anchorages Warwick Clay.
Imray
Landfalls of Paradise Earl Hinz

New Caledonia

There is bareboat and skippered charter out of Noumea and normal itineraries go to the Loyalty Islands or the Isle of Pines to the south. One-way itineraries are possible. The island is a French Overseas Colony and much of the charter is organised by French companies. In fact it was from here that French secret agents chartered a yacht to sail to New Zealand to sink the Greenpeace boat *Rainbow Warrior*. The climate is typically tropical and the winds are the prevailing SE trades. There are international flights into Noumea and internal flights to many places.

For further information, try French and other sailing magazines or a charter broker.

Sailing Guides

South Pacific Anchorages Warwick Clay.
Imray
Landfalls of Paradise Earl Hinz

Samoa

Samoa is divided into eastern and western Samoa, the eastern group of islands being administered by the USA. The western group has some skippered charter around the islands and reefs, although not a lot. The Samoan Islands, lying between 13°–15°S of the equator, have a tropical climate and, like many of the other south Pacific islands, are blessed by constant trade winds from the southeast. The scenery, anchorages and life ashore are wonderful and every bit as good as other islands in the south Pacific.

For more information, see the sailing magazines or a charter broker.

(For temperatures and climate see the chart for Tonga.)

Sailing Guides

South Pacific Anchorages Warwick Clay.
Imray
Landfalls of Paradise Earl Hinz

Fiji

Fiji has a huge cruising ground with an estimated 300 or more islands. These are volcanic and steep-to with wonderful fringing coral reefs. It has some skippered and bareboat charter although companies seem to come and go. The continuing friction between the Fijian and Indian populations and the coup by the army in 1987 under Colonel Rabuka unsettled tourism in Fiji and this persists to the present day in the larger urban settlements. Fortunately most yacht charter is well out of the way of this.

Charter yachts operate from Suva and Musket Cove in the Malolo group of islands. There are also a number of small, usually one or two yacht operations, in other places like Lautoka and Nadi. There is enough cruising around the islands and reefs off the western side of Viti Levu to keep anyone happy. This is also the leeward side of the prevailing easterly trades and, consequently, the drier side as most of the rain falls on the easternmost islands. The wind has also lessened by the time it gets to the western side of the group and is mostly 10–15 knots from the NE–SE.

By law you must have a local guide on board to navigate you through these reef-strewn waters. A brief look at the chart will convince you that this is no bad thing. There are reefs and bombies (coral heads) everywhere. Yachts normally cruise around the Mamanutha group and the Yassawas lying more or less north-south on the western side of Viti Levu.

There are few facilities apart from the resort at Musket Cove and a few other resort hotels where there are restaurants. It is customary in Fiji to go ashore to meet the head of the village. This affords a good introduction to island life and you may just get invited for dinner. Needless to say the diving is superb around the islands and the fishing is good.

The best season is May to October and care is needed during the cyclone season from November to March. There are international flights to Nadi International Airport on the western side of Viti Levu and internal flights to Suva and Musket Cove. Bareboat charter (with a guide) and skippered yacht charter are available. For more information, see the sailing magazines, the Moorings, or a charter broker.

At Suva

	Av max °C	Av min °C	Highest recorded	Relative humidity	Days 1mm rain	Sea temp °C
Jan	29	23	35	74%	18	27
Feb	29	23	36	76%	18	27
Mar	29	23	37	76%	21	27
Apr	29	23	34	77%	19	28
May	28	22	34	79%	16	28
Jun	27	21	32	74%	13	27
Jul	26	20	32	73%	14	26
Aug	26	20	32	74%	15	26
Sep	27	21	32	73%	16	26
Oct	27	21	34	73%	15	26
Nov	28	22	34	74%	15	27
Dec	29	23	36	74%	18	27

Further reading

A Yachtsman's Fiji Michael Calder. Cruising Classroom. Distributed by Imray

South Pacific Anchorages Warwick Clay. Imray

Landfalls of Paradise. Earl Hinz

Australia

FOR

- Long sailing season and near-tropical temperatures in the Whitsundays
- Good steady sailing winds over most of the season
- Some of the world's best diving over coral off the Barrier Reef
- Friendly and helpful locals
- Good seafood and cosmopolitan cuisine around Sydney

AGAINST

- Long flight times from most destinations
- Internal flights necessary to get to the Whitsundays
- Shorter season at Sydney

Types of charter

- Sailing in company
- Bareboat
- Skippered
- Luxury

Australia has several established charter areas, but it is only recently that the notion of chartering in Australia for those in the northern hemisphere has become popular. The main charter area is around the Whitsunday Islands, lying within the Great Barrier Reef about halfway along the Queensland coast. These encompass some 70 islands, counting the very small ones, and really form the only cruising area in Australia where you can sail around a group of islands and find secure anchorages. The Whitsundays lying just north of the Tropic of Capricorn have a tropical climate and the season is year round. There are also charter bases at Sydney and Brisbane where the climate is less equatorial and more geared to the seasons.

When to go

Whitsundays The season is year round and high season tends to be geared to peak holiday periods: Easter, school holidays, and Christmas and New Year. In the Whitsundays you get higher temperatures

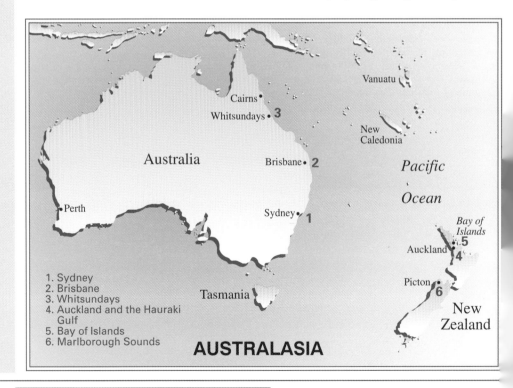

1. Sydney
2. Brisbane
3. Whitsundays
4. Auckland and the Hauraki Gulf
5. Bay of Islands
6. Marlborough Sounds

AUSTRALASIA

during the southern hemisphere summer from November to April (around 26–30°C) and slightly less wind than the winter. From May to October, temperatures are slightly less than the summer (around 22–28°C) but the winds are, on average, slightly stronger than in the summer.

Brisbane/Sydney Further south, at Brisbane and more so at Sydney, the summer and winter periods are more pronounced and the southern hemisphere summer (November to April) is the favoured period.

At Townsville (just N of Whitsundays)

	Av max °C	Av min °C	Highest recorded	Relative humidity	Days 0·25mm rain	Sea temp °C
Jan	31	24	40	70%	15	25
Feb	31	24	43	68%	12	25
Mar	30	23	35	68%	10	25
Apr	29	21	36	62%	6	24
May	27	18	32	60%	5	23
Jun	25	16	31	60%	4	22
Jul	24	15	29	58%	3	21
Aug	25	16	32	59%	3	20
Sep	27	19	34	61%	2	20
Oct	28	22	34	64%	4	21
Nov	29	23	38	66%	5	22
Dec	31	24	38	69%	12	24

Getting there

There are numerous scheduled flights to Sydney from most large international airports around the world. There are internal connections to most other major destinations in Australia. There are also international flights to Cairns and Brisbane. To get to the Whitsundays most people opt to fly to Prosperine or Hamilton Island where a bus, taxi or water taxi will take you to the charter base. Some charter companies may deliver the boat to Hamilton Island. It is also possible to take a hire car to the adjacent mainland or get a coach or train to Prosperine. Flight times from Europe are around 20 hours and, from the USA, around 10–12 hours. In my experience it is best to have a brief stopover somewhere en route rather than flying direct. A stopover will usually diminish the effects of jet-lag commonly found on long flights from Europe to Australia.

Eating and drinking

Eating out in Australia is excellent with considerable influence from the major immigrant groups from Southeast Asia and Europe. In the larger centres, good Thai, Malaysian, Japanese, Vietnamese and Chinese food will be found along with European-orientated restaurants including Italian, Greek, Spanish and French. Many of these influences have been 'Aussified' with interesting mixes of ingredients and cooking styles. The basis – the raw ingredients for the different cuisines – is excellent with an especially good variety of seafood. One excellent Australian invention resulting from the once draconian licensing laws is the BYO (bring-your-own) restaurant which allows you to bring along your own wine or other alcoholic beverage and, for a small corkage fee, drink it in the restaurant with the meal.

Australians are known as beer drinkers although, in fact, Australian beer is over-rated being mostly of the bland lager type common in Europe and the USA. Australian wine is excellent, as most people know. It is keenly priced so you can sample excellent wines at reasonable prices.

Provisioning

Provisioning is easy almost everywhere although, in the smaller places, you will obviously not get the choice available in larger towns with supermarkets. Most of the charter companies can arrange a provisioning service and will provide a list of items before you get to the boat so that you can select what you want to have on board before arriving.

Costs

The overall cost of living is average, perhaps slightly below the European average. Eating out depends on where you are and can vary from around £10 a head to double that for a good restaurant. Remember that, with BYO restaurants, you substantially reduce the overall cost by avoiding the high mark-up most restaurants put on beverages. Eating out is mostly good value. Beer is around 60p a bottle and wine around £4–£6.

Local transport is average for coaches and internal flights. Taxis are moderate. Hire cars cost around £18–£20 a day.

Crime and personal safety

Australia is a safe country to travel in and the likelihood of violence or robbery away from the large cities is remote. Theft from boats is infrequent and few precautions are necessary, especially around the Whitsundays.

Sailing guides and charts

There are numerous guidebooks on cruising in Australian waters and on specific areas. The following may be useful.

Australian Cruising Guide Alan Lucas. Imray. A general guide to cruising around Australia

Cruising the Coral Coast Alan Lucas. Covers the area inside the Barrier Reef in detail

100 Magic Miles (including chart). Produced by Whitsundays charter operators, covers the area in detail. Video also available

Australian charts provide excellent coverage and there are also a series of charts with aerial photographs of harbours and anchorages which are widely available.

Essential information

Time zone
East coast UT +10

Language English and 'Strine'

Telecommunications Automatic dialling. Country code 61. Phone cards in many places. Fax service from agencies and charter operators.

Health Immunisation is only required if coming from an infectious area. Australia has strict quarantine laws and you are not allowed to bring in many foodstuffs or even transport them between states.

Whitehaven Beach in the Whitsundays.
Photo Pat Collinge

There are good medical services in even quite small places and efficient land and air ambulance services. It is essential to take out private medical insurance that includes repatriation in case of major illness. Although medical fees are not excessive, costs will mount up over time and a medical insurance policy is only sensible.

Money The unit of currency is the Australian dollar and rates of exchange have been reasonably stable over the last five years. There is little point in obtaining Australian currency before you enter the country.

Banks are open from 1000–1600 Monday to Friday. Money can often be exchanged in other places, such as travel agents or charter operators. All major credit cards and charge cards can be used in the larger towns and tourist resorts. ATM machines can be found in the cities and larger resorts and work with most credit cards.

Documentation All visitors to Australia require a valid visa which must be obtained before arrival. Visas are normally easily obtained within a short time.

There are no requirements for personal documentation on charter boats although a certificate of competence might prove useful. Other relevant paperwork for the charter yacht will be prepared by the charter company on your arrival and a full briefing on the yacht and area will be given.

Charter areas

Whitsundays
Situated on the east coast of Australia near the southern end of the Great Barrier Reef and just over 400 miles north of Sydney and 200 miles north of Brisbane. There are said to be 70 islands in the group although, realistically, there are only just over a dozen that can be usefully used along with the adjacent mainland coast. Many of the islands now have resorts on them although a number have been designated as nature reserves and are deserted. Consequently you can mix and match your cruising to take in anchorages where you must rely on your own resources along with resorts where there are good facilities and restaurants. The Whitsundays make up arguably the best cruising area in Australia with an archipelago of islands that you can sail around and a good number of anchorages of all types offering protection depending on the wind. Trips to the Great

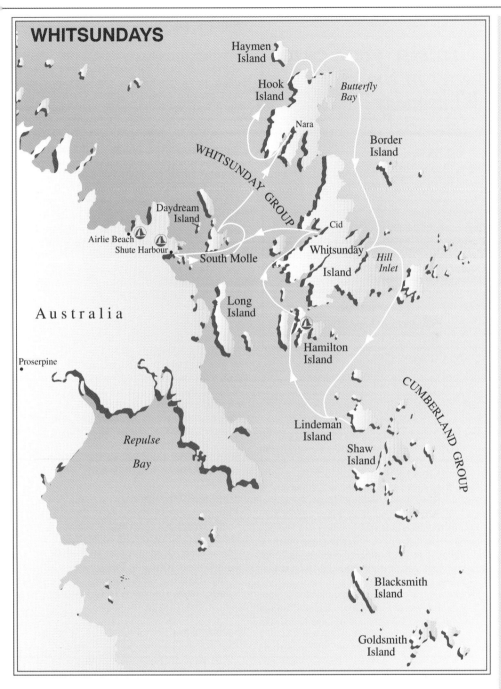

WHITSUNDAYS

Haymen Island
Hook Island
Butterfly Bay
Nara
Border Island
WHITSUNDAY GROUP
Daydream Island
Airlie Beach
Shute Harbour
South Molle
Cid
Whitsunday Island
Hill Inlet
Long Island
Australia
Hamilton Island
Proserpine
Lindeman Island
Shaw Island
CUMBERLAND GROUP
Repulse Bay
Blacksmith Island
Goldsmith Island

Barrier Reef can be organised by hired boat or seaplane. Like any ideal sailing and charter area, you will not be on your own.

Wind and sea

With the Great Barrier Reef protecting the area of sea sandwiched between the reef and

the mainland there are no really big seas rolling in. However, even across the sea area between the reef and the islands, the regular southeast trade wind can at times cause sufficient seas to make some anchorages untenable. The southeast trades are predominant although they blow at varying

strengths and may be interrupted by northerly winds. During the dry season (from March to October) the southeast trade winds are most regular at around 15–20 knots. Often, the southeast trades will blow for a week or more before dying down for a few days when northerlies may blow. March to May is the windiest time when the trades blow strongly and there is the possibility of gale-force winds at times. The occasional cyclone sometimes cuts through the area at this time.

Between November and April, the southeast trades are less prevalent and not as strong at around 10–15 knots and there will be northerly winds as well at around 10–15 knots. There are also days of calm weather. This is the traditional wet season although most rain falls at night. During this time there are more usable anchorages around the Whitsundays because of the alternating winds and the likelihood of more days of calm.

Suitable for . . .

The area is suitable for intermediate to experienced sailors although the charter companies cater for everyone here and can organise an itinerary for the less experienced and provide a guide/skipper for a few days until you feel comfortable. The dry season from March to October when the southeast trades are stronger and predominant is for more experienced sailors as the number of safe anchorages is reduced during this period and the sailing is somewhat harder.

Harbours and anchorages

There are few harbours as such and, for the most part, you will be on moorings or at anchor. A number of the resorts and the charter companies have jetties or moorings for visitors and you will be advised on these by the charter company. As indicated, anchoring options depend on the wind and, again, the charter companies are well versed in detailing safe anchorages depending on wind and sea. There are a number of all-weather anchorages around the islands as well. Contrary to popular opinion you will not be anchoring on coral around the Whitsundays with most of bottom being sand or mud and this is in many ways a blessing for the charterer as anchoring amongst coral is pretty much a 'no-no' to avoid damaging reefs. If you want to go diving on the reef a dive-boat or seaplane is the sensible and environmentally sound option.

Main charter bases

The main charter bases are at Shute Harbour on the mainland coast and at Airlie. However yachts can be delivered to Hamilton Island where there is an airport. It is about a 45-minute transfer from Prosperine Airport to Shute Harbour and around a 15-minute transfer from Hamilton Island Airport to the boat if delivered to the island.

Sailing area

The Whitsundays make up a cruising area in which you can easily sail between the islands in a short time and change your mind and head off somewhere else should the weather or your ideas on where to go change.

A typical seven-day cruise is as follows.

Shute Harbour–Shute Harbour
(Total 80–90 miles)
South Molle Island Moorings available off South Molle Resort. Good walking ashore. Restaurant.

Hook Island/Nara Inlet Fjord-like inlet. Sea eagles and waterfalls after rain.

Whitsunday Island/Hill Inlet Sail around Hook Island. Anchor at Butterfly Bay for lunch. Bring up in Hill Inlet for the night. Wonderful beach and oysters.

Hamilton Island Stop in the Lindemans for lunch. Restaurants and facilities ashore at Hamilton.

Sea-plane tour to the Barrier Reef Bottles can be arranged or snorkel and reef-walk.

Whitsunday Island/Cid Harbour

Shute Harbour

Land excursions

Most charterers should spend some time looking around the wonderful landscape that is Australia. The flora and fauna is spectacular and unique and the country as a whole shatters the senses with its immensity. To see the well-known sights, an organised excursion is easiest as this is a big, big country. If you are short on time, flying is the only way to get around. If you have more time don't omit less well-known sites which can be every bit as spectacular and generally more interesting than the well-known bits of Australia like Ayers Rock or Alice Springs. And don't omit to spend some time in Sydney which is a lively cosmopolitan place sited on a wonderful complex of harbours.

Other areas

Brisbane There is some limited bareboat and skippered charter out of Brisbane.

Sydney There is limited bareboat and skippered charter out of Sydney, principally from Pittwater Harbour, 15 miles north of Sydney. The area comprises Pittwater Harbour itself, Cowan Creek and the Hawkesbury River. There is ample opportunity to cruise around the three-headed area with many indentations and creeks although a one-week cruise or less is probably best. It does not, of course, offer the clear water and tropical conditions of the Whitsundays.

New Zealand

FOR
- Magnificent, dramatic scenery and wide open spaces afloat and ashore
- Settled summer season with semi-tropical temperatures
- Friendly and helpful people ashore
- Good fishing and good seafood ashore if you fail to catch your own

AGAINST
- Long flight to get there (28 hours flying time from the UK, 12 hours flying time from west coast USA)
- Unsettled conditions in the spring and autumn
- It rains more than the locals admit

Types of charter
- Sailing in company
- Bareboat
- Skippered

Despite the fact there are more yachts per head of population than anywhere else in the world, chartering in New Zealand is relatively new. Most of this has to do with the distances to these two islands tucked between Australia and Antarctica and the flying time involved to get there from the northern hemisphere. It doesn't really matter whether you go eastabout or westabout to get there from

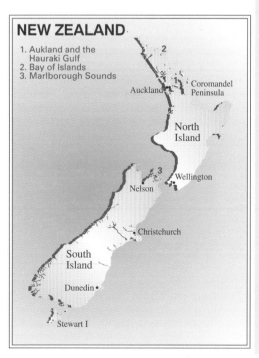

NEW ZEALAND

1. Aukland and the Hauraki Gulf
2. Bay of Islands
3. Marlborough Sounds

Coromandel Peninsula

Auckland

North Island

Wellington

Nelson

Christchurch

South Island

Dunedin

Stewart I

Britain as the flying time is approximately the same. But, with the increasing popularity of holidays in New Zealand over the last decade, yacht chartering has also increased in popularity and there are now a number of yacht charter companies in several locations. The main charter areas are in the North Island around Auckland and the Hauraki Gulf, the Bay of Islands further north, and in the South Island within the Marlborough Sounds. The climate in the north is semi-tropical with the season running through the southern hemisphere summer from November to April and, in the South Island, a slightly shorter season.

When to go

The season around Auckland and the Bay of Islands runs for the southern hemisphere summer between Mid-October and mid-April. The season in the Marlborough Sounds is tighter with the charter season operating from November to March.

Early season Mid-October to end November. Temperatures are around 16°–20°C with temperatures dropping in the evening to 10°–14°C.

High season December to end of February. Around Christmas is the most popular period. Temperatures are around 21–24°C in the day although, at times, they will get up to 30°. The southern sun is fierce and seems hotter than closer to the equator. Temperatures at night are around 15–17°C. Wind patterns are most predictable with sea breezes at around 10–15 knots prevailing.

Late season March to mid-April. Temperatures start to drop to spring levels of around 15–20°C and the wind can be bitingly cold at times. There is a chance of gales coming in off the Southern Ocean.

At Auckland

	Av max °C	Av min °C	Highest recorded	Relative humidity	Days 0·25mm rain	Sea temp °C
Oct	16	9	22	66%	17	16
Nov	19	12	27	64%	15	17
Dec	21	14	32	64%	12	19
Jan	23	16	32	62%	10	20
Feb	23	16	32	61%	10	21
Mar	22	15	30	65%	11	20
Apr	19	13	27	69%	14	17

Getting there

There are numerous scheduled flights to Auckland from most large international airports or onward flights from Sydney, Australia. There are internal connections to other parts of the country. For Auckland the international flight dumps you 45 minutes from the harbour. For the Bay of Islands you can fly to Kerikeri and get a shuttle bus to Paihia or hire a car and make a leisurely trip over a couple of days to Paihia or Russell. For the Marlborough Sounds you can fly to Nelson or Wellington and connect from there. Flight times from Europe to Auckland are around 26–28 hours and, from the USA, around 12–14 hours. It is best to have a short stopover somewhere en route to dilute the effects of jet-lag.

Eating and drinking

Eating out in New Zealand is good with wonderful raw ingredients and some influence from immigrant groups. By and large cuisine away from the cities and large resorts tends to the English model – meat or fish and three veg – although the superior ingredients make it more tasty than in England. In some places there are some excellent fish restaurants and some interesting kiwi variations on the standard cuisine. Like the Australians, New Zealanders are known as beer drinkers although the beer just isn't that great. New Zealand wine, particularly the white, is world class.

Provisioning

Provisioning is easy almost everywhere although, in the Bay of Islands and Marlborough Sounds, you will be away from it all for much of the time so it is essential to provision up when you can. Most of the charter companies can arrange a provisioning service and will provide a list of items before you get to the boat so that you can select what you want to have on board before arriving.

Costs

The overall cost of living is slightly below the European average and is generally good value for money. Eating out depends on where you go and varies from around £8 a head in simple establishments to £20 a head in a good restaurant. Wine is around £8 a bottle in a restaurant but BYOs mean you can buy a reasonable bottle for £4–£5 in a 'bottle-store' and take it along yourself. Beer is around £1 per half-litre. Provisioning is relatively cheap with local variations on hard and soft cheeses, good cured meats and other processed items. Fresh fruit and vegetables are amongst the best in the world and

Bay of Islands in northen New Zealand.
Photo Yachting World

inexpensive. Fresh meat (including the ubiquitous mutton) and fresh fish is available everywhere, as are oysters and mussels. Public transportation is mostly by bus or minibus and is reasonable. Taxis are moderate in cost. Hire cars start at around £16 a day. Mountain bikes can be hired in many places.

Crime and personal safety

New Zealand is a safe country to travel in and the likelihood of violence or robbery away from the large cities is remote. Theft from boats is infrequent and few precautions are necessary.

Sailing guides and charts

There are a number of locally produced guides.

Royal Akarana Yacht Club Coastal Cruising Handbook Produced by the Royal Akarana Yacht Club

Northland Coast: A Fishing and Cruising Guide William Owens. David Bateman

Hauraki Gulf: A Fishing and Cruising Guide William Owens. David Bateman

New Zealand Cruising Guide – Central Area Murray and Koh

The New Zealand Hydrographic Office produces good scale charts of all areas and these are widely available in New Zealand.

Essential information

Time zone UT +11

Language English and Kiwi

Telecommunications Automatic dialling. Country code 64. Phone cards in many places. Fax service from agencies and charter operators.

Health Immunisation is only required if coming from an infectious area. New Zealand has very strict quarantine laws and you are not allowed to bring in many foodstuffs or animal products, including some souvenirs made from animal skins etc.

There are good medical services throughout the country and efficient land and air ambulance services. Private medical insurance should be taken out in case of an accident involving an extended stay in hospital.

Money The unit of currency is the New Zealand dollar and rates of exchange have been reasonably stable over the last five years. There is little point in obtaining New Zealand currency before you enter the country.

Banks are open 1000–1600 Monday to Friday. Money can sometimes be exchanged at travel agents or charter operators. All major credit cards and charge cards can be used in the larger towns and tourist resorts. ATM machines can be found in the cities and larger resorts and work with most credit cards.

Documentation All visitors to New Zealand require a valid visa which must be obtained before arrival. Visas are normally easily obtained within a short time.

There are no requirements for personal documentation on charter boats although a certificate of competence might prove useful. At present, New Zealand is going through some radical changes regarding attitudes to pleasure boats so there may be some changes in the future. Other relevant paperwork for the charter yacht will be prepared by the charter company on your arrival and a full briefing on the yacht and area will be given.

Charter areas

Auckland and the Hauraki Gulf

The much-indented natural harbour around Auckland and numerous off-lying islands is the heart of sailing in New Zealand. There are numerous races and it is also the stopover point for the Whitbread Race. The Americas Cup challenge series will be held here at the turn of the millennium. There are several marinas and a whole host of anchorages around the coast and islands. At the hub is Auckland with a wide choice of restaurants and bars.

Wind and sea

The prevailing winds in the summer are land and sea breezes. The sea breeze fills in from the NNE–N by lunchtime and generally gets up to 10–15 knots. At night a southerly land breeze may blow, rarely getting above 10 knots. Nights are often calm. If you have to get somewhere, remember that mornings are often calm and you will be able to motor. In the spring and autumn, depressions coming off the sea can cause strong winds, and gales can be expected at the very edges of the season.

Seas are reasonable although tidal streams in the channels can raise vicious seas when there is a wind-against-tide situation.

Suitable for . . .

The area around Auckland is suitable for inexperienced to experienced sailors. There is sufficient sheltered water for inexperienced sailors to get about safely and a good choice of safe anchorages. The charter companies can provide a guide/skipper for a few days, if necessary, until you feel comfortable. On the whole, experienced skippers will prefer the expanse of the Bay of Islands.

Harbours and anchorages

There are only a few marinas around the Auckland area. After that there are anchorages everywhere with good all-weather spots available. Some anchorages have moorings, but mostly you will be anchoring. The bottom is mostly mud or sand.

Main charter bases

Westhaven Marina Right in the heart of Auckland. The main charter base for the Hauraki Gulf.

Gulf Harbour Marina At Whangaparoa about an hour's drive north of Auckland.

Sailing area

The cruising area around the Hauraki Gulf includes a mix of populated areas and steep-to coast covered in native bush.

A typical seven-day cruise itinerary is as follows.

Auckland, Westhaven Marina – back to Westhaven Marina

(150 (Great Barrier) or 100 NM)

- Leave Westhaven Marina for lunch at Islington Bay on Rangitoto. Overnight at Onetangi Bay on Waiheke Island. Restaurant and wonderful walks ashore on the island.
- *Coromandel Peninsula* Anchor overnight at Te Kouma harbour.
- *Great Barrier Island/Port Fitzroy* Good diving. Seafood restaurants with good crayfish, scallops, mussels, etc.
- *Great Barrier Island* Port Fitzroy or go to Tryphena or Whangaparapara.
- *Kawau Island* Overnight at Bon Accord Harbour. Visit Governor Grays Mansion House. Good walks through the bush.
- *Gulf Harbour Marina/Whangaparoa* Restaurants.
- *Westhaven Marina*

(For a shorter itinerary, the leg to Great Barrier Island can be omitted.)

Land excursions

There are numerous organised tours to sites like Rotorua to see bubbling mud pools and geysers, white-water rafting in North Island rivers, trekking, bungee-jumping (NZ is the home of this particular madness) or just tour around to see the sites. New Zealand probably has the greatest geographical diversity of any country I know. Alternatively, hire a car or camper-van and make your own way around.

Bay of Islands

The Bay of Islands is just what its name states: a large bay, really a gulf, with around 140 islands dotted about it. It is blessed with a sub-tropical climate and there is diving aplenty and wonderful walks through the native bush ashore. In 1978 the Bay of Islands was formally declared a maritime and historic reserve and this has ensured that development has not blighted it. There are a few restaurants scattered around but mostly you are on your own and must cater for yourself. This is an area for those who like to go sailing and get away from it all.

Wind and sea

In the summer proper the prevailing winds are land and sea breezes. The sea breeze will fill in mid-morning from the NNE–E and usually gets up to 10–15 knots by mid-afternoon. At night there may be a light S–SW land breeze but it rarely gets above 5–10 knots. There may sometimes be a sea fog when warm tropical air meets the cooler seas around the east coast. In spring and autumn things are less settled and, at the edges of the season, there are likely to be gales. Often the wind will suddenly turn from the NE to the SW and blow with some force.

Seas in the area are generally fairly flat and there are more sheltered anchorages than you can shake a stick at. In some of the more exposed areas there can be a big swell coming up from the south, but on the whole it is possible to get behind an island or islands and out of the swell. There may also be a swell that lasts through the night from the NE sea breeze, but there are so many well-sheltered anchorages that this shouldn't be a bother.

Suitable for . . .

Intermediate to experienced sailors. There are a lot of places to go to and it is relatively simple to tailor an itinerary that covers as much or as little ground as you want.

Harbours and anchorages

There are no marinas in the Bay of Islands. There are few harbours and, in most of these, you will have to anchor off or pick up a mooring anyway. Some care is needed entering river harbours where the bar at the entrance and depths over it change over time. There are anchorages everywhere. The bottom is generally sand or mud.

Main charter bases

Opua This can be reached by car, bus or internal flight from Auckland to Kerikeri and shuttle bus from there.

Sailing area

A myriad choice of bays and inlets. The area is tidal so some care is needed over tidal ranges (around 3m at springs) but depths are such that you will have no problem anchoring safely in most bays and creeks. Islands like Urupukpuka, Motorua, Robertson, and Motuatohia all have all-weather anchorages. More adventurous sailors can go north to Cavalli Island and Whangaroa Harbour.

Other areas

Marlborough Sounds Most charter yachts operate out of Picton which is the only marina in the area. The Marlborough Sounds are well sheltered but can be subject to severe gusts off the high land and to katabatic winds at night. The scenery and surroundings are outstanding with few comparable places in the world. Most of the steep hills are covered in native bush. There are a few restaurants scattered around the area but, on the whole, you must cater for yourself – the fishing incidentally is superb. They also produce some of the best Sauvignon Blanc in the world here. The season is slightly shorter than in the sub-tropical north with Christmas again the most popular time.

You can get an internal flight to Picton or Blenheim from major cities or there is a ferry from Wellington to Picton.

Thailand

FOR
- Spectacular islands and coast with sheer limestone pinnacles covered in tropical jungle
- Good, sheltered sailing area with lots of anchorages
- Tropical temperatures and warm waters for swimming
- Exotic and welcoming culture ashore
- Good food although too spicy for some

AGAINST
- Moderately long flights from Europe and USA
- Crowded with tripper boats around popular places like Ko Phi Phi
- Too humid for some
- Waters often murky with river silt making swimming uninviting in some areas

Types of charter
- Sailing in company
- Bareboat
- Skippered
- Luxury

A relatively new charter area with all charter centred around Phuket on the west coast. Although the west coast of Thailand is relatively short, the much-indented coastline and numerous islands combine to make up an extensive cruising area. While it is possible to cruise during either the northeast monsoon (November to April) or the southwest monsoon (May to October), the northeast monsoon period is the favoured time for sailing in Thailand and charter companies will probably close down for part of the southwest monsoon period. The attractions of sailing in Thailand are evident to anyone who has seen photographs of the area or read even a little about the country and its culture. The geography is spectacular, the people are gentle, the culture and cuisine exotic but accessible, and the sailing not at all bad.

When to go

There are two distinct seasons corresponding to the two monsoon periods, although some divide up the year into three periods with the cool dry season from November to February, the hot season from March to June and the rainy season from July to October. The favoured season is during the northeast monsoon between November and April and the less favoured is the southwest monsoon between May and October.

Northeast monsoon November to April. This is the dry season and consequently the least humid season. Average temperatures range from around 31–32°C in November and December to 34–38°C in April. Temperatures are only a few degrees less at night around Phuket. The average humidity at midday is around 50–58 per cent over the season. The northeast monsoon will have settled down by mid-November and lasts through until mid-April with a consistent pattern. The best months are reckoned to be December, January, and February.

Southwest monsoon May to October. This is the wet season and those unused to the tropics will find the humidity difficult to handle. Average temperatures range from 34–38°C in May to 31–32°C in October although temperatures will often reach 35–37°C. The average humidity is around 58–70 per cent over the season. Although the humidity figures appear not to be that much higher than those of the Mediterranean countries, or countries lying in the far northern or southern hemisphere, the actual effect is most uncomfortable during the height of the rainy season. The worst months are reckoned to be July, August and September.

At Phuket

	Av max [C	Av min [C	Highest recorded	Relative humidity	Days 0}1mm rain	Sea temp [C
Jan	31	24	34	57%	5	28
Feb	32	24	36	54%	3	28
Mar	33	25	36	56%	6	29
Apr	33	25	36	61%	12	29
May	31	25	36	68%	21	28
Jun	31	25	34	68%	19	28
Jul	31	25	34	68%	19	28
Aug	31	25	34	68%	20	28
Sep	30	24	34	70%	22	27
Oct	30	24	34	70%	23	28
Nov	30	24	34	67%	16	28
Dec	31	24	33	62%	9	28

Note Phuket actually has a double rainy period with most rain falling in May and again in October. On average it will rain for

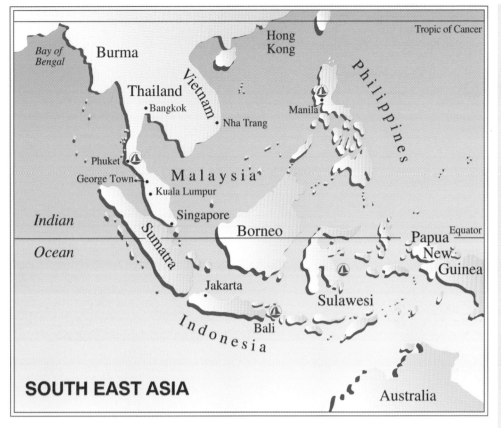

more than 20 days per month during these two months.

Getting there

There are numerous scheduled flights to Bangkok international airport from most major European and American airports and also from most major airports around the Pacific rim. Few charter flights operate as most of the major airlines flying scheduled flights can provide competitive prices for long-haul flights. There are also some international flights from Phuket to Europe including some charter flights. Direct flight times from Europe are around 12 hours, from the USA around 10–12 hours, and from Australia around 8 hours.

To get from Bangkok to Phuket there are regular daily internal flights which take around an hour for a direct flight. Getting there by air is really the best way as, by bus, it is a 12–14 hour trip.

Eating and drinking

Some love Thai food and others are not so keen. I'm a big fan of Thai food for it's variety and freshness though I usually ask for a tourist version without the hot peppers. In general it is spicy and often hot with a lot of garlic and small fiery peppers called *phrik khii nuu* ('mouse-shit' peppers!). Ask for hot soups and curries without hot peppers unless you like exceptionally hot dishes. In most places, even on street stalls, the food will be cooked freshly to order and you can often point out what you would like to go into it. Dishes often contain chicken, beef, pork or fish. Around Phuket there is an excellent choice of seafood and it should not be missed. Dishes are often flavoured with lemon grass, ginger, coriander, lime juice and coconut milk. There is a great deal of Chinese influence on much of the food to be found. Rice is the normal accompaniment although noodles are also popular.

Beer and rice whisky are the two most frequently found drinks. Most visitors tend to stick with the beer of which the most popular brand is *Singha*. Rice whisky is not expensive,

Phantasmagorical seascape in Phangna Bay.
Photo Yachting World

tastes marginally like white rum, and should be tried before you order a bottle.

Provisioning

Most provisions can be found in and around Phuket island and, where there is any concentration of charter yachts, the entrepreneurial Thais offer a provisioning service. It is worth going ashore in a settlement of any size to wander around the market and you can usually buy fish off passing Thai fishermen. Most yachts should take on basic provisions – bottled water, fruit and vegetables, juices, beer, a few staples and canned goods – for just three to five days, as you will probably eat out for the rest of the time.

Costs

The overall cost of living is low. To a large extent it depends on where you eat out. A meal at a street stall (and they can be excellent) can cost as little as £1·50 per head while a meal in an upmarket restaurant or hotel can be £10–£15 per head. In general meals in hotels tend towards a more western approach to food for which you pay over the odds. Small restaurants have excellent local dishes at very reasonable prices. Beer is

around £1·50–£2 a bottle. Whisky is around £3·50–£5 a bottle.

Local transport is very cheap in Thailand. It may be by *tuk-tuk*, the three-wheeler furies which charge around, by *songthaew*, small pick-up trucks with bench seats, or by normal taxi. Normal bicycle rickshaws are also found. Whatever method you choose, establish the price before you get in and haggle over the driver's initial price. Hire motorbikes are around £3–4 a day although this is a dangerous way to get around. Larger motorbikes (lethal) and hire jeeps and cars are also widely available.

Crime and personal safety

In general you will have few problems in Thailand as long as you stick to the Phuket area. Piracy off the Thai coast has been mentioned in the past, but this is mostly off the east coast and no recent incidents have been reported off the west. Some of the crew on Thai fishing boats in the area may look piratical, but they are a friendly lot who will help rather than hinder your cruise. Theft from boats is relatively infrequent, but take all precautions and lock the yacht securely when going ashore.

Ashore there have been some incidents of drugged cigarettes, drinks or sweets being offered to people who wake up sometime later minus their possessions but, on the whole, little of this goes on around Phuket. Nonetheless precautions are in order in some of the bars.

Sailing guides and charts

Several guides afford information on cruising in Thailand. The following may be useful.
Sail Thailand Thai Marine Leisure. Artasia Press. Covers the area around Phuket
Indian Ocean Cruising Guide Rod Heikell. Imray. Covers the area around Phuket
Admiralty charts cover the area around Phuket just adequately. Thai charts provide more detail but the text is in Thai.

Essential information

Time zone UT +7
Language Thai. Some English spoken in tourist areas
Telecommunications Automatic dialling in the larger centres. Country code 66. From smaller towns telephoning internally is straightforward, if slow at times. Making international calls is more difficult. Fax service from some agencies. Mobile phones with a GSM card work in many places.
Health There are no immunisation requirements but the following vaccinations should be obtained: cholera, typhoid, tetanus booster, hepatitis A (preferably *Havrix* or otherwise gammaglobulin).

The incidence of malaria in Thailand has increased in recent years with some resistant strains in the north. This does not affect Phuket where the incidence of malaria is low to non-existent. If advised to do so, take an appropriate malaria prophylactic.

Medical services range from adequate or good in cities and tourist resorts to poor in out-of-the-way places. It is essential to take out private medical insurance and, if the charter operator cannot arrange this, then most of the larger travel agents or other agencies can. Ensure that the insurance covers repatriation in the case of major illness.
Note AIDS and HIV-related illnesses have increased dramatically in Thailand in recent years and given Thailand's reputation for easily obtained sexual favours, all precautions should be taken and safe sex practised.
Money The unit of currency is the *baht* and rates of exchange have been stable over the last five years except for a recent dramatic drop in the value of the currency. There is no point in obtaining *baht* before you go as you will get as good a rate of exchange in Thailand as anywhere else.

Banks are open 0830–1530 Monday to Friday. Exchange offices and travel agents operate outside these hours. Traveller's cheques and cash can be exchanged in many places as well as banks. All major credit cards and charge cards can be used in the cities and larger tourist resorts.
Documentation All visitors to Thailand must have a valid visa. Visas are not difficult to get and may be issued at the airport on proof of an onward ticket. However it is best to obtain a visa in advance. A transit visa is good for 30 days, a tourist visa for 60 days, and a non-immigrant visa for 90 days.

At the moment the situation regarding documentation for charter boats is in flux and there are no official requirements for certification. In the future this may well change and you should ask the charter company for details on certification. It will arrange documentation for the yacht before you leave. You are unlikely to be asked for any paperwork in the area around Phuket.

Charter areas

Phuket

Situated on the west coast of Thailand, Phuket is used as a generic name to cover Phuket Island, Phang Nga Bay and the islands scattered around this area. It is a spectacular area with high limestone cliffs, steep-to islands and lush tropical forest. The area offers a mix of resorts and deserted unspoilt bays. Some of the islands and anchorages are simply spectacular, fantastic jutting pillars topped by dense jungle and undergrowth. Ashore, the resorts vary from chic exclusive hotels to more downmarket affairs and, anywhere there are a few tourists, a restaurant will be found nearby.

Wind and sea

The prevailing wind in the area depends on the monsoon season.

The wind blows from the northeast during the northeast monsoon and with the wind off the land this is the favoured time to sail in this area. It has a diurnal component and generally gets up around midday, blows at Force 4–6, and dies at night. With the wind off the land, seas are small and rarely get over

Lunch stop in Phang Nga Bay.
Photo Rod Heikell

a metre in height. There may be days of calm at the beginning and end of the season, but otherwise there is little disruption to the pattern.

The wind blows from the southwest during the southwest monsoon period and there can be squalls and thunderstorms at times. The southwest wind can blow consistently day and night and push a heavy sea onto the coast across the Indian Ocean. At other times the SW monsoon winds blow only fitfully over the area. Many of the anchorages along the coast are dangerous to use during the southwest monsoon. During July–August there is a small risk of a typhoon affecting the area.

Suitable for . . .

During the northeast monsoon, when wind patterns are settled and predictable, the area is suitable for intermediate and experienced sailors. A small flotilla operates from near Phuket and this is a good way to get to know the area. Within Phang Nga Bay there is ample cruising for a two-week period in well-sheltered waters. For bareboat charterers who want to go further afield there is the west coast of Phuket and the Similan and Surin Islands.

During the southwest monsoon cruising is much restricted and most yachts will content themselves with a cruise around those parts

of Phang Nga Bay that afford shelter from the southwest wind. This period is for more experienced sailors.

Harbours and anchorages

There are few harbours as such and, for the most part, you will be on moorings or at anchor. The area is mostly fairly shallow and approaches to anchorages require some care over navigation. A number of rivers empty into or near Phang Nga Bay and this makes the water a milky green and the bottom difficult to see. Out amongst the islands the water is clearer and you will more easily see the bottom and pick up dangers to navigation like shallows, rock and coral. The anchorages are mostly fairly shallow and you will have no problem with the holding which is predominantly mud or sand.

The anchorages are spectacular and vary from steep-sided cliffs to white sand beaches. They are not to be missed.

Main charter bases

The main charter bases are around Phuket, with yachts at the Boat Lagoon Marina near Phuket and at Yacht Haven in the north. Phuket is around one hour from Bangkok on a direct flight and it is about 15 minutes to Yacht Haven and 30 minutes to the Boat Lagoon from the airport.

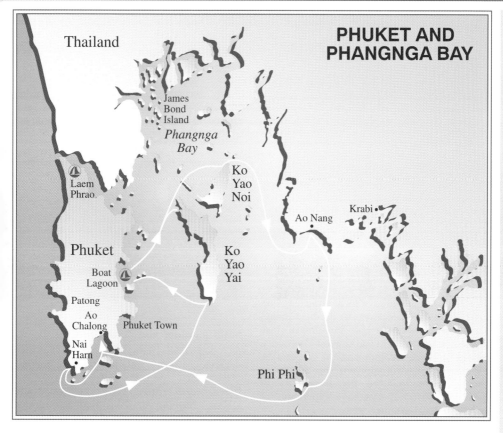

PHUKET AND PHANGNGA BAY

Sailing area

The sea area between Phuket on the west and the mainland on the east makes up the main cruising area. The coast is much indented and the bay is peppered with islands. Most yachts will do a circuit of the bay and islands and then can extend the cruise to the west coast of Phuket and the Similan and Surin Islands if more sea miles are wanted. One of the features of the area are the *hongs*, rock tunnels, caves and chimneys eroded from the cliffs. There are many which can be explored by dinghy from nearby anchorages.

A typical 10-day cruise (allowing time for transfers to and from Bangkok and some sightseeing) is as follows.

Boat Lagoon (Phuket) to Boat Lagoon
(Total 110 miles)
- *Koh Yao Noi* Anchor off the NW side of the island.
- *Ao Nang* Anchor off the beach. Restaurants.
- *Lay day* – Cruise around Krabi and the Koh Dam group of islands

- *Phi Phi Islands* Anchor for the night in Tonsai Bay. Restaurants.
- *Ao Chalong* A large bay on the bottom of Phuket. A long row ashore. Restaurants and nightlife.
- *Nai Harn Bay* Good for swimming. Phuket Yacht Club ashore offers upmarket restaurants and bars or there are less expensive restaurants.
- *Lay day*
- *Koh Yao Yai or Koh Rang.* Good beaches. *Boat Lagoon*

Land excursions

Most charterers flying in through Bangkok will want to spend a couple of days here on the way to or from Phuket. There is much to see and do here, much more than you can cram into a couple of days and that's not counting just wandering around the markets and shops or going upriver in a longtail boat. If you have more time, there are many other excursions with the trip to the northern highlands at Chiang Mai being one of the most popular.

Indian Ocean

Red Sea – Egypt

Yacht charter in Egypt is exclusively in the Red Sea and is as much to do with diving as sailing. Marine life over the coral reefs along the Egyptian Red Sea coast is world renowned with some authorities baldly stating that there is nothing like it anywhere else. Whatever the arguments, there is no doubt that it has some of the top diving sites in the world.

Charter yachts operate mostly from Hurgadha and, to a lesser extent, from Safaga. Nearly all charter is skippered and, given the difficult nature of these coral-strewn waters, this is the best way to go. It also gives you a source of local knowledge on board who can direct you to the best diving sites, the most comfortable anchorages close to the diving sites, and can suggest alternative sites should the weather prevent you getting to a chosen place or prevent you anchoring there. There may be the possibility of bareboat charter if you have experience of sailing in coral in other areas.

Sailing in this area can be rewarding, but can also be a battle against the strong prevailing northerlies. Navigating amongst the coral is complicated because of the extent and irregular nature of the reefs which are quite different in the Red Sea to the more common outlying reefs around islands and typical atoll patterns found in the Caribbean, Indian Ocean and Pacific. In addition the islands and coast are low-lying in many places and, because visibility is often bad when the wind whips sand off the desert to create hazy conditions, navigation between reefs and islands is difficult to say the least.

The season in the northern Red Sea is virtually all year round, with high season in the northern European winter when temperatures in this area are more moderate. It can even be cold at night.

All of the yacht charter companies here can arrange diving courses, advanced instruction, and of course take you to the reefs to go diving. In the end this is the only real reason to come here as the sailing, while challenging, is not really good enough on its own. The diving, though, is superlative.

For further information, consult sailing and diving magazines, the Moorings, or a charter broker.

At Eilat (Northern Red Sea)

	Av max °C	Av min °C	Highest recorded	Relative humidity	Days 0·1mm rain	Sea temp °C
Jan	21	10	27	39%	1	20
Feb	23	11	31	40%	1	21
Mar	26	14	34	38%	2	22
Apr	31	18	41	30%	1	23
May	36	17	44	28%	0.1	24
Jun	38	24	44	20%	0	25
Jul	39	26	47	13%	0	26
Aug	40	26	46	24%	0	27
Sep	37	25	43	27%	0	26
Oct	33	21	39	34%	0	25
Nov	28	16	37	38%	1	24
Dec	23	12	31	42%	1	21

Sailing guides and charts

Red Sea Pilot Elaine Morgan & Stephen Davies. Imray. Detailed pilotage for the Red Sea

Wonders of the Red Sea David Fridman and Tony Malmqvist. ISIS. Red Sea marine life. Published and available in Egypt

A number of locally produced books on dive sites and marine life are available in the larger tourist areas.

Seychelles

Until recently there was only really skippered charter around the Seychelles. Now, with the introduction of a bareboat fleet, it is possible to sail yourself around the islands. All charter is out of the capital and principal port Victoria on the main island of Mahe. There are numerous scheduled flights into the capital from most parts of the world and tourist facilities on the island are already extensively developed so there is no problem getting around and finding somewhere to eat out.

The Seychelles are made up of over 100 islands ranging from the larger granite-based islands to typical coral atolls. There are basically two seasons: the hot season from December to May and the cool season from June to November. The Seychelles are within the Intertropical Convergence Zone (ITCZ) which means that the full effect of monsoon winds and trade winds do not affect them, although they do influence the wind strength

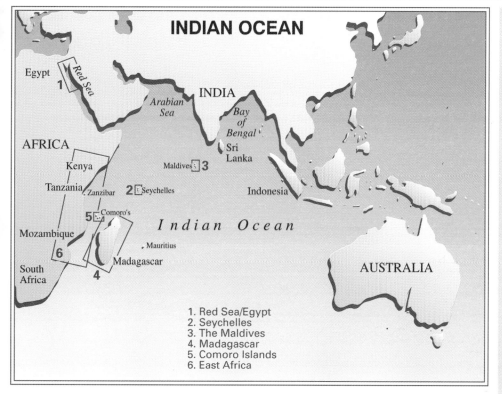

INDIAN OCEAN

1. Red Sea/Egypt
2. Seychelles
3. The Maldives
4. Madagascar
5. Comoro Islands
6. East Africa

and direction around the islands. The hot season coincides with the NW monsoon or Cross Monsoon and the cool season with the SE trades. The prevailing direction of the wind in the hot and cool seasons effectively determines which anchorages can be used and which reef entrances are safe.

Bareboat charterers will sail around the group of islands to the north of Mahé, including Praslin and La Digue. Longer trips to the coral atolls around the Amirantes and Aldabra groups will be by skippered charter and usually only on the larger and faster superyachts because of the distances involved. Apart from Port Victoria, there are only a few piers at the large hotels to tie up to and, for the most part, you will be anchoring off on white coral sand.

The attractions of the Seychelles are many. In the equatorial region, air and sea temperatures vary only a little through the year as can be seen from the accompanying chart. Winds here are normally a pleasant 10–20 knots and gales are rare. The beaches are superb white sandy swathes, the vegetation is that fecund tropical abundance edged by palms, the birdlife is unique in places, the diving is superb, the food is wonderful and the Seychellois warm and friendly. The only drawback is that it can be expensive for services and eating out but, on a boat, you can mix and match eating on board and eating out to even things up.

For further information try sailing magazines, Sunsail, or a charter broker.

At Port Victoria

	Av max °C	Av min °C	Highest recorded °C	Relative humidity	Days 0·1mm rain	Sea temp °C
Jan	28	24	31	78%	15	28
Feb	29	25	32	76%	10	28
Mar	29	25	32	74%	11	27
Apr	30	25	33	74%	10	27
May	29	25	33	74%	9	27
Jun	28	25	32	75%	9	26
Jul	27	24	30	76%	8	26
Aug	27	24	31	75%	7	26
Sep	28	24	31	75%	8	26
Oct	28	24	31	75%	9	26
Nov	29	24	32	74%	12	27
Dec	28	24	33	78%	15	27

Sailing guide

Indian Ocean Handbook Rod Heikell. Imray. Has a small section on the Seychelles

Mahe in the Seychelles. *Photo* Pat Collinge

Maldives

Like the Egyptian Red Sea coast, the Maldives are a sail-dive destination rather than a straight yacht charter destination. All charter here is skippered and the yacht is used as a base to get between diving sites. This gives divers a big advantage over hotel-dive holidays as you can get around a number of sites taking everything you need with you.

The Maldives are a string of atolls stretching for over 450 miles north to south. They are all atolls and, indeed, the word atoll comes from the Maldivian language. There are international flights to the capital Male and most charter is based here and operates around the atolls to the north and south of the main island.

The diving here is superb and this is what people come here for. The locals are friendly, the atolls attractive in a low-lying atoll sort of way (the islands are rarely more than 2·5 metres high), and the food adequate to good. The climate varies between the cool season from November to April and the hot season from June to October, but it rains here quite a lot of the time with May–June and November being the wettest months. The monsoon season roughly corresponds with the cool season during the NE monsoon and the hot season during the SW monsoon. During the SW monsoon it can get very rough getting between the atolls so if you are prone to seasickness pick the NE monsoon period.

For further information try sailing and dive magazines or a charter broker.

INDIAN OCEAN

Sailing guide

Indian Ocean Handbook Rod Heikell. Imray.
    Has a small section on the Maldives

Madagascar, Comoro Islands and East Africa

A number of skippered and crewed charter yachts shuttle around this part of the world, taking in Kenya, Zanzibar, the Comoros and Madagascar. Usually you join the yacht for part of the trip depending on the season. The Seychelles are also often included in this charter patch.

Facilities in this part of the world are not everywhere well developed for tourism with the exception of Kenya. Consequently you really need a large and well-found yacht that can carry most things it needs and has an experienced skipper. Large catamarans are frequently used, partly because of their ability to get in close to the shore in coral-fringed anchorages and also to make use of some reef entrances which could be tricky for deep-draught yachts.

Details on charter in this area can be obtained from a number of the more prestigious charter companies which are agents for large skippered yachts.

For further information try the sailing magazines or a charter broker.

Sailing guide

East Africa Pilot Delwyn McPhunn. Imray.

Some unusual and far-flung charter destinations

The following brief collection of unusual destinations are scattered around the far-flung corners of the globe. There are probably a lot more and it surprises me still to find yacht charter operating in some places where I have voyaged or stopped over while on overland treks. Recently I came across a sail-dive charter yacht in Massawa in Eretria on a voyage down the Red Sea. And, on a visit to Vietnam, I came across a skippered charter junk operating out of Nha Trang on a sail-dive basis and, during the NE monsoon, around the Mekong River. Many of these charter operations are fragile affairs run by cruising yachtsmen who have taken a liking to some exotic location and who set up for a year or two before moving on. Others are well-established operations that have been in place for years.

To track down some of these far-flung charter operations takes time and effort. Often there are no packages and there isn't always a good contact office for booking the charter. For those interested I suggest one of two options. Take some time, a fair amount of time usually, and telephone and write to whatever contact numbers you can get for the area. The Internet is also useful for looking for this sort of thing and you get not only a contact number but also some idea of what is on offer in a particular place. Some areas – like Alaska and Canada – appeal more to the nearby American market and so feature in American sailing magazines. Others like New Caledonia and Tierra del Fuego appeal (for some reason) to the French market and will be found advertised in French sailing magazines. Eventually you will track down something tangible and finally you will be able to establish what is going on and who to book with. There are a number of small agencies and brokers with their finger on the pulse of this sort of far-flung charter and, if they cannot help directly, they may be able to suggest someone who can. The second option for the adventurous traveller is just to get on a plane and go and see what is there. This is not a secure option, it may get no result whatsoever, but you will have a grand adventure looking for that elusive charter destination and you may find some exciting options that are little known outside the country you are in. You will of course need a bit of time.

Great Lakes USA and Canada

(See USA East Coast for information on the USA)
The Great Lakes, straddling the USA and Canada, are home to a sizeable resident population of yachts cruising these waters and also support a good number of charter operations. These vast inland bodies of water are huge and the potential cruising area covers hundreds of miles of coast, not to mention the islands dotted around them. Both Lake Superior and Lake Michigan are close to 300 miles long. There are towns and cities dotted around the Great Lakes but what everyone comes here for is the chance to get away from it all. There are huge swathes of wilderness and the scenery is majestic. Autumn is especially spectacular. There is wildlife aplenty and the fishing is good. The water in many places is crystal clear if not necessarily inviting temperature-wise.

The season in the Great Lakes is compressed into a few summer months. It is possible to cruise here, as the locals do, in spring and autumn, but temperatures either side of July and August are on the cool side and, at night, can drop suddenly to below freezing. Temperatures of -6°C have been recorded in May and -2°C in September in Duluth, although this is unusual.

Most charter in this area is based near well-known cruising areas such as the Apostle Islands or Thunder Bay in Lake Superior or out of the larger cities or their commuter ports – Port Clinton in Lake Erie or Toronto in Lake Ontario. Getting to the charter base is easy enough, either through internal flights and a transfer, by rail or coach, or by hire car. Most of these charter operations are small

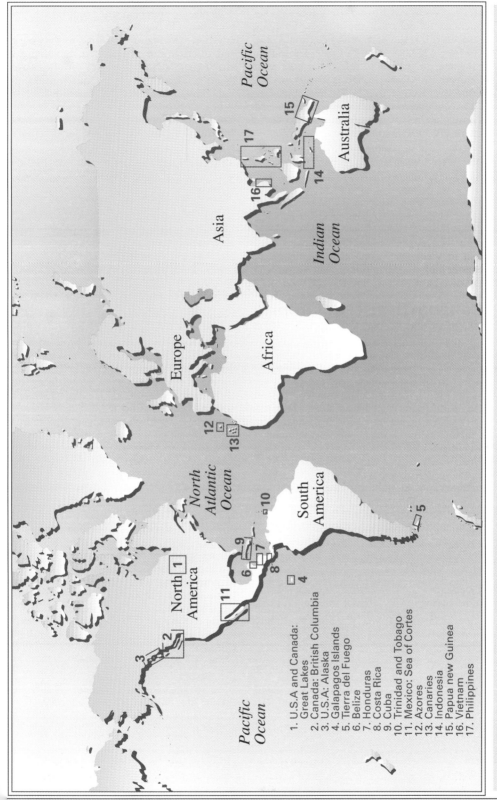

1. U.S.A and Canada:
   Great Lakes
2. Canada: British Columbia
3. U.S.A.: Alaska
4. Galapagos Islands
5. Tierra del Fuego
6. Belize
7. Honduras
8. Costa Rica
9. Cuba
10. Trinidad and Tobago
11. Mexico: Sea of Cortes
12. Azores
13. Canaries
14. Indonesia
15. Papua new Guinea
16. Vietnam
17. Philippines

affairs, often with two or three yachts operated on behalf of the owners. In many respects this is the best way to go because the operator will have a fund of local knowledge on where to go hiking, fishing, or collecting blueberries. Most charter is bareboat, but some skippered charter is also available.

Anyone interested in the Great Lakes will find the addresses and telephone numbers of operators in Compuserve's *Sailing Forum*. Alternatively try American sailing magazines or a charter broker.

At Duluth (USA)

	Av max °C	Av min °C	Highest recorded	Relative humidity	Days 0·25mm rain
May	13	3	35	60%	12
Jun	19	9	36	66%	13
Jul	23	12	41	65%	12
Aug	22	12	36	65%	11
Sep	17	8	34	69%	11

Canada: British Columbia

British Columbia has a large number of resident yachts, mostly based around Vancouver and Vancouver Island, and yacht facilities are consequently well developed. The mainland coast is enclosed by Vancouver Island and, further up, Queen Charlotte Island. Sprinkled along the coast are a whole cluster of islands and islets. Most charter is between Vancouver and Vancouver Island amongst the Gulf Islands and also the Anacortes a short distance down the coast in the USA (see USA West Coast). The large outer islands protect the waters from the Pacific swell and there is wonderful sailing to be had here. The marine life is prolific and there are seabirds everywhere. There are sheltered anchorages everywhere and sufficient marinas and yacht harbours for provisioning and eating ashore in the area.

The season is pretty much compressed into the short summer from June to August. In the spring and autumn it can be distinctly chilly at night and there is a good possibility of depressions coming in across the Pacific. Fog is also a factor to be reckoned with. There are also lots of mosquitoes and midges.

Most yacht charter companies are based around Vancouver itself or on the southern end of Vancouver Island. Most are fairly small affairs with a few boats, although there are some larger companies with a good choice of sail and power boats.

There are bareboat and skippered yachts available. Getting there is fairly easy with international flights arriving in Vancouver and internal and some international flights arriving at Victoria Airport on Vancouver Island. There are good ferry links to Vancouver Island from the Anacortes.

For contacts and information try the Canadian Tourist Office, the Internet, American sailing magazines, or a charter broker.

At Vancouver

	Av max °C	Av min °C	Highest recorded	Relative humidity	Days 0·25mm rain	Sea temp °C
May	18	8	28	63%	12	11
Jun	21	11	33	65%	11	13
Jul	23	12	33	62%	7	14
Aug	23	12	33	62%	8	14
Sep	18	9	29	72%	9	13

USA: Alaska

Yacht charter in Alaska revolves almost exclusively around exploring this huge wilderness. The peaks are capped in snow throughout the summer and glaciers calve into the sea all over the place. The glacial retreat in evidence in most places is a result of the retreat of the Little Ice Age which only occurred here around 1750. The scenery is like little you will see elsewhere. The marine life is close to a cocktail of every cold-water species going. Many people go on charter in these waters to watch whales of which you are likely to see orca (killer whales), humpbacks and minke. Ashore you will see moose, deer and bears. Birdlife includes eagles and gulls. It is a spectacular place and one which impresses everyone who goes there.

The season is obviously short because of the temperatures. Either side of May and September the temperatures slump to way below freezing at night. Even in May and September temperatures can fall to below freezing at night. This means being prepared for cold weather and biting winds even in the summer.

Charter here is all skippered and usually the skipper (and hostess) are well versed in where to look for the abundant wildlife and marine life. For contacts and information try American sailing magazines, the Internet, or a charter broker.

At Anchorage

	Av max °C	Av min °C	Highest recorded	Relative humidity	Days 0·25mm rain
May	12	2	22	49%	5
Jun	17	7	33	57%	6
Jul	18	9	27	63%	10
Aug	18	8	28	65%	15
Sep	14	4	23	66%	14

Galapagos

Most trips around the Galapagos are nature-trail trips looking at the animals that gave Darwin the tip-off for his theory of natural selection and the time-bomb of evolution that was to so drastically change our way of looking at things. Charterers fly in from Quito in Ecuador (to which the Galapagos belong) and are then ushered on to yachts for the trip around the islands. Trips are from two to ten days depending on how long you want to spend surveying the islands and their inhabitants. Everything is catered for on the yachts (which are all fairly large) and either the skipper or crew will be on hand to show you around.

For information try general travel and geographical magazines, the Internet, or a charter broker.

Tierra del Fuego/Antarctica

There were at least six charter boats operating in this area at the last count. These range from the sort of charter where you are pretty much a guest to the other end of the spectrum where you share duties and crew the yacht. Obviously in this climatically hostile bit of the world the seasons very much determine where and when you can go and, even during the southern summer, bad weather can hold up a charter. Itineraries are more like suggestions of what could happen if the weather permits. Going on charter in this area is very much an adventure into a region which few see. Getting about by yacht is really the only way to do it and the reward is scenery and sights that will astound. There are glaciers, peaks to climb, and marine life (including whales and seals, seabirds and furry things like beaver ashore).

Trips to Antarctica by yacht are not as unusual as you might think with around 25 yachts visiting in 1996. While not hazardous it *is* arduous, not least because of the temperatures and winds in the area.

Yacht charter in the area between the bottom of South America and Antarctica revolves around not only getting there, but trips ashore to climb mountains and glaciers, trekking around the coast, visiting the Horn itself, ice diving (if you are so inclined), and watching the marine life and the flora and fauna ashore.

Most of the charter yachts seem to be either French or American. Charter yachts operate out of Punta Arenas, Ushuaia, Puerto Williams and the Falklands depending on the time of year and intended destinations. There are international links to Santiago and connections to Punta Arenas, Puerto Williams and Ushuaia, and international links to the Falklands. For information try general geographical magazines, the Internet, or a charter broker.

At Punta Arenas

	Av max °C	Av min °C	Highest recorded	Relative humidity	Days 1mm rain
Oct	11	3	19	65%	5
Nov	12	4	24	65%	5
Dec	14	6	24	67%	8
Jan	14	7	30	68%	6
Feb	14	7	26	64%	5
Mar	12	5	24	69%	7

Central America

Along the eastern seaboard of central America there is some yacht charter, mostly concentrating on sail-dive charter or a combination of sailing and exploring the rainforest ashore. Only Belize has bareboat charter where you can go off on your own and explore the cays and reefs.

Belize Belize was formerly British Honduras and so, for English-speaking charterers, has the advantage that most people speak English. It has been described as the bit of the Caribbean that got removed to the coast of South America. The offshore barrier reef is second in size only to the Great Barrier Reef in Australia. The waters are unpolluted and teeming with marine life and, ashore, there is abundant rainforest and the creatures that live in it. The area is politically stable but there are few facilities and, for the most part, you must look after yourself.

Bareboat and skippered charter are available from Moho Cay near Belize City. There are flights from some major American Airports in the south to Belize City and Moho Cay is a short boat ride away. The season is primarily in the northern winter as hurricanes do hit Belize from time to time.

At Belize City

	Av max [C	Av min [C	Highest recorded	Relative humidity	Days 1mm rain
Nov	28	20	35	91%	12
Dec	27	20	33	90%	14
Jan	27	19	32	89%	12
Feb	28	21	34	87%	6
Mar	29	22	35	87%	4
Apr	30	23	36	87%	5
May	31	24	36	87%	7

Honduras In the Bay Islands off the northern coast of Honduras there is some bareboat and skippered charter. The latter is mostly to do with sail-dive charter. The islands themselves are just what you would expect of a tropical island: palm-fringed with white sandy beaches, but it is the diving over the coral reefs that people come for. There are flights from the southern USA into San Pedro and then internal flights to the coast or road transport.

Costa Rica Yacht charter off the Costa Rican coast is exclusively skippered charter. Often the holiday combines trips into the rainforest with some time afloat. Costa Rica

has made moves towards establishing eco-tourism around its coast and, consequently, there are strict regulations governing yacht charter in its waters.

There are flights to Limon on the east coast from where a charter can be picked up or a connection made to the yacht.

Cuba

Once the playground of Americans, it is likely that, in future, Cuba will open up to tourism in a big way. At present Fidel Castro is promoting tourism to attract foreign currency to help out the island's ailing economy. Take American dollars in cash when you go. It should be remembered that Cuba is the largest island in the Caribbean and the indented coast and offshore islands offer a huge cruising area.

At present there are a number of charter companies offering bareboat and skippered charter in a limited area. On the south coast there are charters out of the marina at Cayo Largo and, on the north coast, there are charters from around the resort areas east of Havana. There are few marinas or yacht

Cruising in Cuba *Photo* Nigel Calder

harbours and provisioning and getting fuel and water is done largely via hotels. There are restaurants at the resort areas and others around the coast and larger islands, but there will certainly be more in the future.

What Cuba offers is a huge Caribbean island with all that implies: semi-tropical temperatures and warm waters, reefs and cays, marine life aplenty and good fishing, trade winds, an interesting cuisine and Cuban rum, all with virtually no yachts around at all – for the present anyway. In the future it will undoubtedly become a popular area.

You can fly direct to Havana from Europe although not at present from the USA. Transport within Cuba is by internal flights or by road. For information on yacht charters consult the sailing magazines, the Internet or a charter agent.

Sailing guides

Cuba: A Cruising Guide Nigel Calder. Imray

At Havana

	Av max °C	Av min °C	Highest recorded	Relative humidity	Days 1mm rain	Sea temp °C
Jan	26	18	32	64%	6	23
Feb	26	18	33	61%	4	23
Mar	27	19	33	58%	4	23
Apr	29	21	34	58%	4	24
May	30	22	34	62%	7	25
Jun	31	23	36	65%	10	27
Jul	32	24	34	62%	9	28
Aug	32	24	35	64%	10	28
Sep	31	24	34	66%	11	27
Oct	29	23	34	68%	11	27
Nov	27	21	33	65%	7	26
Dec	26	19	32	64%	6	24

Trinidad and Tobago

Trinidad and Venezuela almost touch each other in the SE corner of the Caribbean. Much yacht charter is on cruising boats which have set up in the area for a few years to earn some pennies, although the area is likely to develop.

The area is tropical and, as such, has large coral reef areas for exploration; although around much of Trinidad the muddy effluent from the Orinoco River restricts visibility and reef development. However on the islands of Tobago and Bonaire there are wonderful dive sites with that around Bonaire regarded as among the best in the world. Ashore, things are tropical with a diverse flora and fauna. There is also the wonderful mix of cultures in Trinidad where African, Indian, European and whoever else dropped by are mingled to produce a cocktail of beauty. This intermingling of cultures, expressed in the Trinidad Carnival in January, is acknowledged by anyone who has been there as the best carnival anywhere.

There are international flights into Port of Spain. For information on yacht charters consult American yachting magazines, the Internet or a yacht charter agent.

Note Venezuela has had some yacht charter but interference from the authorities has all but eliminated it except on an 'unofficial' basis.

(For temperature chart see Windward Islands)

Sailing guides

Cruising Guide to Trinidad and Tobago, Venezuela and Bonaire Chris Doyle. Cruising Guide Publications, distributed by Imray

Cruising Guide to Trinidad and Tobago N C Hoover and G B Gliksman. Cruising Guide Publications

Martinique to Trinidad D M Street Jr distributed by Imray

Mexico

On the west coast of Mexico, just under the border with the USA, lies the huge Golfo de California which most know by the more evocative name of the Sea of Cortez. It is a huge cruising area with more than enough anchorages to satisfy those who want to put in some miles. The landscape is dramatic and there is much sea life and good fishing. For a flavour of the place, read John Steinbeck's *The Sea of Cortez*. Ashore there is Mexico and Mexican food!

The main cruising area is on the western side of the Sea of Cortez. Here there are a number of offshore islands and mainland anchorages as well. The attraction of the area is the rugged rocky mountains and clear waters and just being in Mexico. There is bareboat and skippered charter. There are flights into La Paz or it is possible to fly into Los Angeles or San Diego and get connecting flights down to the Baja. For further information try American sailing magazines, the Moorings or a charter agent.

(For climate, see the chart for San Diego in USA West Coast)

Puerto Ballangra in the Sea of Cortez.
Photo Yachting World

Sailing guides and charts

Cruising Guide to the Sea of Cortez edited by
Nancy and Simon Scott (research: Kees
Fransbergen). Cruising Guide
Publications
Charlie's Charts West Coast of Mexico
distributed by Imray

Atlantic Islands

There is some charter around the Azores and
the Canaries although the operations are
relatively small affairs. Part of the reason for
this is that there are no really sheltered waters
for yacht charter around the islands and
much of the time you will be taking on a large
Atlantic swell and also battling against the
windward (little wind as it lifts over the high
land mass) and leeward (gusts off the high
land) effects of the islands.

Azores There is a limited bareboat and
skippered operation out of Ponta Delgada.
Flights from Lisbon to Ponta Delgada. For
further information try a charter agent.

Sailing guides

Atlantic Islands Anne Hammick. RCC
Pilotage Foundation/Imray
Azores Cruising Guide World Cruising

Canaries There is some bareboat and
skippered charter from various bases around
the islands. A number of 'learning to sail'
courses are also offered. The temperate
climate all year round makes this a popular
tourist destination and there are now a
number of marinas scattered around the
islands which makes cruising easier. There
can be a substantial swell in places and gusts
off the lee side of the islands and in the
channels. There are flights from all over
Europe to the Canaries. For further
information try sailing magazines or a charter
agent.

Sailing guides

Atlantic Islands Anne Hammick - RCC
Pilotage Foundation. Imray

Africa

There is some yacht charter around the
African coast although much of it is on an ad
hoc basis. Charter options currently around
at the time of writing are catamaran-safaris
on Lake Kenya and day charter out of
Capetown. For further information try the
sailing magazines or a charter broker.

Southeast Asia

Apart from Thailand, where charter is well
developed, there are a number of small
operations in other Southeast Asian
countries. Some of these are on converted
traditional craft like the *pinisi* or *bugis* in
Indonesia or the junks of Vietnam. Some of
the charter is just about getting away from it
all and cruising through seascapes that are
like nothing else in the world, while others
concentrate on sail-dive. For information on
charter in the area try a charter broker or one
of the following Southeast Asian boating
magazines.

Asian Boating Sai Kung PO Box 116, Hong
Kong
Asian Marine No 18 Upper Cross St,
Singapore 058332
Action Asia (travel magazine distributed
worldwide) 8/F Al Aqmar House, 30
Hollywood Rd, Hong Kong

Malaysia A charter area on the west coast of Malaysia centred around Langkawi Island just under the Thai border. There are said to be over 100 islands in the Langkawi group, but only if you count some very small islets. The cruising area actually extends south to Penang and further south to Port Klang near Kuala Lumpur, if you want to put some sea miles in. While it is possible to cruise during the southwest monsoon period (May to October), the northeast monsoon (November to April) is the favoured time for sailing in Malaysia and you will find charter companies will probably close down for part of the southwest monsoon period. The attractions of sailing in this area are many, with spectacular islands, friendly people and excellent cuisine .

Langkawi is the principal charter area. It is a spectacular area with high cliffs, steep-to islands and lush tropical forest. Penang is the peninsula formerly known as Georgetown to the south of the Langkawi group. Apart from Penang there are few large centres of population and most of the other settlements can fairly be described as villages. Kuah on Langkawi island is the closest you get to a town after Penang. The islands and anchorages are spectacular with jutting pillars of rock, fjord-like inlets dripping with vegetation, and deserted white sandy beaches. Ashore, things vary between chic exclusive hotels with hot and cold running everything to simple fishing villages.

Almost all charter here is skippered or luxury on a piecemeal basis with no large companies operating. At one time there was a bareboat operation here but bareboat charter seems to have all but disappeared.

Indonesia There are a number of small charter operations here. The converted *bugis* schooner *Duta Bahari* cruises the coast around Nusa Tenggara, the Moluccas and Sulawesi. There are other operations out of Bali and from near Jakarta. A few luxury yachts will sometimes do charters around the area depending on demand and there are sometimes smaller skippered charter yachts.

At Amboina (Moluccas)

	Av max °C	Av min °C	Highest recorded	Relative humidity	Days 0·1mm rain
Oct	29	23	33	68%	13
Nov	31	24	34	66%	11
Dec	31	24	36	64%	13
Jan	31	24	36	66%	13
Feb	31	24	36	64%	13
Mar	31	24	35	67%	15

Papua New Guinea There is at least one large motor catamaran and a number of owner-operated charter boats. Sail-dive is popular and mostly operates off the east coast where the diving is said to be world class.

Vietnam The recently built junk *Song Sai Gon* operates sail-dive charters around Nha Trang and, during the NE monsoon, around the Mekong delta. It is fully crewed with a dive instructor and offers a fair degree of comfort and, of course, the chance to sail on a junk-rigged boat.

Philippines There are a number of sail-dive charters operating out of Manila and Bacuit Bay and at least one skippered sailing yacht available for charter in Marina del Nido in Bacuit Bay. The scenery and diving over remote reefs are outstanding.

III. Charter companies in Britain & Ireland

UNITED KINGDOM

1st Choice Yacht Charters
4 Aldworth Road
Compton
Berkshire RG20 6RD
☎ 01635 578383
Fax 01635 578903

Acamar Marine
Capella House
57 Salisbury Road
Burton
Christchurch
Dorset BH23 7JJ
☎ 01202 488030
Fax 01202 475051

Activity Holidays
198 South Road
Hanworth
Middlesex TW13 6UH
☎ 0181 898 2830
Fax 0181 894 5425

Adventure Sailing
Beachley House
Bowerchalke
Salisbury
Wiltshire SP5 5AY
☎ 01722 780141

Alan Gauci Sailing Holidays
and Tuition
198 South Road
Hanworth
Middlesex TW13 6UH
☎ 0181 898 2830
Fax 0181 894 5425
E-mail info@atlantis-
sailing.demon.co.uk

Alan Morgan Yachting
2 The Corner House
Firle Road
Seaford
E Sussex BN25 2HN

☎ 01323 893983
Fax 01323 895250

Alba Sailing
Alba Yacht Services Ltd
Dunstaffnage Yacht Haven
Oban
Argyll PA37 1PX
☎ 01631 565630
Fax 01631 565620
Bareboat
Scotland west coast

Alpha Yacht Charter
Mews Cottage
Carbeth Stables
Killearn
Stirlingshire G63 9QB
Scotland
☎/Fax 01360 550836

Anvil Yacht Charters
Old Mill Yard
The Quay
Poole
Dorset BH15 1HJ
☎ 01202 741637

Appleby Charters Ltd
Crownwood
Emery Down
Lyndhurst
Hants SO43 7GA
☎ 01703 283712
Fax 01703 283713

Arcadian Charters
1 Beechcroft
South Town
Dartmouth
Devon TQ6 9BU
☎ 01803 834896

Armada Yachts
18 Glasdrum Road
Fort William
Inverness-shire PH33 6DD
Scotland
☎ 01397 700008

Artemis Sailing Holidays
40 Park Estate
Shavington
Crewe
Cheshire CW2 5AP
☎ 01270 67556
Fax 0030 661 99005

Associated Scottish Yacht
Charter
Carloonan
Mawcarse
Milnathort
Kinross-shire KY13 7SQ
☎/Fax 01577 862816

Atlantis Sailing
40 Kings Road
Long Ditton
Surrey KT6 5JF
☎/Fax 0181 398 8684

AYC Charters
26 The Maltings
Tingewick
Bucks MK18 4LQ
☎/Fax 01280 847368

BG Marine
169 Skipper Way
Lee-on-Solent
Hants PO13 8HS
☎ 01705 553702

BIII Charter
6 Shorefield Street
London SW3 4BD
☎ 0171 352 7035
Fax 0171 352 7068

Blakes Holidays Ltd
Wroxham
Norwich NR12 8DH
☎ 01603 782141
Fax 01603 782871
Bareboat, Crewed
Managed, Sole Agent
UK: Norfolk Broads,
Scotland, Ireland

Blue Cruise Ltd
87 High Street
London NW10 4NT
☎ 0181 838 0998
Fax 0181 838 1448
Gulet cruises
Turkey 72ft

Blue Peter Sailing
5 Rowley Close
Botley
Southampton
Hants SO3 2FT
☎ 01489 781136
Fax 01489 780887

Blue Sapphire Charters
Blue Sapphire
Littlehampton Marina
Ferry Road
Littlehampton
W Sussex
☎ 01903 723568
Fax 01903 732740

Blue Sea Sailing
☎ 01234 854831
Fax 01234 853980

Blue Water Charter
Neptune Quay
Pegasi
Ipswich
Suffolk IP4 1AX
☎ 01468 936115

BOSS (British Offshore
Sailing School)
Hamble Point Marina
School Lane
Hamble
Southampton SO31 4JD
☎/Fax 01703 456744
Sailing school, Bareboat,
Skippered
UK

Britannia Sailing
The Boathouse on the Quay
Shore Road
Warshash
Southampton SO31 9FR
☎ 01489 577789
Fax 01489 572054
Sailing school, Pre-flotilla,
Flotilla, Bareboat,
Skippered, Racing charter,
Corporate charter

Owned, Agent
UK, Mediterranean,
Caribbean

Bulldog Sailing Centre
Town Quay
Southampton
Hants SO1 2AQ
☎ 01703 230260
Bareboat, Crewed, Owned,
Managed
Northern Europe, Solent,
South Coast, Southampton
10 yachts
33ft to 40ft (sail and motor)

Bumble Bee Cruises
Daavar
Connel
Argyll PA37 1PT
☎/Fax 01631 710729
Crewed
Owned
Scotland west coast
1 yacht
38ft

Bute Sailing School
Canon House
Battery Place
Rothesay
Isle of Bute PA20 9DP
☎ 01700 502819
Fax 01700 505725

Camper & Nicholson
(Mayfair) Ltd
26 Bruton Street
London W1X 7DB
☎ 0171 491 2950
Fax 0171 629 2068
Sole agent, Agent
Luxury charter, Skippered
Worldwide
75 +
Over 16 metres

C J Broom & Sons Ltd
Riverside
Brundall
Norwich
Norfolk NR13 5PX
☎ 01603 712334
Fax 01603 714803

Cardinal Yachts
12A Grafton Court
Grafton Road

Torquay
Devon TQ1 1UP
☎ 01803 212954
Fax 01803 212954

Carefree Sailing
122 Pavilion Gardens
Laleham
Middlesex TW18 1HW
England
☎ 01784 462796
Fax 01784 469081

Carey Yacht Charter
Hillash House
Ledbury Road
Dymock
Gloucestershire GL18 2DB
☎ 01531 890317
Fax 01531 890832

Catamaran Sail-Teach
11 Ulting Lane
Langford
Maldon
Essex CM9 6QB
☎/Fax 01621 855447

Cavendish White
39 Tadema Road
Suite 7
Chelsea
London SW10 0PY
☎ 0171 352 6565
Fax 0171 352 6515
Luxury crewed
Agent
Worldwide

Chameleon Yacht Charters
31 St Marks Road
London W7 2PN
☎ 0181 8403010

Charlie Ward Traditional
Boats Ltd
Tides Reach
Morton
Nr Holt
Norfolk NR25 7AA
☎ 01263 740377
Fax 01263 741424

Charterlease International
Byways
Church Farm Lane
E Wittering
Chichester

W Sussex PO20 8PT
☎/Fax 01243 673800

Charter Party
Florida Yacht Charters Inc
2 Market Place
Ringwood
Hampshire BH24 1AW
☎ 01425 472063

Charter Plus
2 Victoria Road
Mudeford
Christchurch
Dorset BH23 3LF
☎ 01202 478248

Charters International
17 Monks Way
Hill Head
Hants PO14 3LU
☎ 01329 512439

Charter Party
Florida Yacht Charters Inc
2 Market Place
Ringwood
Hants BH24 1AW
☎ 01425 472063

Chichester Sailing Centre
Chichester Marina
Birdham
Chichester
W Sussex PO20 7EJ
☎ 01243 512557
Fax 01243 512570
Sailing school, Bareboat
UK south coast
Classic Cruising

Chief Ivanhoe
4 Spernen Wyn Road
Falmouth
Cornwall TR11 4EH
☎ 01326 317241

Chloe May Classic Charters
Flat 2
51 Harley Street
London W1N 1DD
☎ 0171 636 4465
Fax 0171 636 4286

Classic Cruising
Oak Leys
108 Orchard hill
Little Billing

Northampton
Northants NN3 9AG
☎/Fax 01604 412397

Classic Sailing Ltd
Pantiles
St Mawes
Truro
Cornwall TR2 5AA
☎ 01326 270027
Fax 01326 270092

Club Sail
11 O'Connell Road
Eastleigh
Southampton SO50 9FX
☎ 01703 399860
Fax 01703 328487
Flotilla, Bareboat, Crewed
Owned, Managed
UK south coast, northern
France, Canary Islands
4 yachts
33ft to 45ft

Clyde Argyll Charters
Kip Marina
Inverkip
Renfrewshire PA16 0AW
☎/Fax 01475 520541
Bareboat
Scotland west coast

Clyde Offshore Sea School
Kip Marina
Inverkip
Renfrewshire
Scotland PA16 0AS
☎ 01475 521210
Fax 01475 521572
Bareboat, Racing,
Corporate
Owned, Managed
Scotland

Compass Rose Sailing
School
7 Alexandra Terrace
Exeter
Devon EX4 6SY
☎ 01392 277012
Fax 01392 412481

Conwy School of Yachting
Conwy Marina
Conwy
Gwynedd LL32 8GU

☎ 01492 572999
Fax 01491 572111
Sailing school, Bareboat,
Skippered
Wales

Cookson International
Yacht Charter
Windward House
1-2 Bull Hill
Lymington
Hants SO41 5RA
☎ 01590 670929
Fax 01590 677586

Cornish Adventure Sailing
12 Lansdowne Road
Falmouth
Cornwall TR11 4BE
☎ 01326 314728
Fax 10326 314728
Skippered
UK south coast

Cornish Cruising
Falmouth Yacht Marina
North Parade
Falmouth
Cornwall TR11 2TD
☎ 01326 211800
Fax 01326 318309
Bareboat
Managed
UK south coast

Cornish Day Sailing
Langorrock
28 Gustory Road
Crantock
Cornwall TR8 5RG
☎/Fax 01637 830956

Cosmos Yachting Ltd
74 Kingston Hill
Kingston-upon-Thames
Surrey KT2 7NP
☎ 0181 547 3577
Fax 0181 546 8887
Flotilla, Bareboat,
Skippered
Sole agent, Agent
Northern France, Greece,
Turkey, Corsica, Sardinia,
Italy, Caribbean, Tahiti
500 yachts
28ft to 60ft

Crane Yacht Charters
8 Ardayre Road
Prestwick
Ayrshire KA9 1QL
☎ 01292 75355
Fax 01292 312836

Crestar Yachts Ltd
Colette Court
125 Sloane Street
London SW1X 9AU
☎ 0171 730 9962
Fax 0171 824 8691
Luxury crewed
Agent
Worldwide

Crinan Yacht Charters
The Pump House
Crinan
Argyll
Scotland PA31 8SP
☎/Fax 01546 830260

Cruiseaway Yacht Charter
Maywood
Forest Lane
Wickham
Hants PO17 5DN
☎ 01329 832583

Crusader Yachting
Box Farm Office
Winkfield Row
Bracknell
Berks RG12 6NG
☎ 01344 890941
Fax 01344 890041
Bareboat, Crewed
Owned, Managed
Turkey
10 yachts
26ft to 50ft

Dart Sailing School &
Charters
18 Fairfax Place
Dartmouth
Devon TQ6 9AB
☎ 01803 833973
Bareboat, Skippered
UK south coast

Dartmouth Yacht Cruise
School
Freespirit
37 Higher Street
Dittisham

Devon TQ6 0HT
☎ 01453 731142
Fax 01803 722226
Sailing school, Bareboat,
Skippered
Owned, Agent
UK South coast,
Mediterranean

DC Yachts
8 Coley Grove
Lt Haywood
Stafford ST8 0UW
☎ 01889 881 1453
Fax 01562 746089
Bareboat, Crewed
Owned, Managed
UK south coast, Northern
France
3 yachts
32ft to 35ft

Dolphin Haven Yachting
7 Hurstway Close
Fulwood
Preston
Lancs PR2 9TU
☎ 01772 717379

Dundarg Charters
9 Apsley road
Denton
Manchester M34 3HE
☎/Fax 0161 292439

Earley International
Riddings Court
Hartford
Cheshire CW8 1SB
☎/Fax 01606 783712
Agent
Skippered
Caribbean

East Anglian Sea School
Studio One
Foxis Marina
Ipswich IP2 8NJ
☎ 01473 684884
Fax 01473 780877
Bareboat, skippered

East Coast Offshore Sailing
1 Moory Croft Close
Great Staughton
Cambs PE19 4DY
☎ 01480 861381

Elise
165 Earlsfield Road
London SW18 3DD
☎ 0181 874 1956

Elite Charters
4 Prospect Row
Brompton
Gillingham
Kent ME7 5AL
☎/Fax 01634 845639

Elizabethan Yacht Charter
30 Gages Road
Kingswood
Bristol
Avon BS15 2UG
☎/Fax 01179 615739

Elk Classic Sailing &
Restoration
Dalnaneun
Loch Neil Side
Kilmore
Argyll PA34 4XU
☎ 01631 770209

EME
Marina House
Falmouth Yacht Marina
Falmouth
Cornwall TR11 2TD
☎/Fax 01326 211121
Flotilla, Bareboat, Crewed,
Managed, Sole Agent,
Agent
Falmouth, Mediterranean
40 yachts
24ft to 71ft

Emsworth Sailing School
The Port House
Port Solent
Hants PO6 4TH
☎ 01705 210510
Fax 01705 219827
Sailing school, Bareboat,
Crewed, Owned
UK, Port Solent, Chichester
30 yachts
32ft to 36ft

Enterprise Sailing
36 Hart Street
Henley-on-Thames
Oxon RG9 2AU
☎ 01491 410411
Fax 01491 572497

Bareboat, Owned,
Managed, Sole Agent,
Agent
Mediterranean: Greece,
Turkey, Balearics
300 yachts
30ft to 55ft

Epic Ventures Ltd
120 High Street
Cowes
Isle of Wight PO31 7AX
☎/Fax 01983 291292
Cruising rallies

Euro Sea School (Greece)
124 Northlonsdale Road
Ulverston LA12 9DZ
☎/Fax 01229 586751

Fairview Sailing
Port Hamble
Hamble
Southampton
Hants SO31 4QD
☎ 01703 457023
Fax 01703 457570

Fal Sail
Polkerris
One Wood Lane
Falmouth
Cornwall TR11 4RG
☎ 01326 313208
Sailing school
Falmouth

Falmouth Sea School
John Conyard
'Tamara'
Clijah Lane
Redruth
Cornwall TR15 2NN
☎ 01209 214783

Falmouth School of Sailing
The Boat Park
Grove Place
Falmouth
Cornwall TR11 4AU
☎ 01326 211311/373203

Firstaway Charters
23 Orchardlea
Swanmore
Southampton
Hants SO32 2QZ
☎/Fax 01489 893889

Bareboat, Skippered
UK south coast

First Charters
188 Sutton Court Road
London W4 3HR
☎ 0181 995 5676
Fax 0181 995 6195

Five Star Sailing School
Port Westerly
Shore Road
Warsash
Southampton
Hants SO31 9FR
☎ 01489 885599
Fax 01489 885505
Sailing school, Bareboat,
Skippered
UK south coast

Flamingo Yacht Charters
23 Main Road
Fairlie
Ayrshire KA29 0DW
☎ 01475 568526
Bareboat
Owned, Managed
Scotland west coast
4 yachts

Fort Bovisand Sailing
Centre
Fort Bovisand
Plymouth
Devon PL9 0AB
☎ 01752 482882
Fax 01752 481952
Sailing school

Fowey Cruising School &
Services
32 Fore Street
Fowey
Cornwall PL23 1AQ
☎ 01726 832129
Fax 01726 832000
Sailing school
Bareboat, Skippered
UK south coast, Portugal,
Malta
15 yachts
30ft to 42ft

France Charter
13 Arden Grove
Harpenden
Herts AL5 4SJ

☎ 01582 712441
Fax 01582 620941

Freewinds Yacht Charter
Marisco
Windsor Terrace
Falmouth
Cornwall TR11 3BW
☎/Fax 01326 318101
Bareboat, Skippered
Cornwall, Ireland
24ft to 51ft

Gairloch Marine
Casmufeanna
Gairloch
Ross-shire IV21 2BX
☎/Fax 01445 712163
Bareboat, Crewed
Owned
Scotland
2 yachts
31ft to 36ft

Gallivanter Yacht Charter
Old Bell House
Northfield End
Henley-on-Thames
Oxon RG9 2JG
☎ 01491 574350
Fax 01491 571544

Go Sail Ltd
1 Bucklands Court
Castle Street
East Cowes
Isle of Wight PO32 6RB
☎/Fax 01983 280220

Greek Sails
21 The Mount
Kippax
Leeds LS25 7NG
☎ 0113 232926
Bareboat
Owned, Managed
Greece
40 yachts
30ft to 45ft

Gullivers Yacht Services
Antells Farm
Stour Provost
Gillingham
Dorset SP8 5SA
☎ 01747 838987
Fax 01747 838853

Hamble School of Yachting
Mercury Yacht Harbour
Satchell Lane
Hamble
Hants SO3 5QH
☎ 01703 452668
Fax 01703 456687
Sailing school, Bareboat,
Skippered
Owned, Managed
UK south coast
10 yachts
32ft to 42ft

Hanna Desjardins
International Ltd
22 Blenheim Terrace
St Johnís Wood
London NW8 0EB
☎ 0171 372 2857
Fax 0171 372 2891
Luxury charter
Sole agent, Agent
Worldwide
50ft to 200ft

Hardings of Hardanger
Bell Lane
Broad Heath
Tenbury Wells
Worcester WR15 8QX
☎/ *Fax* 01886 853692
Bareboat, Skippered
Norway, Brittany,
Mediterranean, Caribbean

Hayes Charters
Unit 2a
Europa Trading Estate
Fraser Road
Erith
Kent
☎ 01322 440332
Fax 0860 676867

Hebridean Charter Ltd
Pier Road
Gairloch
Ross & Cromarty IV21
2AH
Scotland
☎ 01445 712458
Fax 01445 712511

H E Hipperson Ltd
The Quay
Gillingham Dam
Beccles

Suffolk NR34 0EB
☎ 01502 712166

Hobo Yachting
13 Alcantara Crescent
Ocean Village
Southampton
Hants SO41 3HR
☎/*Fax* 01703 334574

Hoseasons Holidays Ltd
Sunway House
Lowestoft
Suffolk NR32 2LW
☎ 01502 500505
Fax 01502 514298

Hunters Fleet Ltd
Hunterís Yard
Horsefen Road
Ludham
Norfolk NR29 5QG
☎ 01629 678263

Imperial Motor Yachts Ltd
Flanders House
Silver Street
Lymington
Hants SO41 6DF
☎/*Fax* 01590 681938

Impression Marine
Unit 20
Hamble Yacht Services
Port Hamble
Southampton SO31 4NN
☎ 01703 458307
Bareboat, Crewed
Managed, Agent
Northern Europe, Solent,
Port Hamble, Liverpool,
Poole, Caribbean, Antigua
30 yachts
9·5m to 24m

Inland Waterways Holiday
Cruises
Greenham Lock Cottage
London Road
Newbury
Berks RG14 5SN
☎ 0831 110811
Fax 01635 42884

International Yacht
Charters
Marina House
Falmouth Yacht Marina

Falmouth
Cornwall TR11 2TD
☎ 01326 211121
Fax 01326 311230
Bareboat, Skippered
UK west country,
Worldwide
UK 20+ yachts

Iolair Yacht Charter
12 The Grove
Musselburgh
E Lothian
Scotland
☎ 0131 665 5273
Fax 0131 653 6638

Ionian Sailing
3 Wymeswold Road
Rempstone
Loughborough
Leics LE12 6RN
☎ 01509 880085
Fax 01509 880525

Islander Yacht Charters
6 Park Road
Edinburgh EH6 4LF
Scotland
☎ 0131 552 5886
Bareboat, Crewed
Owned, Managed
Scotland west coast
6 yachts
32ft to 41ft

Islander Yacht Charters &
Sailing School
7 Torinturk
By Tarbert
Argyll PA29 6YE
Scotland
☎/*Fax* 01880 820012

Island Cruising Club
10 Island Street
Salcombe
S Devon TQ8 8DR
☎ 01548 842329

Island Sea School
7 Church View
South Milford
Leeds
W Yorks LS25 5BH
☎ 01977 685394

CHARTER COMPANIES IN BRITAIN & IRELAND

ITC Yachts
Cocorde House
Forest Street
Chester
Cheshire CH1 1QR
☎ 01244 341131
Fax 01244 310255

Jannel Cruisers Ltd
Shobnall Marina
Shobnall Road
Burton-on-Trent
Staffs DE14 2AU
☎ 01283 542718
Fax 01283 545369

Jersey Cruising School and
Yacht Charters
New North Quay
St Helier Marina
St Helier
Jersey Channel Islands
Great Britain
☎ 01534 888100
Fax 01534 888088
Bareboat, Crewed
Managed, Sole Agent
Channel Islands
8 yachts
28ft to 44ft

Johnsonís Yacht Station
Beccles Road
St Olaves
Norfolk NR31 9HE
☎ 01493 488479
Fax 01493 488499

J P C Powles
Staithway Road
Wroxham
Norfolk NR12 8RX
☎ 01603 783311
Fax 01244 310255

Jubilee Sailing Trust
Jubilee Yard
Merlin Quay
Hazel Road
Woolston
Southampton SO19 7GB
☎ 01703 631388
Fax 01703 638625
Adventure sailing holidays
for able-bodied and
physically disabled people

KC Yacht Charters
3 Black Prince close
West Byfleet
Surrey KT12 7ES
☎ 01932 356422
1 Harbour House
Town Quay
Southampton
Hants SO14 2AQ
☎ 01703 333370
Fax 01932 356422

Lamarair
Universal Shipyards
Sarisbury Green
Southampton
☎ 01489 583601
Fax 01582 661037
Bareboat, Skippered

Langstone Yachting Ltd
Southsea Marina
Fort Cumberland Road
Southsea
Hants PO4 9RG
☎ 01705 822719
Fax 01705 822220

Largs Sailing School
24 Castle Park Drive
Fairlie
Largs
Scotland KA29 0DF
☎ 01475 568080
Bareboat
Scotland west coast

Leisurebase International
12 Carlton Road
Kibworth
Leics LE8 0LZ
☎/Fax 0116 279 2932

Liberty Yachts Ltd
Queen Anneís Battery
Coxside
Plymouth
Devon PL4 OLP
☎ 01752 227911
Fax 01752 229122
Bareboat
Managed
UK south coast, Brittany,
Greece
65 yachts
20ft to 44ft

Liz Fenner Worldwide
Yachting Holidays
Fairfax Place
London NW6 4EJ
☎ 0171 328 1033
Fax 0171 328 1034
Agent

Loch Ness Yacht Charters
Dochgarroch
Inverness IV3 6JY
Scotland
☎ 01463 861303
Fax 01463 86353

Lymington Cruising School
24 Waterloo Road
Lymington
Hants SO41 9DB
☎ 01590 677478

Holiday Malta Co
314 Upper Richmond Road
Putney
London SW15 6TU
☎ 0181 785 3222
Fax 0181 780 0833

Marinair Yacht Charter
Services
188 Northdown Road
Cliftonville
Kent CT9 2QN
☎ 01843 227140
Fax 01843 228784
Free ☎ in UK 0800
220763

Marwin Charters Ltd
7 Somerset Square
London W14 8EE
☎/Fax 0171 6020111

McCulloch Yacht Charter
60 Fordwych Road
London NW2 3TH
☎/Fax 0181 983 1487
Crewed
Agent
Mediterranean: Turkey,
Greece
42 yachts
36ft to 160ft

McFarlane Billington
Yachting
Seaforth House
Lymington
Hants SO41 3RW
☎ 01590 688220
Fax 01590 688221

Melfort Pier Ltd
Kilmelford
By Oban
Argyll PA34 4XD
☎ 0185 22333
Fax 0185 22329
Bareboat, Crewed
Owned, Managed, Sole
Agent
Scotland west coast,
Bahamas
4 yachts
30ft to 60ft

Mevagissey Sailing School
Inner Moorings
Lamledra Hill
Gorran Haven
St Austell
Cornwall PL26 6JR
☎/*Fax* 01726 842383

Minorca Sailing Holidays
58 Kew Road
Richmond
Surrey TW9 2PQ
☎ 0181 948 2106
Fax 0181 332 6528
Dinghy sailing, windsurfing
Mediterranean
150 boats/150 boards

Minotaur Charters
204 Altham Grove
Harlow
Essex CM20 2PW
☎/*Fax* 01279 830478
Greece 0645 928854
Bareboat
Owned, Managed
Greece, Ionian
7 yachts
27ft to 36·5ft

Moonfleet Sailing
Cobbs Quay Marina
Poole
Dorset BH15 4EL
☎ 01202 623911

Multihull Cruising
18 Truro Lane
Penryn
Cornwall TR10 8BW
☎ 01326 373365

Multihull International
27 The Slipway
Port Solent Marina
Portsmouth
Hants PO6 4TR
☎ 01705 200123
Fax 01705 214123
Multihull charters,
Bareboat, Skippered
UK south coast

Multihull Marketing
Parkstone
Poole
Dorset BH14 8EE
☎/*Fax* 01202 744501
Multihull specialist,
Skippered, Crewed
Owned, Agent
UK south coast, Channel
Islands, Brittany
Mediterranean Cyprus,
Tunisia
4 yachts
26ft to 34ft

Multihull Sailing School
275 Swanwick Lane
Swanwick
Southampton
Hants SO31 7GT
☎ 01489 589971

National Federation of Sea
Schools
Staddlestones
Fletchwood Lane
Totton
Southampton SO40 7DZ
☎ 01703 869956
Fax 01703 869956
Sailing school representative

Nautilus Yachting
4 Church Street
Edenbridge
Kent TN8 5BD
☎ 01732 867445
Fax 01732 867446
E-mail charter@nautilus-
yachting.co.uk

Flotilla, Bareboat
Agent
Mediterranean, Caribbean,
Pacific

Nelson Charter Services Ltd
Nelson House
Jordans Way
Jordans
Bucks HP9 2SP
☎ 01494 874064

Neptune School of Yachting
Ltd
Camper & Nicholsons
Marina
Mumby Road
Gosport
Hants PO12 1AH
☎ 01705 511461
Fax 01705 504447
E-mail
neptune@athene.co.uk
Bareboat, Skippered
UK south coast, Greece,
Turkey, Portugal, Canaries

Newhaven Marina Ltd
The Yacht Harbour
Newhaven
E Sussex BN9 9BY
☎ 01273 513881
Fax 01273 517990

New Hebridean Cruising
Co Ltd
Kilmelford Yacht Haven
Kilmelford
Oban
Argyll PA34 4XD
☎ 018525 200511
Fax 018525 324

Nigel James Yacht Charter
30 Enfield Road
Brentford
Middlesex TW8 9PB
☎ 0181 568 8562
Fax 0181 569 8409
E-mail
nj-yacht@dircon.co.uk
http://www.users.dircon.co.u
k/nj-yacht/
Bareboat, Skippered,
Crewed
France, Greece, Turkey,
Caribbean

Norfolk Broads Yacht Co
Ltd
Southgate Yacht Station
Lower Street
Horning
Norfolk NR12 8PF
☎ 01692 631330

Norfolk Broads Yacht Co
Albatross Quay
Riverside
Fritton
Great Yarmouth
Norfolk NR31 9HG
☎ 01493 488479
Fax 01493 488499
Bareboat, Crewed
Owned
Norfolk Broads
30 yachts
24ft to 60ft

North Haven Motor
Cruising
71 Tatlam Road
Salterns Marina
Poole
Dorset BH15 2DP
☎/Fax 01202 386761

North Sea Yachting
Coles Lane
Walton-on-the-Naze
Essex CO14 8SL
☎ 01473 232221/01255
851613

Oban Sea School
Mount Stuart
Gallanach
Oban
Argyll
Strathclyde PA34 4QH
Scotland
☎ 01631 562013

Ocean Spirit Sailing
Charters Ltd
5 Foss Street
Dartmouth
Devon TQ6 9DW
☎/Fax 01803 832186
Sail-dive
Maldives

Odysseus Yachting Holidays
33 Grand Parade
Brighton

E Sussex BN2 2QA
☎ 01273 695094
Fax 01273 688855

Osprey Cruising Ltd
Royal Oak Inn
Laxfield
Woodbridge
Suffolk 1P13 8DH
☎ 01986 798446

Pace Charter
131 High Street
Lymington
Hants SO41 9AQ
☎ 01590 677450

Peculiar Yachts Ltd
Haslar Marina
Haslar Road
Gosport
Hants PO12 1NU
☎/Fax 01705 589953

Pembrokeshire Cruising
Cleddan House
Milford Marina
Milford Haven
Pembrokeshire SA73 3AF
☎/Fax 01646 690285

Pembrokeshire Sailing
School
Neyland Marina
Milford Haven
Pembrokeshire
☎ 01646 601677

Pharos Yacht Charter
Craobh Haven Marina
By Oban
Argyll
Scotland
☎/Fax 01852 500351

Philip Marshall Sailing
Beechborough
Park Lane
Twyford
Winchester
Hants SO21 1QU
☎ 01962 712160

Plain Sailing
Brixham Marina
Berry Head Road
Brixham
Devon TQ9 5RX

☎ 01803 853843
Fax 01803 866621

Plymouth Sailing School
Queen Anneís Battery
Coxside
Plymouth PL4 0LP
☎ 01752 667170
Fax 01752 257162

Port Edgar Marina &
Sailing School
Shore Road
South Queensferry
West Lothian EH30 9SQ
Scotland
☎ 0131 331 3330
Fax 0131 331 4878

Port Solent Yachting
3rd Floor
Arundel House
54 Arundel Street
Portsmouth PO1 1NL
☎ 01705 200939
Fax 01705 826770

Portway Yacht Charters
(Dartmouth)
Noss House
Bridge Road
Kingswear
Devon TQ6 0EB
☎ 01803 834100

Portway Yacht Charters
(Dittisham)
Cornerways
Church Street
South Brent
Devon TQ10 9AB
☎/Fax 01364 73624

Portway Yacht Charters
(Falmouth)
Falmouth Yacht Marina
North Parade
Falmouth
Cornwall TR11 2TD
☎ 01326 212320

Portway Yacht Charters
(Hamble)
Hamble Point Marina
School Lane
Hamble
Southampton
Hants SO31 4JD

☎ 01703 457110
Fax 01703 458410
E-mail
enquiries@yacht_charter.co.
uk

Portway Yacht Charters
(Haslar)
Haslar Marina
Haslar
Gosport
Hants PO12 1NU
☎/Fax 01705 520099

Portway Yacht Charters
(Hayling Island)
Sparkes Yacht Harbour
Wittering Road
Hayling Island
Hants PO11 9SR
☎ 01705 467786

Portway Yacht Charters
(Lymington)
Maycroft
Tweed Lane
Boldre
Hants SO41 8NF
☎/Fax 01590 677612

Portway Yacht Charters
(Plymouth)
Mayflower International
Marina
Richmond Walk
Plymouth
Devon PL1 4LS
☎ 01752 606999
Fax 01752 607309

Portway Yacht Charters
(Suffolk)
Woolverstone Marina
Woolverstone
Ipswich
Suffolk IP9 1AS
☎ 01473 780008
Fax 01473 780007

Portway Yacht Charters
International
Office 1
The Chandlery Building
Hamble Point Marina
Hamble
Southampton
Hants SO31 5NB

☎ 01703 452100
Fax 01703 452122

Power Waves - Sunseekers
Charters
Hythe Marina Village
Hythe
Southampton
Hants SO45 6DY
☎ 01703 840011
Fax 01703 840088

Prestige Power Ltd
Marina Services Area
Maritime Walk
Ocean Village Marina
Canute Road
Southampton
Hants SO14 3TL
☎ 01703 230089
Fax 01703 224165

Professional Charter
Association
Willows
Rookwood Park
Horsham
West Sussex RH12 1UB
☎ 01403 253275
Fax 01403 276375

Puffin Yachts
Fastmet
9 Mary Vale
Godalming
Surrey GU7 1SW
☎ 01483 420728
Bareboat, Skippered
UK south coast

Rainbow Sailing School
14 Cambrian Place
Swansea Marina
Swansea
West Glamorgan SA1 1UH
☎ 01792 467813
Fax 01792 467804

Ramsgate Yacht Brokerage
and Charter Agency
The Smack Boys Home
Miltary Road
Ramsgate
Kent CT11 9QL
☎/Fax 01483 592973
Bareboat, Skippered
UK east coast, Florida,
Balearics

Rhodos Yachts Ltd
10 Abbey View
Mill Hill
London NW7 4PB
☎ 0171 485 1015
Fax 0171 267 6934

Richardson Cruising
42 Croydon Road
Caterham
Surrey CR3 6QB
☎ 01883 340525
Fax 01883 344000
Flotilla, Bareboat, Crewed
Agent
Turkey

Rockley Point Sailing
Centre
Hamworthy
Poole
Dorset BH15 4LZ
☎ 01202 655309
Sailing school, Skippered
Owned, Managed
UK south coast

Roy Yacht Charter
18 Ferndale Crescent
Cowley
Uxbridge
Middlesex UB8 2AX
☎ 01895 671841

Rozel Marine
59 Western Road
Lymington
Hants SO41 9HJ
☎/Fax 01590 671841
Skippered
UK south coast

Sail & Stay Holidays
Orchard House
Dodwells Road
Hinckley
Leics LE10 3BZ
☎ 01455 234601

Sail Australia Ltd
Dolphin Cottage
The Street
East Clandon
Surrey GU4 7RX
☎/Fax 01483 222890
Bareboat, Skippered
Australia, Kenya
Sailaway Sea School

Ballochmartin Bay
Millport
Isle of Cumbrae
Ayrshire KA28 0HQ
☎ 01475 530040
Fax 01475 530317

Sailing Holidays Ltd
105 Mt Pleasant Road
London NW10 3EH
☎ 0181 459 8787
Fax 0181 459 8798
Flotilla, Bareboat
Owned
Greek Ionian Islands
70 yachts
Size 27ft to 41ft

Sail Northwest
Cornmill Cottage
43-45 Ingrow Lane
Keighley
W Yorks BD22 7BU
☎/*Fax* 01535 602133

Sailing Opportunities
Hambleside
Swanwick Shore Road
Swanwick
Southampton SO3 7EF
☎ 01489 885345
Fax 01489 885845
Bareboat, Crewed
UK south coast
2 yachts
31ft to 34ft

Sail Scotland Ltd
7 Alexandra Parade
Dunoon
Argyll
Scotland PA23 8HJ
☎ 01369 705533
Fax 01369 705588

Sail Training Association
2a The Hard
Portsmouth PO1 3PT
☎ 01705 832055
Fax 01705 815769
Sailing school
Tall ships
Winter sun
Canaries

Salen Jetty
Salen Jetty
Acharacle
Adnamurchan
Argyll PH36 4JN
Scotland
☎ 01967 431333

Saxonia Charters
22-28 Tower Street
Brightlingsea
Essex CO7 0AL
☎ 01206 302863
Fax 01206 305858

Scottish European Charters
Mid Auchentiber
Ayrshire KA13 7RR
☎ 01294 85278

Sea Jay Charters
24 Cobb's Quay
Hamworthy
Poole
Dorset BH15 4EL
☎ 01202 660974
Bareboat, Crewed
Owned, Agent
UK south coast,
Mediterranean Greece
30 yachts
28ft to 44ft

Seaquest Holidays
9 Grand Parade
Green Lanes
Haringey
London N4 15X
☎ 0181 800 8030

Sea Ventures Ltd
Hamble Point Marina
School Lane
Hamble
Southampton
Hants SO41 4JK
☎ 01703 455333
Fax 01703 455553
Flotilla, Bareboat
Owned, Managed, Sole
Agent, Agent
UK: Lymington, Hamble,
Plymouth
40 yachts
20ft to 60ft

Sea Ventures Yacht Charter
Lymington Yacht Haven
Lymington
Hants SO41 3QD
☎ 01590 672472
Fax 01590 671924

Seaway Sailing
Shamrock Quay
William Street
Southampton SO1 1QL
☎ 01703 234666
Fax 01703 234270

Sea West Scotland Charters
St Germain Street
Catrine
Ayrshire KA56RH
☎ 01290 51621

Secret Charters
Pippins
Abberton Road
Layer-de-la-Haye
Colchester
Essex CO2 0JX
☎ 01206 734727

Setsail Holidays
Victoria Chambers
16–18 Strutton Ground
London SW1P 2HP
☎ 0171 799 2333
Fax 0171 976 8137
Flotilla, bareboat
Greece, Turkey

Shakespeare International
Marine Ltd
Station Road
Hartlebury
Worcs DY11 7YJ
☎ 01299 250685
Fax 01299 250509

Shire Cruisers
The Wharf
Sowerby Bridge
West Yorks UX6 2AG
☎ 01422 832712
Fax 01422 839565

Shotley Marina Sea School
Shotley Gate
Ipswich
Suffolk IP9 1QJ

☎ 01473 788982
Fax 01473 788868
Sailing school, Skippered

Simanda Yachting Services
8 Grovelands
Lower Bourne
Farnham
Surrey GU10 3RQ
☎ 01252 714919
Fax 01252 737634

Sinbad Charters
Aidenkyle House
Aidenkyle Road
Kilcreggan
by Helensburgh
Dunbartonshire G84 OHP
☎/*Fax* 01436 842 247
Crewed
Scotland
1 yacht
36ft

Skyesail Charters
36 Bernisdale
Portree
Isle of Skye IV51 9NS
Scotland
☎ 0147 032413
Fax 0147 032466
Crewed
Owned
Scotland, Canaries
1 yacht
58ft

Sleat Marine Services
New Building
Ardvasar
Isle of Skye IV45 8RU
☎ 01471 844216
Fax 01471 844387
Bareboat, Skippered
Owned, Managed
Scotland
6 yachts
34ft to 40

Smart Yachts International
39 Maple Close
Barton-on-Sea
Hants BH25 7AR
☎/*Fax* 01425 614804

Solent Yacht Charter
Haslar Marina
Haslar Road
Gosport
Hants
☎/*Fax* 01705 602708
E-mail
Solenty@interalpha.co.uk
Bareboat
UK south coast, Greece

South Cornwall Yacht
Charter
Mylor Yacht Harbour
nr Falmouth
Cornwall TR11 6UF
☎ 01326 374204
Fax 01326 377768
Bareboat, Skippered
Owned, Managed
UK south coast
16 yachts
26ft to 41ft

Southeast Sailing
The Historic Dockyard
Chatham
Kent
☎ 01634 402518
Skippered
UK east coast

Southern Sailing School
305 Swanwick Lane
Swanwick
Southampton SO31 7GT
☎ 01489 575511
Fax 01489 578828
E-mail
sailing@southern.co.uk

Southern Yacht Charters
43 Gravel Hill
Wimborne
Dorset BH21 1RW
☎ 01202 842877
Bareboat, Crewed
Owned, Managed, Sole
Agent
UK south coast
12 yachts
8·5m to 14m

Start Point Sailing
Cover House
113 Bewdley Road
Kidderminster
Worcs DY11 6RX

☎ 01562 748635
Fax 01562 746089

Staysail
The Old Rectory
Llangwn
Haverfordwest
Pembrokeshire SA62 4GA
☎ 01437 890078

St Blanes Yacht Charter
Crofton Cottage
Ascog
Rothesay
Isle of Bute PA20 9LN
☎ 01700 503108
Scotland

Steve Bedford's Yacht
Charter
15 The Ridings
Steyning
West Sussex BN44 3PX
☎ 01903 813630

Suffolk School of Yachting
and Motor Cruising
Wherry Lane
Wherry Quay
Ipswich
Suffolk IP4 1LG
☎/*Fax* 01473 288111
Bareboat, Crewed
Owned, Managed, Sole
Agent, Agent
UK east coast
7 yachts
33ft to 40ft

Sula Charters
Laga Marine Services
Laga Bay
Acharacle
Argyll PH36 4JP
Scotland
☎/*Fax* 019724 218

Sundeck Charters
Hamble Point Marina
School Lane
Hamble
Southampton SO3 5NB
☎ 01703 457733
Fax 01703 457551

Sunfleet Yacht Charter
Haven Quay
Mill Lane

Lymington
Hants SO41 9AZ
☎ 01590 670041
Fax 01590 679080

Sunsail Ltd
The Port House
Port Solent
Portsmouth
Hants PO6 4TH
☎ 01705 222222
Fax 01705 219827
Sailing school, Flotilla,
Bareboat, Skippered
Owned, Managed
UK south coast, Scotland,
Northern France, Canaries,
Mediterranean Spain,
France, Greece, Turkey,
Caribbean, USA, Bahamas,
Seychelles, Thailand, Pacific
Australia, New Zealand,
Tonga
700 yachts
Size 30ft to 55ft

Sunshine Charters
Greenfield House
Dowlands Lane
Copthorne
West Sussex RH10 3HX
☎/*Fax* 01342 718671
Bareboat, Crewed
Owned, Managed, Sole
Agent, Agent
Mediterranean: Greece,
Turkey, France, Corsica,
Balearics
Caribbean: BVI,
Martinique, St Lucia
New Zealand, Australia
600 yachts
26ft to 55ft

Sunworld Sailing
120 St Georgeís Road
Brighton
East Sussex BN2 1EA
☎ 01273 626284
Fax 01273 626285
http//www.sunworld-
sailing.co.uk.sunworld
Flotilla, Bareboat
Greece, Turkey
Owned
70 yachts
28ft to 34ft

Swan Sail Yacht Charter
Ltd
PO Box 77
Bury
Lancs BL9 7YE
☎ 0161 705 2288
Fax 0161 797 2518

Tangaroa Yachting
Town Quay Marina
Town Quay
Southampton
Hants SO14 2AQ
☎ 01703 636878
Fax 01703 636879

Teign Sailing Enterprise
54 Torridon Way
Hinckley
Leics LE10 0UH
☎ 01455 238985

Telegraph Charters
6 Church Row
Wandsworth Plain
London SW18 1ES
☎ 01428 751845

Templecraft Yacht Charters
33 Grand Parade
Brighton
East Sussex BN2 2QA
☎ 01273 695094
Fax 01273 688855
E-mail
tc@templecraft.telme.com
Flotilla, Bareboat,
Skippered
Sole agent, Agent
Mediterranean France,
Italy, Greece, Turkey
Caribbean
30ft to 55ft

Tenrag Yacht Charters
Freepost 986
Wingham
Canterbury
Kent CT3 1AR
☎ 01227 721874
Fax 01227 721617
E-mail
tenrag@compuserve.com
Flotilla, Bareboat, Crewed
Managed, Sole Agent,
Agent
Europe: Norway, Brittany,
Ireland, Holland, Canaries

Mediterranean: Cyprus,
Greece, Turkey, Malta,
Corsica, France, Spain,
Gibraltar
Caribbean: BVI, St Martin,
Guadeloupe, Antigua,
Martinique, St Vincent
Florida
Pacific: Tonga, Tahiti,
Australia, New Zealand
9m to 50m

The Algarve Sea School
Henfaes Uchaf
Llangurig
Llanidloes SY18 6SN
☎ 01686 440227
Fax 01686 440398

The Challenge Business Ltd
Trepen House
Menheniot
Liskeard
Cornwall PL14 3PN
☎ 01579 348387
Fax 01579 347255
E-mail
101372.150@compuserve.
com

The Island Yachting Co Ltd
8 St Michael's Place
Brighton
East Sussex BN1 3FT
☎/*Fax* 01273 735254
Skippered, Crewed
Caribbean

The Owners Syndicate
79 Balham Park Road
London SW12 8EB
☎ 0181 767 7926
Bareboat, Skippered
Caribbean

The Solent School of
Yachting
The Quay
Warsash
Southampton
Hants SO31 9FR
☎ 01489 583066
Fax 01489 572054
Sailing School

The Moorings
188 Northdown Road
Cliftonville
Kent CT9 2QN
☎ 0800 220763
Fax 01843 227140
Sailing in company,
Bareboat, Skippered and
Crewed. Owned and
Managed. Brittany
Mediterranean: Spain,
France, Greece, Turkey
Caribbean: Virgins,
Leeward, Windwards
USA: Florida
Bahamas, Mexico
Pacific: Australia, Fiji,
Tonga, New Zealand,
Tahiti.
10m to 25m.

The Yacht Club Charters
Ltd
Docklands Business Centre
10-16 Tiller Road
Docklands
London E14 8PX
☎ 0171 3081122/4735140

Top Cat Cruising School
c/o Seahaven Voyager
Yachts
Southdown Quay
Millbrook
Plymouth
Devon PL10 1HG
☎ 01752 823360

Top Deck Marine Services
14 Forresters Gate
West Common
Blackfield
Southampton
Hants SO45 1S
☎ 01703 810610
Fax 01703 337939

Topsail Charters
22 Church Street
Maldon
Essex CM9 5HP
☎/Fax 01621 857567

Top Yacht Charter
Andrew Hill Lane
Hedgerley
Bucks SL2 3UW

☎ 01753 646636
Fax 01753 645539
Owned, Managed
Bareboat, Skippered
Turkey, Greece, Italy
31ft to 51ft

Transworld Yachting
16 Cheltenham Crescent
Lee on Solent
Hants PO13 9HH
☎/Fax 01705 553702

T W Allen & Son (Yachts)
Ltd
Ash Island
East Molesey
Surrey KT8 9AN
☎ 0181 9791997
Fax 0181 9412553

UKSA (United Kingdom
Sailing Academy)
West Cowes
Isle of Wight PO31 7PQ
☎ 01983 294941/290154
Fax 01983 295938

Ulster Cruising School
Marina Carrickfergus
County Antrim
Northen Ireland BT38 8BE
☎ 01960 368818
Bareboat, Crewed, Owned
Irish Sea, West coast of
Scotland
No of Yachts 2
Size 32ft

Victoria Yachts Ltd
Stone Pier Yard
Warsash
Southampton
Hants SO31 9FR
☎ 01489 885400

Viking Afloat
Lowesmoor Wharf
Worcester
Worcs WR1 2RS
☎ 01905 610660
Fax 01905 616715

Voltair Charters
Lagg Cottage
Dervaig
Isle of Mull
Argyll PQ75 6QY

Scotland
☎/Fax 01688 400380

Wave Yacht Charters
Castlecary Castle
Walton Road
Bonnybridge
Stirlingshire FK4 2HP
Scotland
☎/Fax 01324 841330
E-mail
bobhunter@easynet.co.uk

West Coast Yachts
15 Forties Road
Crosslee
Johnstone
Renfrewshire PA6 7JP
Scotland
☎/Fax 01505 690728

WG Yachts
PO Box 3000
Coulsdon
Surrey CR5 3ZP
☎ 01737 552885/557020
Fax 01737 556877
Bareboat, Skippered,
Crewed
Managed, Agent
Europe: England, France,
Germany, Ireland
Mediterranean: France,
Italy, Spain, Portugal,
Greece, Turkey, Malta,
Cyprus
Caribbean: Antigua,
Grenada, Virgin Islands,
Martinique, French Islands,
St Lucia, Grenadines
Malaysia, USA, Thailand
300 yachts
25ft to 90ft

West Country Charters
c/o Plymouth Sailing School
Queen Anne's Battery
Plymouth PL4 OLP
☎ 01752 667170

Westfleet
Neyland Marina
Milford Haven
Pembrokeshire
Wales
☎ 01646 601677
Bareboat, Skippered
Wales

West Highland Marine Ltd
Badachro
Gairloch
Ross-shire IV21 2AA
☎ 01445 712458
Fax 01445 83215
Bareboat, Crewed
Owned, Managed
Scotland west coast
5 yachts
24ft to 41ft

Windsport International
Mylor Yacht Harbour
Falmouth
Cornwall TR11 5UF
☎ 01326 376191
Fax 01326 376192
E-mail
windsport.international@
btinternet.com

Windward Sailing
15 Spencer Glade
Rhyde
Isle of Wight PO33 3AJ
☎ 01983 612800
Fax 0421 942393
Bareboat, Skippered
UK south coast

Windward Yachts Ltd
29 Eastern Parade
Fareham
Hants PO16 ORL
☎ 01329 236920
Fax 01329 823577

World Crews
52 York Place
Bournemouth
Dorset BH7 6JN
☎/Fax 01202 431520

Worldwide Yacht Charter
Steeple Cottage
Easton
Winchester
Hants
☎ 01962 779317
Fax 01962 779458
E-mail
pkellie@yachtors.u-net.com

Yacht Charter Association
11 Bassett Close
Bassett
Southampton

Hants SO16 7PE
☎ 01703 768941
Fax 01703 767896
E-mail
geoff@yatchcharterassn.
demon.co.uk

Yacht Charter Ecosse
9 Muirfield Crescent
Dundee
Tayside DD3 8PS
Scotland
☎ 01382 827831

Yacht Connections Ltd
The Hames
13 Church Road
South Ascot
Berkshire SL5 9DP
☎ 01344 24987
Fax 01344 26849
Crewed, Luxury
Agent
Mediterranean: Greece,
Turkey, Sardinia, France,
Spain
Caribbean: Virgin Islands,
Leewards and Windwards
Pacific: Tonga, Tahiti
Indian Ocean
Seychelles, Kenya,
Zanzibar, Comoro Islands
New Zealand, Red Sea,
Thailand
200 yachts
40ft to 200ft

Yacht Corryvreckan
Dal An Eas
Kilmore
Oban
Argyll PA34 4XU
Scotland
☎/Fax 01631 770246

Yachting Partners
International
28-29 Richmond Place
Brighton BN2 2NA
☎ 01273 571722
Fax 01273 571720
Luxury crewed
Agent
Worldwide

Yachts International Ltd
Marina House
Falmouth Yacht Marina
Falmouth
Cornwall TR11 2TD
☎ 01326 211121
Fax 01631 770246
E-mail
101612.1320@compuserve.
com

IRELAND

Atlantic Adventures
Frances Street
Kilrush
Ireland
☎ 065 52133
Fax 065 51720

Celtic Cruise Lines Ltd
5 Main Street
Co Kerry
Ireland
☎ 068 21235
Fax 068 22057

Dingle Sea Ventures
Seventh Wave
Milltown
Dingle
Co Kerry
Ireland
☎ 066 52244
Fax 066 51325

Hibernian Cruising School
94 Merrion Village
Merrion Road
Dublin 4
Ireland
☎ 01283 9035
Fax 01283 9185

Ireland Sailing Holidays
67A Upper Georges Street
Dun Laoghaire
Co Dublin
Ireland
☎ 01284 6819
Fax 01280 5990

John Greaney
Dingle Sea Ventures Ltd
6 Grey Street
Dingle
Co Kerry
Ireland
☎ 066 51694
Fax 066 51325
Bareboat, Crewed
Owned, Managed, Agent
Ireland southwest
8 yachts
30ft to 40ft

North West Cruising
Windward Upper Rosses
Point
Co Sligo
Ireland
☎ 071 62467
Fax 071 69488

Rossbrin Yacht Charters
Rossbrin Cove
Schull
West Cork
Ireland
☎ 028 37165
Skippered
Owned
Ireland west coast
1 yacht
36ft

Sailing Holidays in Ireland
Trident Hotel Marina
Kinsale
County Cork
Ireland
☎ 021 772927
Fax 021 774170
Bareboat, Crewed
Owned
Ireland southwest
15 yachts
36ft to 43ft

Sail Northern Ireland
Carrickfergus Marina
Roagers Quay
Carrickfergus
☎ 01960 366666
Fax 01960 350505

Sail West-Seol Siar
Leitir Ard
Caiseal
Co Galway
Ireland
☎ 095 33546
Fax 095 33457
Bareboat, Skippered
Ireland west coast

**Shannon-Erne Waterway
Holidays**
Blaney
Enniskillen
Co Fermanagh
Ireland
☎ 01365 641507
Fax 01365 641734

Shannon Sailing Ltd
New Harbour
Dromineer
Nenagh
Co Tipperary
Ireland
☎ 067 24295
Fax 067 33488
Bareboat
Owned, Managed
Ireland
19 yachts
18ft to 35ft

Ulysses Yacht Charters
Bellmount House
Ballinea
Mullingar
Westmeath
Ireland
☎ 044 43558

Index

INDEX

INDEX